Narcissus and Echo

To Paul

NARCISSUS AND ECHO:

women in the French *récit*

Naomi Segal

Manchester University Press

Distributed exclusively in the USA and Canada by St. Martin's Press, New York

Copyright © **Naomi Segal** 1988
Published by **Manchester University Press**
Oxford Road, Manchester M13 9PL, UK
Distributed exclusively in the USA and Canada
by **St. Martin's Press, Inc.**, 175 Fifth Avenue, New York, NY 10010, USA
British Library cataloguing in publication data
Segal, Naomi
    Narcissus and echo: women in French récit.
    1. French fiction — History and criticism
    2. Women in literature
    I. Title
    843'.009'352042   PQ637.W64

Library of Congress cataloging in publication data
Segal, Naomi.
    Narcissus and Echo : women in the French récit.
    Bibliography: p. 238.
    Includes index.
    1. French fiction—History and criticism.
    2. Women in literature. 3. Women and literature—France—History.   I. Title.
    PQ637.W64S44 1988   843'.009'352042   87-31345

ISBN 0-7190-2362-9 *hardback*

Typeset in Jansen
by Koinonia Ltd, Manchester
Printed in Great Britain
by Billings of Worcester

Contents

Acknowledgements

This book was first written during a nine-month sabbatical leave at Cambridge University; I want to thank Queens' College for awarding me this leave, and St. John's College for giving me the opportunity to take it up. As always, I owe a real debt to students and colleagues, who provide constant stimulus and interest; and above all to my friends and colleagues in the 'Not the Julia Kristeva Reading Group': Ann Caesar, Liz Guild, Teresa Brennan, Morag Shiach, Judy Davies, Sarah Kay and others. Special gratitude goes to Paul Hamilton and Morag Shiach, who looked at the typescript in progress, and especially to Teresa Brennan, whose support and detailed comments have been invaluable.

This book is dedicated to my husband, living proof that a man can be a feminist; it also goes with much love to my mother Leah and my daughter Rachel, between whom I am proud to be placed.

N.S.

Chapter 1: Narcissus and Echo

'I was afraid I might cloud the magic mirror
that cast me back her image'
(Nerval)

Ovid's story begins with a prologue on Olympus. 'It chanced that Jove . . . while warmed with wine, put care aside and bandied good-humoured jests with Juno in an idle hour'.[1] The casual banter is about men and women. Jupiter maintains that women have the greater pleasure in lovemaking. 'She held the opposite view' (p. 147). They call in Tiresias to arbitrate. Tiresias knows 'both sides of love', for 'once, with a blow of his staff he had outraged two huge serpents mating in the green forest; and, wonderful to relate, from man he was changed into a woman, and in that form spent seven years'; in the eighth year, seeing the same serpents, he struck them again to reverse the spell, and was changed back into a man. Now, invited to decide 'the playful dispute of the gods' (pp. 147-9), he sides with Jupiter. Juno grieves 'more deeply than she should and than the issue warranted' (p. 149) and strikes Tiresias blind. 'But the Almighty Father (for no god may undo what another god has done)' compensates this loss of sight by granting Tiresias the gift of prophecy, 'lightening the penalty by the honour'.

The tale that follows is presented as an instance of the infallibility of Tiresias's prophetic speech. 'The first to make trial of his truth and assured utterances was the nymph, Liriope' who, having been raped by the river-god Cephisus, brought forth a beautiful child and named him Narcissus. She questions Tiresias whether Narcissus will live to ripe maturity and he replies: '"If he ne'er know himself"'. The meaning and accuracy of the enigmatic saying is proved in time. Narcissus at fifteen or sixteen 'might seem either boy or man. Many youths and many maidens sought his love; but in that slender form was pride so cold that no youth, no maiden touched his heart.' One day, while hunting, he is seen by 'a certain nymph of strange speech . . . resounding Echo, who could neither hold her peace when others spoke, nor yet begin to speak till others addressed her'.

We learn how Echo came to be like this; she too has suffered from the anger of Juno:

1

Up to this time Echo had form and was not a voice alone; and yet, though talkative, she had no other use of speech than now – only the power out of many words to repeat the last she heard. Juno had made her thus; for often when she might have surprised the nymphs in company with her lord upon the mountain-sides, Echo would cunningly hold the goddess in long talk until the nymphs were fled. When Saturnia realized this, she said to her: 'That tongue of thine, by which I have been tricked, shall have its power curtailed and enjoy the briefest use of speech.' By her actions she confirmed her threat.[2] All she does is to repeat the sounds of speech and to return words that she hears. (pp. 149-151)

Echo follows Narcissus and the nearer she gets to him, the more her passion burns. 'Oh, how often does she long to approach him with alluring words and make soft prayers to him! But her nature forbids this' (p. 151): she has to wait for Narcissus to speak first. He has become separated from his friends, and calls out: '"Is anyone here?" and "Here!" cried Echo back.' In amazement, unable to find the owner of the voice, he calls 'Come!', and '"Come!" she calls him calling'. Still seeing no-one, he cries 'Why do you run from me?' and again Echo repeats his words. 'He stands still, deceived by the answering voice, and "Here let us meet" he cries'.

Echo, never to answer other sound more gladly, cries: 'Let us meet'; and . . . she comes forth from the woods that she may throw her arms around the neck she longs to clasp. But he flees at her approach and, fleeing, says: 'Hands off! embrace me not! May I die before I give you power o'er me!' 'I give you power o'er me!' she says, and nothing more. (pp. 151-3)

Spurned and ashamed, Echo 'lurks in the woods' (p. 153), hiding among foliage or in lonely caves. Her 'love remains and grows on grief', but her body disappears: 'her sleepless cares waste away her wretched form; she becomes gaunt and wrinkled and all moisture fades from her body into the air'. All that remains of her is an unfading voice and bones said to have turned to stone. She is no longer to be seen but 'all may hear her, for voice, and voice alone, still lives in her'.

Echo is not the only one to be spurned by Narcissus: he mocks all his admirers, male and female. One of these puts a curse on him: 'so may he himself love, and not gain the thing he loves!' The curse is answered.

There was a clear pool with silvery bright water, to which no shepherds ever came, or she-goats feeding on the mountain-side, or any other cattle; whose smooth surface neither bird nor beast nor falling bough ever ruffled. Grass grew all around its edge, fed by the water near, and a coppice that would never suffer the sun to warm the spot.

Here Narcissus, worn out by hunting, comes to drink, and falls in love with his reflection. 'Unwittingly, he desires himself; he praises, and is himself what he praises; and while he seeks, is sought; equally he kindles love and burns with love' (p. 155). He tries to kiss and embrace what he sees, but it cannot be clasped. The beloved seems to be reaching up to him, 'eager to be embraced' (p. 157), and at last he realises it is his own image. Yet this knowledge is no advantage; if he already has what he desires, he can have no encounter with it: 'the very abundance of my riches beggars me . . . would that what I love were absent from me!'

Such self-love is a wish for annihilation. 'Wasted with love . . . slowly consumed by its inner fire', he melts like wax or hoar-frost: 'scarce does his form remain which once Echo had loved so well'. She watches him decline, echoing his laments of 'Alas dear boy, vainly beloved!' and, finally, 'Farewell!' Then 'death sealed the eyes that marvelled at their master's beauty'. Even in Hades he continues to 'gaze at his image in the Stygian pool'. On earth, his body disappears and is replaced by a narcotic yellow-and-white flower.

The title of my book is borrowed from this story, and I have retold it in some detail in order to extract themes which will concern me in the study that follows. Plenty of writers have taken up the myth – 'narcissism' is a popular as well as a psychoanalytic term – and a deconstructive analysis of it by John Brenkman received a lengthy exposition in Jonathan Culler's *On Deconstruction*. But Laplanche's comment is fairly typical: 'the position of narcissism [is] outside the situation of sexual difference and also outside language. Echo, that "personification of the acoustic self-reflection" (Rank) is herself disqualified, for she brings in a first element of symbolisation or difference'.[3] In this view, which leans on Freud's definition of 'primary narcissism' as an originary, pre-linguistic and pre-sexual mode, Echo does not properly belong in the story at all. Another recent study, by Caren Greenberg, concentrates on the figure of Echo as standing for the 'female text' or female reader within the text.[4] But a more extended analysis is needed to bring together the two figures in their setting and restore the sexual politics of their desire.

If we go back to the prologue, we find ourselves in a heaven populated by domestic units modelled most exactly on social structures herebelow. Cheerful philanderer Jupiter baits his crabby wife Juno, who lacks a sense of humour about the things he finds amusing. The text stresses his relaxed *bonhomie* and the casualness of the subject of banter with such turns of phrase as 'it chanced that . . . warmed with wine . . . put care aside . . . bandied good-humoured jests . . . in an idle hour'; even the dispute is 'playful'. All these terms warn us that Jove's viewpoint will be both lighthanded and iron-fisted. Is Juno 'warmed with wine'? Presumably not. The bandying of goodhumoured jests is one-sided, and joviality very precisely located. After all the stress on the arbitrariness of the subject-matter, it turns out, like a nagging symptom, to be the question of sexual pleasure.

Who has greater *jouissance*, men or women? This is no simple question of pleasure (if that could be simple) but rather one of knowledge. Jupiter starts where Freud and Lacan stop, on the question of what women desire and what women know. Can one person, metonym to her sex, know her own pleasure or speak that of the whole group? Or is the outsider the 'objective' witness to what the insider merely experiences? Lacan has a phallic knife to cut the Gordian knot: 'quite simply, the women don't know what they are saying, that's the whole difference between them and me'.[5]

In this view, women fail to speak the truth and men must speak it for them. This is what Jupiter does. His unexpected (joking?) judgment that women have greater pleasure in lovemaking than men is no compliment to Juno; we learn tersely that 'she held the opposite view'. It is perhaps not so much that what he says annoys her as the fact that he asserts his knowledge of *her* pleasure. His drunken certainty provokes a denial from her which is either brief or at least of brief importance to the narrator.

Tiresias is called in because he, 'throbbing between two lives', as *The Waste Land* gives it, has lived both as man and as woman. Eliot's note carefully arranges a hierarchy of plurals: 'all the women are one woman, and the two sexes meet in Tiresias'.[6] But if we look carefully at the narrative of Tiresias's metamorphosis we see how stringently his actually being a woman is excluded. The act that changes him is thrice-phallic: the *huge serpents* caught in coitus are *struck* by his *staff*. This 'outrage' results in a change of sex – clearly a punishment. Metamorphosed, he never takes on womanhood as his substance ('in that form spent seven years'); it is, rather, a skin he can slough off when, this time voluntarily, he calls up the magic again and becomes 'as he had been born'. There has been no change of face. Looking like a woman, he has never seen as a woman, but assumed the female state like a garment from inside which he can speak.

When the divine couple call him in, even though the dispute is supposed to be mere banter, he takes sides, and once again Juno is displeased, chiefly perhaps by the fact that, in the very act of asserting women's gifts, the two men have grouped together against her. In the triangle they form, Tiresias, instead of being Eliot's supposed in-between, composes a couple with Jupiter which, familiarly, makes the wife cuckold. She makes the mistake of all injured minorities and cannot take a joke, striking Tiresias blind for the arrogance of the falsely assumed viewpoint.

In this pantheistic paradise, human squabbles are reproduced but authority (unlike that in Judeo-Christianity) is severally distributed. Jupiter, the humourist and drunkard, has no more power than his wife. Like the last fairy at Sleeping Beauty's christening, he cannot undo, but only amend, her curse – although the narrator works hard to present his act as much more significant than hers: 'the *Almighty Father* . . . gave Tiresias the power to know the future, lightening the penalty by the *honour*' (my italics).

If women have pleasure, then, men alone have a knowledge of that pleasure which can be spoken; and if women have power it lacks decorum, neither light enough to show measure (for the politics of laughter makes her irritation, in Bergson's terms, 'an effect of inflexibility . . . a curvature of the soul')[7] nor effective enough to escape being superseded. Ovid, Eliot *et al.* agree that Tiresias's physical blindness does not matter since he acquires insight and the pleasure of penetrating what others cannot see.

The story of Narcissus and Echo is introduced as proof of the insight of Tiresias and the superior effect of Jupiter's might over that of Juno. If Tiresias is right here, then he was right also about the pleasure of women, and his knowledge then is like his knowledge now; Juno's punishment will have been proved as ineffectual as its motive was disproportionate.

The second female to enter the tale is a 'beauteous nymph . . . whom once the river-god, Cephisus, embraced in his winding stream and ravished, while imprisoned in his waters' (p. 149). When she consults Tiresias, the latter subverts the Greek maxim by replying '"si se non noverit"' (p. 148), if he does not recognise himself.

Narcissus and Echo

Narcissus is beloved by both men and women, but feels nothing for either. Throbbing between ages, he is the object of a plural, bisexed passion. This adolescent is the obverse, the mirror-reflection of Tiresias: each a speaking male, each knowing or not knowing only out of a male body, but defined as intermediate, double and self-dependent in a way that specifically excludes the knowing, the seeing and the pleasure of the female.

At this point, as it were tangentially, the narrative turns to Echo. She alone of all the main characters has no parents and belongs to no place;[8] she is, one might say, already subsumed in the thing we call by her name, whereas Narcissus's identification with the flower appears only as a postscript to his story.

When was Echo a whole person? The narrator never tells us. Unlike the other figures, she is never shown in a state before her metamorphosis. When we first hear of her, she has already suffered punishment and can only speak by repetition. Her disabled state is given as her reality, her 'nature' (p. 151). Even before she becomes only voice, she is mainly voice, and her voice is powerless. Her speaking is never an act of choice or initiative. She must follow, not chase; catch fire and not inflame.

'Talkative', 'resounding' and 'cunning', Echo once had creative powers: she spun out the talk with Juno till the nymphs with whom Jupiter was dallying had time to disperse. Here, a woman was the catcher not the caught; but only to catch another woman, and on behalf of a man whose prey her sisters were. She appears to have had no part in the jovial sport but, parked as sentinel, marked the divide-and-rule of women which kept Jupiter's pleasure intact: she spoke and did not enjoy, and her speech was the border between legitimate and illegitimate women. Echo's freest speech, then, was brilliant but obedient, and it is attributing too much autonomy to her to suggest, as Victoria Hamilton does – 'like Teiresias, Echo interferes in the "parental" marriage between Hera and Zeus by her deliberate aiding and abetting of Zeus' adultery'[9] – that she was the third party in the disrupting of a couple. Her utterance in those days was already conditional on her not partaking in pleasure (if pleasure it is; Jupiter thinks so) and representing no wish of her own.

Humourless Juno punishes Echo by 'curtailing' the power of her tongue, reducing it to 'the briefest use of speech', an emblematic castration parallel to that of Tiresias. As before, Juno is free not only to speak but to act – 'by her actions she confirmed her threat' – but again her power is undermined by the Ovidian narrator, who shows us, with some virtuosity, how even within the bounds of repetition, Echo will manage to speak her desire.

The power of Juno and the desire of Echo (mother's voice and daughter's voice) cannot coexist, unlike the doubling of Jupiter and Tiresias, Tiresias and Narcissus, or Narcissus and his beloved reflection. The minimal speech of the two women, curtailed and delimited as it is, remains, however, as the power that the men cannot 'undo'.

The key image of Echo's passion is the familiar trope of fire. Watery Narcissus is desired by an 'inflamed' girl who pursues him and 'the more she followed, the more she burned by a nearer flame; as when quick-burning sulphur, smeared round the tops of torches, catches fire from another fire brought near'. The simile implies that her desire catches on his flame, though nothing else in the description of Narcissus endorses this; proximity is not the flame 'brought near' but more accurately the forward-motion of Echo herself. Narcissus is a hunter and frightens deer into his nets, but he is the prey of Echo. She approaches him unseen; she wishes to use language to draw him towards her: 'oh, how often does she approach him with *alluring words* and soft *prayers*' (my italics); but by language she can only chase, not bring another to her. 'Her nature' – for Echo you remember, unlike Tiresias, never really was what she was before her metamorphosis – 'forbids this'.

In repeating the ends of Narcissus's phrases, Echo contrives to express a good part of her feelings. But I disagree here with Brenkman, who comments: 'what could have been the mere play of significations left unattached to a speaker, a character, a consciousness, becomes the other side of an actual dialogue between autonomous speakers, between two equally realized characters'.[10] This, precisely, does not happen. Echo's linguistic captivity is all the more pitifully emphasised; we are never unaware that the cleverness, assistance in her distress, belongs to the narrator, who is duping her as much as Narcissus when he lets her pick up Narcissus's verbal leavings as the food and drink of her desire.

Narcissus's position here is strange. How can he be 'deceived by the answering voice' if, as we are told, that voice is Echo's? The implication is that the sound he hears has lost its female timbre and become recognisable (by him at least) as a male tone. Echo's speech is, then, doubly displaced: not only are her words initiated by the man, but even her sound is appropriated by an angle of hearing which expects, and therefore receives, a man's voice.

Echo's phrase 'I give you power o'er me!' turns the grammar of Narcissus's utterance: here, for the last time in this dialogue, she casts off the opening phrase, with its rhetorical suicide, inverts the remaining clause to make it an offering rather than a curse, and appropriates (as she has the signifiers) the dying to herself. Her decline is described as a survival and a growth; her body desiccates but, in a sort of gestational symbiosis with nature, gives forth her life to the landscape. Stone, caves and mountains replace foliage as her habitat. She occupies the mineral base, lesser than the organic, but more or less eternal.

It is very soon after this that Narcissus comes upon his shady pool. Fire and stone imagery, the air drying out Echo's body, are superseded by the water that will be his doom. If we look again at the description of the pool, we will find certain oddities in it: the water has no liquid quality, no person or animal drinks from it, its surface is as smooth as glass. It is surrounded by grass, but totally obscured, and never warmed by the sun. Narcissus arrives, all mobility and heat, to embrace his obverse.

This is where the uncanny story of Narcissus's fate begins. Let me quote Freud here, for a clue to the fascination of this water which is somehow not water.

> This *unheimlich* place . . . is the entrance to the former *Heim* [home] of all human beings, to the place where each one of us lived once upon a time and in the beginning. There is a joking saying that 'Love is home-sickness'; and whenever a man dreams of a place or a country and says to himself, while he is still dreaming: 'this place is familiar to me, I've been here before', we may interpret this place as being his mother's genitals or her body. In this case too, then, the *unheimlich* is what was once *heimisch*, familiar: the prefix *'un'* ['un-'] is the token of repression.[11]

Where Narcissus finds love is that place where he sees himself reflected: the hole shadowed by long grass and hidden away, where he comes for refreshment and rest, to which he is drawn away from the chase. His mother conceived him while entrapped in a swirling male current – he finds the prenatal self preserved immobile in the stilled image of her captivity. Thus, and we shall find this repeatedly demonstrated in the fictional instances that follow, the narcissist seeks his own image within the frame of the mother's body.

Brenkman stresses the difference between Echo's passion for 'another like herself' (p. 297) and Narcissus's for 'his mirror image'. But Echo, the marginalised female who has no origin in either birth or intact selfhood, loves another who is precisely not like herself. Narcissus is both of the other sex and also a closed, bisexed unit, turned inward towards a self in which the desire of both male and female has been frozen. The difference between Narcissus and Echo is that he is given as suicidally complete, while she always remains the detached part of an inconceivable whole, having neither life nor, finally, death.

The relationship of Narcissus with his double is both dreadfully frustrating and at the same time wonderfully reciprocal. This is not consummation but it is love. Recognising, as he dies, that 'now in the death of one two hearts shall die together', he is acknowledging the perfect circle that his doubleness makes. Not so suprising, then, that the double, and the gazing love, are continued in Hades. What remains of Narcissus on earth is the mimetic emblem of the bending flower, whereas what remains of Echo is a haunting unspeaking voice, with no home except everywhere.

The only winner in this gloomy tale is Tiresias, the double-sexed figure of the 'subject presumed to know', Jupiter's envoy in language. Juno's curse, his lack of sight, is turned into Narcissus's repetitious gaze on himself; Jupiter's honour, the speech and knowledge that arrogated women's pleasure, has become Echo's unfinished voice.

In this book, I shall be looking at a sub-genre of French fiction that I call the confessional *récit*. Like any other generic definition, this one is a matter of family resemblances rather than strict codification: most of the texts I am interested in contain most of the following motifs. They are first-person narratives, usually embedded in a frame-narrative, in which a male protagonist tells the story of his failed life to another man or men. Somewhere in the tale there is a woman and she is crucially implicated in the protagonist's failure, whether by being too strong or too weak, loved too much or too little, in the right or in the wrong; whatever role she plays, she usually ends up dying, while the man lives on to tell 'his' tale. Most of my examples are taken from the nineteenth century, for of course this is a recognisable Romantic genre, but others were written in the eighteenth and twentieth centuries. Most of them are in French, but I shall point to some English and German analogues; it will, for instance, be clear to anyone familiar with the Novelle that the *récit* has a great deal in common with that much-debated genre.[12]

Many more confessional *récits* exist than I shall be analysing; for reasons of space, I have chosen to limit extended discussion to a selection of ten: chronologically, Prévost's *Manon Lescaut* (1731), Chateaubriand's *René* (1805), Constant's *Adolphe* (1816), Gautier's *Mademoiselle de Maupin* (1835-6), Musset's *La Confession d'un enfant du siècle* (1836), Mérimée's *Carmen* (1845), Nerval's *Sylvie* (1853), Fromentin's *Dominique* (1863), Gide's *L'Immoraliste* (1902) and *La Porte étroite* (1909). I have chosen these as the best-known and most widely read, not just by students of Modern Languages or scholars of Romanticism, but also by non-specialist readers, for whom I have translated all quotations into English. My discussion of these texts is mainly chronological, but is also designed to highlight a succession of themes. Chapter 2 begins with an analysis of *Manon Lescaut*, in which we find the woman playing the part of a *femme fatale*, and then leaps more than a hundred years to compare the same role in *Carmen*. Chapter 3 analyses the two earliest nineteenth-century texts, *René* and *Adolphe*, concentrating on the oedipal motif of the mother's child-bed death. Chapter 4, on texts by Gautier and Musset, focuses on the themes of surface and masks, the woman's costume and the man's epistemological pursuit. Chapter 5 looks at two fictions of nostalgia in which regret takes the place of desire. And Chapter 6, which moves into the twentieth century, finds in Gide two narratives of undesire both for the woman and also, more surprisingly, for the image of the self in other men. My last chapter concludes by way of a broad analysis of the themes that emerge from the discussion of these texts, viewed through the perspective of feminist-psychoanalytic theory: male and female narcissism, the man's mirror, the woman's voice, who looks and who speaks. . .

The decision to neglect those many *récits* that have disappeared from publisher's lists despite great popularity in their day has, unsurprisingly, meant leaving out many texts written by women, who produced large numbers of highly acclaimed *romans intimes* in the eighteenth and nineteenth centuries, as in our own.[13] In opting to analyse male-authored as well as male-narrated texts, I am examining the *récit* specifically as a confession in the male voice, a communication from man to man. In an earlier book, I suggested that this form of communication between men, which has woman as its subject, can fruitfully be compared with Freud's model of the 'smutty joke'.[14] He argues that smut occurs when the desire felt by a man for a woman is refused and he turns her refusal against her by sharing a joke at her expense with the male rival – for Freud an indispensible cause of the woman's 'inflexibility' (6, p. 142). This collusion of men is premised first on the woman's refusal, and secondly on her exclusion and silence, for Freud insists that 'at higher social levels' (6, p. 143) at least, the jokes begin only when the woman is absent: 'the men save up this kind of entertainment, which originally presupposed the presence of a woman who was feeling ashamed, till they are "alone together"'. I take this as a model for the communication of the *récit* for I believe that the marginalisation and suppression of the woman, for all her centrality, is essential to it. She is the object, not the subject, of its speech, and to the pattern of male doubles within the text there corresponds, essentially, an implied author and an implied or intended reader who are also male. What I want to examine in this book is the place of the woman in this genre that seems to conspire to exclude her.

I shall have more to say in a moment about the difference between the protagonist's relationship to his doubles and his relationship to the woman who seems to be the heroine of the narrative; and also about the suppression of her story into his, by which his act of looking into memory subsumes her lost act of speech. This brings us back to the Narcissus and Echo story, from which there are a few more key points to be extracted. What is the link between this benighted couple and those in the confessional *récit*?

The first obvious analogy is between the protagonist and Narcissus: both conceive of the self as perceptible and direct their desire devotedly and attentively to that object. All else, in the end, is ignored. The narrator's speech is inevitably a lament, not for the incompleteness of the self, but that it cannot be possessed as other. Behind this, the woman's desire is barely audible, it becomes in the ears of the hero translated into what he wishes to hear. Thus when Manon or Carmen concedes to her status as *femme fatale*, or Marceline loses her faith, they are speaking and acting the words and gestures assigned to them by the hero's self-desire. Yet at the same time, something of the woman's strength survives and surfaces in the man's text.

Narcissus and Echo

The woman's status in the *récit* is always both marginal and essential. She is occasionally, though not usually, introduced first like Echo and often her name is given as the title, but the story is by definition not hers. The connexion with the outside world of the frame narrative, the significance of the story, belong – just as that of Narcissus is contextualised and made significant by its proof of Tiresias and men's truth – to the hero who speaks, not to the heroine who dies. Apropos of these definitions, it might be objected that in Ovid's text the fate of the two protagonists is exactly the opposite of this, for Narcissus dies and enters Hades, while Echo has an audible immortality; but I want to twist the Narcissus and Echo story a little, in order to suggest why the heroine is not only marginal but also essential.

First of all, in the *récit*, the death of the woman is, like Echo's, only provisional. It is the climax of the tale told by the protagonist, but his unconscious motive for telling the story is the enigma of the woman's unresolved meaning, her intention as generative of his utterance. If she, as we glimpse her in his narrative, is reduced to echoing the words he lends her, nevertheless he too is haunted by her stifled self and unspoken will. She remains everywhere present, even in the mirror where he looks for himself. This Narcissus must echo the undead Echo's wish-to-speak, just as surely as she, in his text, is trapped by the conditions he sets upon language.

In Ovid's text, there is another figure besides Echo who can never speak anything but Narcissus's utterances. This figure is the mirror-image with whom Narcissus falls in love. As Brenkman points out, Narcissus, in his lament, lends the response a brief time-lag that logically it would not have, and this brings it closer to the essential lapse of Echo's repetition. In this and other ways, Narcissus's love-object is another Echo as much as another himself. I have already suggested that he finds, in the shady motionless secret pool, a last home reminiscent of the mother's genital – that door at which, according to Freud, children first seek the truth of human origin, later cultivate the delusion of female castration, and finally, as adults, confront the return of the repressed in the 'uncanny'. Gazing into this 'gaping object' he finds the Sartrean obscenity of an 'appeal to being';[15] himself as object, compliant but silent: 'the lips open, but the sound does not reach my ears.' Self-love, then, also does not exactly and uncomplicatedly repeat the text it is dictated – after all, a reflection is always a lateral distortion, a Lacanian fiction. But more than this: the image Narcissus perceives in the pool is not simply an adaptation of tday's gazing self, it is a past self conceivable only through the mediation of the image of the mother's body. In seeking and desiring himself, he turns to the mother and desires to have/to be her. The narrator of the text confronts his past self as he confronts the remembered woman. The speech and actions of the reflected self have a similarly attenuated status to those of the woman: both are dictated, represented and intercepted by the confessional desire of the narrator. In other words, there is a complex mirroring at the heart of these texts, in which the narcissist seems to be looking at himself but is actually haunted by the face of the woman, the mother he requires to return him a whole reflection, the enclosed, bisexed, complete self that is narcissism's crucial myth.[16] It is this magical reflection that Nerval's narrator is thinking of when he says, of the actress: 'I was afraid I might cloud the magic mirror that cast me back her image'.[17] He needs to keep her image under control because it is the mirror in which he seeks his own reflection.

A mirror is something in which we ordinarily look for our own face. Used as a term in literary theory, it is, oddly, mostly taken to refer to a mimetic reflection of the world outside the self: thus a text is said to be a mirror 'held up to nature' or one which 'walks along a high-road',[18] rather as if it had its own legs. In fact, as the imagery of the Narcissus and Echo myth shows, there is no mirror which does not present to the gaze both the gazer's own face and also a perhaps ill-assorted external world. If it is in the frame of the mother's body that Narcissus looks for his desired wholeness, then it is an Echo of her that he finds, haunting the self-image he cannot quite possess.

In the sexual asymmetry of the Narcissus and Echo narrative, the men are full – Tiresias and Narcissus bisexed, Jupiter 'almighty' – and they support and extend each other, each one endorsing, even if suicidally, the same structure of true and justified speech. Like them, the male doubles in the *récit* (frame-narrator and protagonist/narrator, implied author and implied reader, the many father- and brother-figures) are grouped around the central self that, though problematic, earnestly seeks a deserved wholeness. The women, on the other hand, carry (as in psychoanalysis) the perceptible burden of incompleteness, that castration which he wants to place elsewhere.

Juno, queen of Olympus, is no wife and no friend to her sire; she mishears, misknows and cannot even utter what the men know to be her truth. She is powerful but her power is petty in motive. Like Echo or the woman of the smutty joke, she is outside verbal or sexual play. Liriope, helpless woman and well-intentioned mother, disappears to become the trap that kills her beloved son. Echo was once clever – at the price of knowing no pleasure – but her real 'nature' is to be disabled, both voiceless and incapable of silence; her desire is so intense (flame-like) that somehow she utters it, but she can never love, since she is condemned to chase after one who refuses to be pursued: Narcissus is water to her fire, cannot hear her prayer, stays immobile but never gets any nearer, and always looks away, towards himself.

In the confessional *récit*, the central woman carries the burdens I have outlined in my analysis of Juno, Liriope and Echo. In isolating her and stressing her uniqueness, the protagonist makes her represent in one body the dead mother, Nature or the 'sister soul', and mark the flaw in the world that disrupts his desired consummation of self. Female plurality is abhorrent but, as we shall see, it appears also more obliquely, as the ghost in the machine.

I want to close this introductory discussion by presenting two pairs of ideas that will run right through this book. The first pairing is between the 'double' and the 'mirror', the second a pairing of 'speech' and 'sight'.

I want to distinguish first between a 'double' which, following Otto Rank,[19] I would define as the shadow-figure of *Peter Schlemiehl*, the film *Der Student von Prag* or such Gothic fictions as *The Confessions of a Justified Sinner* or *Dr Jekyll and Mr Hyde*. In each of these instances, a figure close to the original, but understood as a piece of self masquerading as other, acts for him and carries his inadmissible impulses for him. This figure is always male, as the protagonist is male, and may resemble him physically in more specific ways, though with an essential element of distortion, such as the automaton of *The Cabinet of Dr Caligari* or the enlarged and grotesque monster of Frankenstein. Rank's analysis stresses the psychological insecurities which the double embodies: fear of impotence or infertility, terror of growing old, an inability to love or (which is the same) an inordinate longing for love, all the symptoms of narcissism, which are then expressed either in a horror of deeds performed by the double, or in the

14

emblematic loss of the shadow or mirror-image. Doubles used in fiction can, of course, play a positive role vis-à-vis the protagonist, as figures who abet his legitimate desire or present models of what he wishes to be; we shall see many examples of both kinds in the *récits* of this study. But whether the function of the double is ostensibly positive or negative, the protagonist's relation to 'him' is always ambiguous. Essentially, as I have argued elsewhere, fictional doubles serve to mark the limits of a text's realism, and provide the protagonist with a kind of self-dissemination that is always both increase and loss. This ambiguity will be discussed further in Chapter 7.

I want to suggest a key difference between the function of the [same-sex] double and the [other sex] mirror. Departing from the practice of Rank and the Lacan of the 'mirror phase', I shall use the term 'mirror' only for the special use made of the female figure in her relation to the male protagonist. She is not his shadow or imitator; she stands opposite him and is, before she is made anything else, other and known as other. The urge to make her his mirror-image, exemplified in the quotation from Nerval that heads this chapter, is intrinsically different from the dissemination of the self into doubles. A double may wilfully be distorted: that is what makes Frankenstein's gall-eyed monster or François Seurel's lightly-moustached Meaulnes into an obvious misshaping of the original self. But a mirror-image is always primarily outside and distinct from the self: it never truly resembles, just as lateral inversion means that the face we see in the glass is not the one we look out of, and is framed in something that is not us. In this way, as we have seen, Narcissus loves something that is not so much a double (another himself, projected outward) as a mirror-image (the self sought in the body of the woman). In all the *récits* I shall be examining, the protagonist tries to bend the woman to serve him as mirror, but her otherness remains as the residue that distinguishes her – and his need of her – from his doubles.

The second key pairing is between 'speech' and 'sight'. These are so commonly run together in literary theory that we hardly baulk at such a mixed metaphor as 'narrative viewpoint'. In Chapter 7 I shall end by bringing them back together in the figure of the pre-oedipal mother, but until then it is useful to see how they are separated by a gender distinction already evident in the tale of Narcissus and Echo. Juno castrates Echo's speech and Tiresias's sight. Jupiter compensates the latter's blindness by a super-strength of speech, so that bereft of the use of his eyes he gains linguistic 'insight'. Tiresias is the figure said to carry both genders. The usual gender distinction is to consider women the passive object of sight and men the active lookers and speakers. Women present themselves to the view; men pursue, look and write. But in the couple Narcissus and Echo, we see the sight all on the man's side – he looks and is seen – and speech both passive and active the prerogative of the woman. Echo is only, suffers from and survives as speech, Narcissus is locked into a tragedy of sight. In the *récit*, the male protagonist owns speech, since the whole text is his (and the male author's); so the issue of the woman's speech is particularly urgent, a specially essential way for us to seek the traces of her autonomy. The passive quality of being-seen, which we would expect to find invested in the woman, is the protagonist's secret vice, his interest in himself, the narcissism by which he is to be diagnosed. In *Manon Lescaut*, for example, Manon's letter and the scene of the mirror that traps the protagonist in a momentary idyll of self-viewing are the keys to understanding them against the text's demand and towards its covert desire. Again, this gender-split will be taken up in Chapter 7, and linked to the first pairing to show how men's mirror and women's voice can be reread in theoretical terms.

The texts I have brought together under the heading of confessional *récits* have often been grouped in works of criticism, under a variety of rubrics: as the 'personal' or 'autobiographical novel' or the 'novel of the individual', the work of 'French introspectives', instances of 'short fiction in France', contexts for 'the hero in French Romantic literature' or 'the "Adolphe" type'; most large- or small-scale studies of European Romanticism mention them at least in passing. Jean Paulhan, for instance, argues that 'whoever wishes to define the nature of French literature or attempts to mark its "centre", thinks first of all of the *récit*'; Pierre Lafille, more cynically, quotes R. Doumic as believing that 'the "personal novel" is the form of novel taken up by writers who are not novelists'.[20] In general, the claims made by the protagonist/narrators, so anxious to be heard with the severe sympathy owing to confessions, are obligingly met by the critics, who tend to swallow whole the special pleading if not of René, Octave and Don José, then of Chateaubriand, Musset and Mérimée under the guise of irony or self-critique. A few examples will show how the premises of the *récit* are accepted just as they are offered:

the critic lends his understanding, even if sometimes laced with asperity, to the enterprise of confession; he rarely expresses suspicion, veering rather between delight and impatience. Often, this is combined with a failure to distinguish between fiction and the life (again, a direct response to the demands embodied in the blurred 'I' of the text). Joachim Merlant, in his massively comprehensive study, defines the 'autobiographical novel' in the broadest terms, as 'the collection of emotions and melancholy moods that lyrical writers dip into' (p. 400).[21] Jean Hytier defines the 'novel of the individual' as a 'novel concerned above all with the metaphysics of man considered in himself, rather than man in society', adding, after particular examples: 'they have not only expressed their metaphysics of human existence but divulged their own individuality' (pp. 22-3) – the meeting of general and particular 'human' perspectives creating a synthesis which makes differences simple decoration. P. Mansell Jones sums up his 'introspective' type as 'the being who by his very deficiencies, his limitations, his defeatism seems best qualified to tell us what we are like *from within*' (p. 101); here the distinction between author and character is buried still deeper beneath an I-thou idyll very like the one Narcissus died for. Who are 'we', in this analysis? Why, the intended male readers who take up the position of father confessor, listening to what is said and thereby to what is asked. Other critics are less lenient. To N. H. Clement, 'some men – at a certain period of, or often throughout, their lives – are too sensitive, too subjective, too imaginative to be able to see reality whole and entire, to see it as it is, and accordingly are prone to indulge in the analysis and expression of their own ego' (p. 295). Henri Peyre finds the genre largely outdated: 'posterity is inclined to smile at the personal novels of Chateaubriand . . . the tone is too consistently lyrical, the invocations to nature and solitude bombastic; the sorrows of René baffled by his sister's mysterious attachment to him . . . bear the imprint of the *style Empire* a little too markedly' (p. 167). In the studies of the romantic hero by George Ross Ridge, Glyn Holmes and Lloyd Bishop, typical characteristics are carefully listed and compared, but the exceptional status of the protagonists, their right to speak, is accepted and reiterated without question.

In general, all these readers consent to play the part marked out for them by the texts, for the latter anticipate both the irritation and the admiration that the confession deserves, and cannot be undermined by either the dismissive response of a Père Souël or the sympathetic hearing received by the protagonists of *Carmen* or *Dominique*. They willingly join in the round-dance of doubles which the clever directness of the text's appeal choreographs for them. Only a reader at whom the confession is not directed, who could never have the paternal status of the required hearer of its speech, only, that is, the unintended reader, can stand outside the dance, excluded from the joke, and say no to the text. By mishearing (as Juno mishears) the tone of the confession, we can perhaps begin to reappropriate (as Echo briefly does) the language of the confession. This means ignoring the demand and seeking out instead the unconscious desire embodied in speech, 'clouding' the mirror and looking for the female presence that pervasively echoes in the text.

Chapter 2: *Manon Lescaut* and *Carmen*

'She was lying, monsieur, she did nothing but lie'
(Mérimée)

'In art, don't you see', Gide reports Oscar Wilde as saying, 'there is no *first* person!'[1] In this he would seem to agree with the more sober Emile Benveniste, for whom the first person is tied inseparably to the second, and both belong to a present moment of speech, defined only by itself.[2] But when it comes to narrative forms, Benveniste distinguishes between two systems, each of which can be found in both speech and writing: that of 'story' or *récit* and that of 'discourse'. The first system tends towards the third person and preterite tense, the second generally uses first and second persons and perfect tenses, the common markers of spoken language. Benveniste's definition of the 'I' as tied both to a 'you' and to a present time and place of discourse makes it seemingly impossible for a story to be told in the conventional 'past historic' (preterite) and in the first person. The term *récit* as I shall use it in this book and as it is used, say, by Gide of his own writings, is precisely a consistent use of Benveniste's system of 'discourse' in a text not marked grammatically as a version of speech. It helps, perhaps, to view the structure of first-person narrative within a system of doubles. Both author and reader are, of course, only implied. Their relationship is mutually dependent but never fixed, since each 'actual' person, at a moment that is equally unfixed, conjures up the counterpart in a sort of daydream of present speech.

The narrator of the confessional *récit* speaks both to the reader and also to someone within the fiction: thus the reader is expected to adopt the position of Michel's friends, Dominique's house-guest, Des Grieux's Man of Quality.[3] The implied reader is expected to be not only the double of the implied author, but also that of the fictive receiver of the narrative. Further, of course, the implied reader is required to serve as double for the protagonist, who is presented as a model of what not to be, a man to watch, 'a terrible example of the power of passion' who provides 'a moral treatise pleasantly transformed into a practical example'.[4]

The structure of doubles into which we (as implied reader) are inserted is designed to ensure that we render up some of our individuality in order to make the fiction work. We are required to become

figures enough like the hero (for instance in our gender) to be able
to take him on and off like a suit of clothes. Both our assent to him
and our critique of him fit into this scheme. The relation of 'I' and
'you' which appears in the text, then, when the protagonist tells his
tale to a fictive hearer or hearers, is set up as an analogue to the
required relation of the reader to the utterance of the protagonist,
of the frame-narrator and, by extension, of the author who is 'really'
addressing us.

The confessional *récit* stands at the borderline between speech and
writing, and between the two systems outlined by Benveniste. It is
a first-person story in which the conditions of present discourse seem
to be fulfilled even though it is a preterite truth; it says 'je fus'.
Exemplary even or especially in his wrongness, the speaking protagonist settles language into narrative. It is in this context that we
must understand the convention (well established in the eighteenth-
century *mémoire*) that the frame-narrator can remember word-for-
word a speech of many hours' length and can also be trusted to
reproduce it without distortion.

All the protagonists of the *récit* are telling the truth as best they
can: even Gide's heroes are not guilty of deliberate deception – the
irony would not work if they were. It is only insofar as Des Grieux
and Don José are truthful that the uncertainty of Manon's and Carmen's intentions can become an issue. The frame-narrator believes
Des Grieux and Don José; so must we if we are to play the implied
reader; only if we do can we perceive the lying and betrayal of their
ladies.

What I am leading to is the idea that the text depends for its
apparent Romantic indeterminacy on the establishment of a mirroring couple who stand before the reader: the truth-telling protagonist
and the woman whose speech is exactly the opposite, unreliable,
enigmatic, perhaps simply a lie. The truth of the protagonist is established by the presence of the frame-narrator who vouches for what
he receives. By 'Romantic indeterminacy' I mean the apparent freedom left to the frame-narrator, and thus to the reader, to condemn
or condone, to be irritated or sympathetic: each of these reactions,
seemingly so different, endorses the truthfulness of the speaker and
the reliability of his speech. Père Souël's critique of René amounts
no more to disbelief than Chactas's embrace: they both accept his
speech as justified in itself.

The justified speech of the man is underpinned by the unjustified speech of the woman. We first see Manon, through the eyes of the Man of Quality, outside a sordid inn in Pacy. An old woman's cry of horror has whetted his appetite to view a group of prostitutes bound for deportation, "'a sight . . . fit to melt the heart'" (p. 11). He finds a group of twelve girls, chained by the waist, in a sad state of disarray. One of them strikes him as exceptional: '[her] look and face were so ill-fitting her situation that in any other state I should have taken her for a person of the noblest rank' (pp. 11-12). In other words, Manon is an enigma; her appearance gives two inconsistent messages: beauty and an apparent innate breeding combined with a humiliated position and the marks that signify 'whore'. Des Grieux, too, presents inconsistent signs: he is first perceived as 'her brother or her lover'; he clearly belongs neither to the deportees nor to their captors; he accepts money but will not tell his story. But whereas Manon's few modest words to the Man of Quality cause him to '[ponder], as I walked away, on the incomprehensible nature of women' (p. 15), Des Grieux provides a reassuring sense of recognition: 'he was dressed very simply, but one can distinguish a man of birth and breeding at the first glance . . . I perceived, in his eyes, his face and every movement, such a refined and noble manner that I felt instinctively disposed to wish him well [lui vouloir du bien]' (p. 13) This 'bien' is reified literally as money, though the Man of Quality does not, at this stage, get to hear the story he has paid for. That only comes two years later, when Manon is dead.

From the first, then, we find the conditions of existence of the two central figures marked out by their reception in the eyes of the frame-narrator. Manon is already, for all her simplicity, naturalness and modesty, her charm and sweetness, intrinsically enigmatic, impossible to trust. Des Grieux, found in the strangest of contexts and refusing to give away even his name, is reliable, pitiable and noble. We can see, if we know a little about the frame-narrator, whose 'memoirs and adventures' this tale concludes, that the latter feels he has found in Des Grieux a double who reproduces himself (and his father before him) in young-manhood: a little wild, passionate, true-hearted but wayward, madly in love. Manon, on the other hand, is so closely bound up with Des Grieux that 'he could not inform me who she was without making himself known at the same time': language ties them together so irrevocably that it is safer not to speak.

Narcissus and Echo

In the opening scene, we have found the two faculties of sight and speech mediated by the Man of Quality's introduction of the two central characters. The very similarities between them are undercut by the politics of his way of looking and hearing. Both afford him a view that is strange and incomprehensible, but Des Grieux's appearance is felt as acceptable and familiar, while Manon's is enigmatic and confusing; both speak, but Manon's words of politeness (which are not given in the text) baffle her hearer, while Des Grieux's refusal of information is rewarded with money and longsuffering trust. In the man, looks and speech 'make sense'; in the woman they are at once 'natural' and offensive to sense.

If the relation of Des Grieux to the Man of Quality is easy and assured, that is because the latter finds in him a younger self on whom maturity can charitably smile. The implied reader (male, able to 'learn from Des Grieux's example') stands in line too as a further double. But the relation of Des Grieux and each of these males to Manon is that of the subject to a mirror-image. This is why the very analogies disturb.

As I have argued elsewhere, the female reader, simply by her situation of gender, is outside the system of doubles and thus 'unintended' by the text. She is, if you like, a potential double for Manon, that ally whom the *femme fatale* is not permitted to find within the text. The unintended reading which a woman reader is in a position to give the *récit* is a way to release the fictional woman from her speechless position as mirror in the narrative to a kind of doubleness of her own.

If Frankenstein's monster or Mr Hyde fatally act out the abhorred impulses of their virtuous masters, the *femme fatale* stands in a rather different relation to the crimes of her adorer. His way to blame her is infinitely more complicated and unembarrassed. The frankly supernatural is replaced by the enigmatic, 'the incomprehensible nature of women'.

In this chapter, I am placing side by side two narratives separated by more than a hundred years. The comparison between them is neither gratuitous nor original: Sainte-Beuve observed that *Carmen* was 'a Spanish and rather spicier *Manon Lescaut*' and more recently Dupouy has called Carmen 'a wild sister of Manon, whose only law is her own caprice'.[5] They are probably the most famous and best-loved (?) of *femmes fatales*, and by this term I mean those fictitious

22

heroines who go their own way, are passionately desired by their narrating menfolk, and somehow are the cause of all the crimes the latter commit, even down to their own murder. Untamed, yet in a strange way entirely submissive, they obediently talk their man's script just before he murders them. Why does Carmen concede to the appellation of 'devil'? Why is she given the lines, quoted by so many critics as wonderfully simple and self-explanatory: 'José, . . . you are asking the impossible. I don't love you any more; you are still in love with me, and that is why you want to kill me'.[6] That she clairvoyantly agrees it is reasonable to murder her is the secret of her fascination for many readers – the wild lady so perfectly, masochistically tame.

When Mario Praz uses the term 'fatal woman', he has something rather different in mind: the vampiric, livid queen of the Swinburnian fantasy of being '"the powerless victim of the furious rage of a beautiful woman"'.[7] Although our *femme fatale* has hints of this 'phallic mother' figure, she is far less the projection of male masochism than Praz's 'cruel sphinx' (p. 231); rather, it is male violence against social norms and especially against women that she is required to embody. In herself, as far as she can be perceived through his narrative (and that is what I shall be trying to do in this book), she is neither pale nor vampiric: both Manon and Carmen strike one as healthy, lively, full of their own sensuality and strength. Let us go back to them.

Two years later and with Manon out of the way, Des Grieux declares himself ready to tell his tale. After promising that he has added nothing to the narrative, the frame-narrator disappears.

Des Grieux does not begin his story, as his nineteenth-century heirs generally will, with his birth, but with the moment of his meeting with Manon – clearly for him a far more essential awakening. He is seventeen, a naive and submissive theology student, 'girlish' in his attitudes, especially towards the father to whom, but for the meeting with Manon he might have taken home 'all my innocence' (p. 19). Des Grieux has never before 'given a thought to the difference between the sexes or cast more than a passing glance at any girl', but at the first sight of this woman, 'I was suddenly inflamed with ecstasy'; she is straight away 'the mistress of my heart'. Manon is younger than Des Grieux, but much more 'experienced' (the narrator knows, whether by retrospection or not, that flighty behaviour is the reason why her family are sending her to a convent). Though her manner is ingenuous, she is clever enough to suggest a way that the young man can rescue her from her fate, promising him in return 'something dearer than life' (p. 21). The narrator, looking back, marks the sudden and total change in his younger self – 'love made me . . . enlightened' (p. 20) – he knows what he wants, has no social or moral scruples and, especially, he can talk: 'I opposed her family's cruel intention with all the arguments that my newborn love and scholastic eloquence could devise . . . Many a time, thinking about it, I have wondered where I got such boldness and ease of expression'. Love, or the woman in whom he finds it embodied, becomes his new deity: it is from this moment and in the speech of Manon that he identifies 'the fatal ascendancy that drew me to my doom'.

The first encounter with the *femme fatale* is crucial, a kind of birth which is also the start of an irrevocable descent. It is primarily an instant of sight, but cited as the moment when the hero acquires language – all at once, as an instrument of deception and apparently contagiously from the desire of the woman. What does Manon want? We are not told, because it does not concern Des Grieux, but presumably her interests are the same as his for the moment: she wants to escape and he wants to run away with her. The bargain suggested by her monetary hint of 'something dearer than life' aptly reflects his attitude to her as an acquisition: 'her family's cruel intention' is frustrating, in Des Grieux's eyes, not so much to her as to him: he wants her for his own.

The superior power of Manon is already made clear at this point in an image which carefully reverses the biological roles of male and female: when it comes to putting his helpful intentions into action, 'my hopes would have been dashed if she had not had enough presence of mind to supplement the sterility of mine' (p. 21). And a moment later, Des Grieux's joy in first speaking to Manon alone is described in the terms of a female orgasm:

> I saw at once that I was less of a child than I had thought. My heart opened up to all sorts of pleasurable feelings that I had never dreamt of before. A sweet warmth spread through all my veins. I was in a kind of ecstasy that for some time robbed me of the use of my voice, and was expressed only through my eyes.

'Less of a child' perhaps but, in phantasy, a woman rather than a man. In experiencing something like female *jouissance*, Des Grieux loses speech and is all eyes, eyes which do the speaking for him, for

24

these are women's eyes, seen rather than seeing. The imagery of 'feminisation' found here is a theme which becomes increasingly central in the course of the text.

From the start of his narrative, then, the narrator prepares a fatality in which the bad end they will both come to is set in motion by the quasi-divine power of the woman's presence. Her body and the desire it provokes are responsible for whatever will follow; nothing will be the hero's fault. The rest of the story consists in the hero's battle against the undomesticated will of Manon. Her independence must, in the end, be bad, for it leaves him feeling abandoned and betrayed. What he does he does for her – to keep her near him at all costs. She is described as the pagan deity that has drawn him away from virtue, his friend Tiberge, a clerical career and peace of mind. Only after she is dead can he return to those paths, welcome Tiberge back, see the light of religious teaching, and tell his tale to the Man of Quality.

The couple get away, '[defrauding] the rights of the Church' (p. 25), and settle in a furnished apartment in Paris. But after some weeks, Manon's discourse proves unreliable. In a poignant scene, Des Grieux, who has come to suspect that she has been getting money from their vulgar neighbour B. . . , examines the signs she emits and finds them enigmatic:

> by the light of the candle standing on the table between us, I thought I perceived a look of sadness in my dear mistress's face and eyes. This thought made me sad too. I observed that her glances were fixed upon me with a different intentness from usual. I could not make out whether this was from love or compassion, though it seemed to me that it was a gentle, listless sentiment. I looked at her with a similar intentness: and perhaps she had no less difficulty in judging from my gaze what was going on in my heart (pp. 29-30)

The last remark can be read as a nostalgic farewell on the part of the narrator to an idyll of reciprocity once enjoyed, or at any rate assumed, by his seventeen-year-old self. He will never again believe it possible to judge the meaning of another's signs in terms of his own. It is not possible for him to know whether Manon is searching the hero's looks for the answers to questions as he is searching hers (one could well imagine she is not, since in this scene she is in the know, and he is in ignorance); what we see here is the breakdown of his initial faith that a mutuality of desire and speech can be adequately evinced by appearance. What do her looks mean? He begins from this point to see Manon as enigmatic at best or deceitful at worst, but he does not deduce from this quality in her signs the probability that the latter, and his own expressions too, could be ambiguous. Truth, love, fidelity, are henceforth located in him, and untruth, unreliability, enigma invested in the woman.

Back in what he now calls the 'prison' of his father's house, he conjures up an image of Manon as unfaithful and treacherous but still desirable: 'I no longer respected her, that is certain; how could I have respected the most flighty and fickle of creatures? But her image, the charming features that I carried deep in my heart, remained unchanged' (p. 36). His own ambivalence is tucked away at the bottom of his heart, internalised beneath the features of Manon; just as his eloquent desire on first meeting her must somehow have originated in her, so now she is made to carry emblematically the complexity and equivocality of his feelings.

Their second meeting occurs in a Paris seminary where she has come to hear him give a public sermon. In this famous 'parlour scene', Des Grieux quickly succumbs to Manon's Mephistophelean charms, once again with gestures of 'feminine' passivity – 'she overwhelmed me with a thousand passionate caresses . . . I responded with langour' (p. 45). He willingly throws up a clerical future for the presence of Manon, who pays for everything (mostly with B. . .'s money) and abducts her prey to safety.

In a phrase intended to show their inequality of interests, Des Grieux also suggests an analogy between them: 'Manon was mad about pleasure; I was mad about her' (p. 50). His dependence on her is no less – rather more – of an addiction than is her taste for pleasure. He is aware of the price of ensuring his fix, but will not admit that it is anything but generosity: 'far from objecting to the prodigal sums she sometimes spent, I was the first to procure her anything I thought might please her'. When their funds run out, Manon's seedy brother (a double who mediates the hero's entry into the world of swindling and later murder) introduces Des Grieux into a card-sharping circle where having 'something in my features which suggested honesty, no one would suspect my artifices' (pp. 62-3). Thus the features which the Man of Quality 'recognised' as proving the worthy birth of the young man are now used unashamedly in a sort of prostitution: the metaphor underlines this behind an intended ironical link between the card-sharping syndicate and a religious order: 'a vote of thanks was passed to M. Lescaut for having procured such a promising novice for the Order' (p. 63). In this nunnery, as 'procured' hints, the pretty young thing will repeatedly sell 'her' virgin charms.

But soon Manon leaves Des Grieux for a second time, for they lose all their money by theft. He finds a letter waiting for him:

> I swear to you, my dear Chevalier, that you are the idol of my heart and the only one in all the world that I could love as I love you; but don't you see, my poor darling, that in the state we have been reduced to, fidelity is a foolish virtue? Do you think one can be truly loving when one has nothing to eat? Hunger might cause me to make some fatal mistake: one day I would breathe out my last, thinking I was uttering a sigh of love. I adore you, believe me, but for a while you must leave the management of our affairs to me. Woe betide whoever falls into my clutches! I am working to make my Chevalier rich and happy. My brother will let you know how your Manon is, and tell you how she wept at having to leave you. . . (pp. 68-9)

I have quoted this letter in full because it is the closest we get in the *récit* to hearing Manon speak. Her discourse is strikingly different from that of Des Grieux; how could it fail to offend and even frighten him? Though she begins and ends with passionate assurances of love, he cannot square these with her easy dismissal of the 'foolish' virtue of fidelity. Des Grieux's separation anxiety – 'I am the one who should be asked what cruel pain is caused by parting from the thing one adores' (p. 70) – and fundamental conventionality make such a dismissal as incomprehensible as her tasteless image of mistaking starvation for passion, or her vulgar 'woe betide whoever falls into my clutches!' She assumes financial responsibility, as earlier and later, and she is not too squeamish to use the term 'work', presumably no euphemism to her but the exact reason for doing what she does. Her plans leave Des Grieux as the 'idiot de la famille': she will go out to earn, her brother will bring messages, he has nothing to do but, like some passive daughter, be taken care of. Above all it is his sense of the decorum of language that is transgressed in her letter. Such lively carelessness, the dashing rhetoric and practical exactness of terms belong to an aesthetic of utterance as play which is very different from his. To Des Grieux, duplicity in language may be used, as is his pretty face, to get what he wants, but it cannot be admitted: truth, like fidelity, requires that words be not signs but solid things; the doubleness of language is something he has covertly invested in

27

Manon. Her letter is funny and messy, but it is not enigmatic; yet if Des Grieux is to preserve the linguistic system on which he now depends, he must find it unreadable.

It is soon after this, when he has agreed glumly to help fleece the rich and licentious G...M..., that Des Grieux looks back elegiacally to his youthful innocence and laments: 'by what fatality ... have I become so criminal? Love is an innocent passion – how did it change, for me, into a source of affliction and vice? Fateful reversal!' (pp. 72-3). Love must at all costs be simple; his own feelings are by definition innocent; his crimes must therefore be someone else's fault.

The dissemination of blame for the protagonist's anti-social acts is a motif common to all the confessional *récits*; it occurs by means of doubles, by direct complaints against 'society' and history or, in the *femme fatale* narrative, in the embodiment of irresistible desire in the person of the woman. Imprisoned within the benign walls of Saint-Lazare, Des Grieux argues, in a famous speech to Tiberge, that the joys of Christian virtue are few compared with the 'perfect joys' (p. 93) of sexual pleasure, while the torments and martyrdom of Christianity compare equally badly with the justified suffering of love. Pity me, I cannot help myself, pleads Des Grieux, with an eye to his friend's purse and a fancy for the role of Racinian hero. In this fatality it is Manon, as witch-deity, who is put in the place of God. Unlike Mérimée, Prévost does not vulgarise this into explicit devil-mongering, but the sense is the same. Love is innocent; then criminality must have been caught from its object, that pesky Manon.

Des Grieux succeeds both in escaping from Saint-Lazare and in abducting Manon from the Hôpital (where he has been appalled to hear that she 'is learning better behaviour' (p. 85), in other words, is made to work) and he is not pursued, even though in the course of these criminal acts he commits both deception and murder.

During a happy interlude, Manon plays a trick which the narrator finds flattering, for it forecloses an insecure moment for the hero. She spends the whole morning dressing Des Grieux's hair; when his rival, an Italian prince, arrives as she has arranged, she drags her lover by his flowing locks to the doorway where she confronts the prince with a mirror, declaring:

'Observe, monsieur ... take a good look at yourself, and give me a fair answer. You ask for my love. Here is the man I love, the man I've sworn to love all my life: judge for yourself. If you think you can compete with him for my heart, I'd like to hear on what grounds – for I declare that in the view of your most humble servant, all the princes in Italy are not equal to one of these hairs in my hand' (p. 123)

I shall look in detail at this scene presently, for it is one in which Manon's function as mirror for Des Grieux is undermined in several ways.

The son of old G. . . M. . . takes a fancy to Manon; Des Grieux agrees to trick him, but for the third time finds himself 'abandoned'. This time Manon makes the tactical error of sending him a pretty girl as messenger. In the structure of the text, the offer of this surrogate double changes everything. For Des Grieux the girl is, at first, no more than 'a pretty little face which was not hers' (p. 134): she is defined simply as not-Manon. But bit by bit he finds he can after all make use of her: in response to his histrionic performance of gestures and words, she approaches, retreats, tries to caress him, speaks badly, and is generally manipulated by a terrorism of the voice as Manon has never been. He emerges armed with the weapons of patriarchy: from this point on, Manon will essentially be silenced, fit only to be seen. His potential feminisation is replaced by a choice of castration, sueing for desire with the powerful fathers, not with the maternal power of Manon. She is no longer the unique deity, the queen of his heart; she has become a metonym for 'a sex that I loathe' (p. 136), and she too can be controlled.

The hero goes to see Manon, and in a scene that goes a step further than the one with her double, he repeats the discourse of oppression; for the first time Manon fails to take charge. She ends by defining in a phrase the relationship that she desires with him: 'I sincerely hoped [the girl] would help to cheer you up for a little while; for the faithfulness I want from you is the faithfulness of the heart' (p. 147). The 'fidelity of the heart' is Manon's version of doubling: she wants a promiscuity of sexual sharing in which her surrogate need be no threat, just as her 'work' of sleeping with rich men is simply a sensible source of finance. But Des Grieux has undercut her gesture: the surrogate girl has made it possible for him to see Manon as just one among women. In refusing to be the passive mirror and instead performing the aesthetic move of self-dissemination into doubles, Manon has gone too far, and henceforth she is progressively suppressed by a narrator who makes it his prerogative to order the doubling of the text. The expression of her own desire that she articulates here is too late to be heard.

It is from this moment that Des Grieux judges Manon (as have countless critics after him) as simple, instinctive and true-hearted in her way:[8] "'she sins without malice", I said to myself; "she is light-headed and foolish, but she is honest and sincere'" (p. 148). The limpid sign, truthfulness and straightness are now her privilege; she has at last become comprehensible to him. Henceforth she will no longer be the *femme fatale* but the suffering penitent for whom he sacrifices all: she will speak in his language and die out of sheer love for him.

When Manon and Des Grieux land in prison for the third time, the latter negotiates his own release by acting out the gestures of castration, persuading his stern father and the other figures of authority that he has merely been young and foolish. But the patriarchate has less pity when, once free, he pleads for Manon. The kindly Lieutenant Général has never seen her but heard of her as 'a danger-ous creature' (p. 160); his father is horrified when the hero tries to soften his heart by comparing her with his mother. As we shall repeatedly see in other texts, women are not to be doubled: the comparison crosses too many oedipal boundaries. Des Grieux's release is granted effectively at the price of Manon's deportation.

It is logical enough. Manon is to be punished because Des Grieux has committed fraud, abduction and murder; she must pay for his misdeeds because, all along, she has been responsible for them. The double standard has it nicely both ways: it is he alone that matters, so he must be saved; but if his crimes are the important ones, his motives are merely childish, his acts harmless – this is the legal version of the castration owed to the symbolic order of the fathers. The real phallus is the woman: Des Grieux must relinquish her if he is to be accepted in the club. He is not quite aware of this. To their double standard, he is both consenting and rebellious: he accepts his own release and sees nothing intrinsically aberrant in Manon's being punished, though it causes him great personal frustration. When the fathers are adamant (for severity against women is an essential element in their male-centred clemency) he resolves to be deported to Louisiana with his beloved.

In America they find love and death; it provides Des Grieux, for a time, with idyllic happiness. For here Manon begins devoutly to echo everything he wishes to hear: "'I know I have never deserved the prodigious affection you have felt for me'" (p. 187), she avows; "'I have been flighty and fickle, and even while loving you desperately, as I always have, I was horribly ungrateful'". Now her signifiers refer not to her feeling but to his: "'my tears, which you have seen flow so often since we left France, were never once shed for my own troubles. I stopped feeling those as soon as you began to share them. I have wept only out of tenderness and sympathy for you'" (p. 188). Des Grieux's apparent sacrifice is nothing of the kind – he after all is addicted to Manon's presence – while here we see Manon making over to him the very act of signification.

But this idyllic state of affairs is shortlived. The Governor's nephew, Synnelet, wants to marry Manon. Des Grieux wounds him in a duel and, leaving him apparently dead, the couple flee into the desert, where Manon quickly succumbs to exhaustion.

Before they can sleep, each outbids the other in acts of nurturing care. Then just before dawn, Des Grieux finds Manon's hands cold and trembling; as he tries to warm them, she feebly swears her last hour has come. At first he does not believe her: 'I took this speech simply for the ordinary language of misfortune, and replied simply with the tender and consoling terms of love' (p. 199). When he perceives that the signs all point to her death, he still insists: 'I received from her the marks of true love even as she was breathing out her last'.

Des Grieux's reaction to Manon's death-throes is to interpret her signs as pure rhetoric, making the very mistake – sighs of love rather than the final breath – that she had mockingly warned against in her letter. He answers what she has not said. As narrator, he again fails to hear anything she might have intended but instead stresses the significance of her devoted death: every mark endorses his sacrifice and her gratitude. Indeed, one can see that Manon is more or less dying of self-abnegation; and whose phantasy is that?

After she has died, Des Grieux (both as hero and as narrator) declares himself empty, powerless and exhausted. Yet the gestures he carefully lists as his personal ritual over her grave chart a curious process of absorption and revival. He first lies prostrate for twenty-four hours, 'my mouth pressed to the face and hands of my dearest Manon' (p. 200). Then, to gain the strength to bury her in order to prevent her being eaten by wild beasts, he drinks some of the liqueurs he was provident enough to bring along. Breaking his sword, he digs a grave and, after gazing for a long time, 'I buried in the bosom of the earth the most perfect and lovable thing it ever bore' – Manon's corpse and with it, the emblems of his castration, the broken sword and all his clothing. After that he lies down on the grave, his face turned to the sand, determined to die. The narrator adds: 'you will find this difficult to believe, but all the time I was carrying out this doleful ministry, not a tear fell from my eyes nor a sigh from my lips' (pp. 200-1). In other words, he is giving nothing away, but preserving in his body, or breathing in the last, of what Manon gave him as she quite literally expired.

Des Grieux is revived by the miraculously restored Synnelet, and soon the original double Tiberge arrives, having sailed the seven seas to find him; he is welcomed into Manon's place in the cabin where the couple had lived. Soon after, Des Grieux, resigned to the ways of righteousness, returns to France and delivers his story to the Man of Quality.

The text contains Manon not just because it tells of her (as its popularised title shows) but because it is in appropriating her *mana* at the moment of her death that Des Grieux is changed from the hero into the narrator. As clearly as his story, and the relinquishment of Manon on which it depends, is his entry-paper into the symbolic order of the fathers, it is also an utterance made up of the virtue that he has sucked forth from the woman. Maman/Manon gives birth twice, first to the doomed boy for whom she plays *femme fatale*, and secondly to the clever narrator, born again to patriarchal virtue, who confines her in the text. Like Echo, she desires, acts, is robbed of her speech, and more or less dies. But her survival informs the narrative, not only in the many traces of her strength and the overheards of her less mediated speech, but also in the feminisation that Des Grieux finds in her mirror.

I want, before turning to the wilder but even more murdered Carmen, to take a closer look at the scene where Manon is momentarily in a real ascendancy, the scene of the Italian prince. I have shown elsewhere how precisely this scene, which was added in the 1753 edition, supersedes and subverts the scene of abduction from the Hôpital, in which Des Grieux appeared to be in charge, and Manon humbled and grateful. In playing out her joke, Manon releases herself from that state of humility. She is the artist, star and director of a performance that she alone understands; she has the last laugh and manages to ridicule not only the ugly Italian prince, who at least leaves the house on his feet, but also Des Grieux, his hair all awry, who (even as narrator) never quite admits how foolish he must have looked. In other words, Manon is inverting the conditions of Freud's 'smut': the two men, originally rivals, are divided not united, and cannot group against her. She is Juno not piqued but triumphantly appropriating the right to make jokes. In undermining the structure of the male pair in the Freudian joke, she has taken away the creative right to doubling which the narrator of the *récit* makes his own. She has shown, in her mirror, what fools the pair are, each in his separate but reproduced ignorance.

This is the opposite of the self-doubling she unwisely attempts soon afterwards, when she sends the surrogate to her lover; in doing that she relinquishes what she has just gained, for it gives Des Grieux ideas that he uses, first against her in the short term and fatally, and second when he becomes the narrator: the discovery that doubling of the self is the writer's imperialism. What Manon does in the mirror-scene is to break into the doubling and replace it by the exposure of mirroring.

Des Grieux seated at her dressing table sees his reflection in her glass and, even more, in her look: 'as she worked, she frequently made me turn my face towards her and, leaning with both her hands on my shoulders, gazed at me with avid curiosity. Then, expressing her satisfaction with a kiss or two, she . . . continued her handiwork' (p. 122).

What is Manon seeing with such greedy curiosity? Surely the man posing as woman, beautified by the cosmetic arts that entrap women by enforced narcissism inside the internalised gaze of the other. She has climbed outside the looking-glass, and he is inside it. This moment of feminisation of Des Grieux takes him dizzily beyond the prescribed narcissism of the narrator's structure, making him Manon's mirror instead of her his. (One wonders what exactly made Prévost, confident apparently that he was merely increasing the 'plenitude' of Manon's character by making her play a flattering trick on her beloved,[9] add into his text something as subversive as this, when it was after all already a closed book.) This state of things is so perilous to Des Grieux that it is rapidly foreclosed by the scene of the surrogate and the silencing of Manon. But it helps us to see how much is really at stake in the figure of Manon, what power she has possessed, and what it is that, in breathing in her mana to make his text, the narrator of *Manon Lescaut* so urgently needed.

'Women', Virginia Woolf wrote in *A Room of One's Own*, 'have served all these centuries as looking-glasses possessing the magic and delicious power of reflecting the figure of man at twice its natural size'.[10] For a moment, in the scene of the Italian prince, Manon reverses the joke by showing Des Grieux his right size and sitting him in the position of women where, briefly, he basks in femininity. Then it is all over.

There is a scene in Mary Shelley's *Frankenstein* (1818) which perfectly demonstrates how a desired woman becomes a *femme fatale*. The monster is telling his creator how, after murdering the latter's beloved brother and removing from his neck a 'portrait of a most lovely woman' (Frankenstein's mother), he came to plant the portrait as false evidence in the clothing of an innocent servant, the aptly named Justine:

> A woman was sleeping on some straw; she was young, not indeed so beautiful as her whose portrait I held, but of an agreeable aspect and blooming in the loveliness of joy and health. Here, I thought, is one of those whose joy-imparting smiles are bestowed on all but me. And then I bent over her and whispered, 'Awake, fairest, thy lover is near – he who would give his life but to obtain one look of affection from thine eyes; my beloved, awake!'
>
> The sleeper stirred; a thrill of terror ran through me. Should she indeed awake, and see me, and curse me, and denounce the murderer? Thus would she assuredly act if her darkened eyes opened and she beheld me. The thought was madness; it stirred the fiend within me – not I, but she, shall suffer; the murder I have committed because I am forever robbed of all that she could give me, she shall atone. The crime has its source in her; be hers the punishment! (p. 411)[11]

The badness in Frankenstein (here displaced onto his misshapen double and, more significantly, offspring) has already expressed itself in the murder of the little brother, darling of the dead mother. The mother's likeness, found on the child, suggests a bliss of recognition that a woman's gaze can give. But the monster, whose aspect has horrified everyone who has looked on him, knows that 'she whose resemblance I contemplated would, in regarding me, have changed that air of divine benignity to one expressive of disgust and affright' (p. 410). Justine, the approximate double of the mother, seems to offer another hope of that mirroring gaze. The beloved's gaze, so ardently desired, becomes the one thing he fears, for it would reveal a physical and moral ugliness innate, it seems, in the poor creature's being. So she must not awake, and her gaze must be stifled. The devious way to do this is not so much to kill her – though that is the foreknown consequence – as to transfer to her the crime he has committed. He does this not only legalistically but also psychologically: the murder of William actually is her fault, in his eyes, because she would not love him. In the final curse, 'the crime has its source in her', the monster-double shows how the woman stands in not only for the mother but also for his creator Frankenstein, his parthenogenic source and the first mirror to reflect him back with horror and repulsion.

Because the woman will not love him exactly as he wants to be loved, 'the crime has its source in her'. Don José argues just the same thing, but his crime is precisely the murder of that desired and blamed woman.

The couple Don José and Carmen are foreshadowed many times in Mérimée's earlier writings. His first publication, the *Théâtre de Clara Gazul*, was a collection of plays dressed up as the work of a Spanish actress who is biographically introduced by a certain Joseph L'Estrange – surely a precurser of the José who is also an outsider even in his native land. Clara's dazzling white teeth, olive skin, long black hair and the 'somewhat wild expression of her eyes' all prefigure Carmen;[12] in addition she claims Moorish blood and gypsy culture. Clara Gazul's first published work is interestingly entitled *Une femme est un diable*.

Interesting in particular because this is not, of course, a woman bad-mouthing her sex but Mérimée more or less literally disguising his misogyny under the face of a woman. The original frontispiece of the book showed a side-glancing young lady in a mantilla with a crucifix on her *décolleté*, which was actually a drawing of Mérimée by his friend Delécluze with some details added and others taken away.[13] Milhaud calls Clara the 'mask of Mérimée' (p. 50), Dupouy, more exactly for my purpose, titles her 'Clara, Mérimée's double and the elder sister of Carmen' (pp. 21-36). What is clear here is that the figure of the Spanish siren so willing to speak herself into the role of sorceress has been conjured as surrogate by the author, who finds a less exciting disguise as the narrator Joseph L'Estrange.

There is another Don José in the early work, and another tigerish girl: here, they are father and daughter, the incestuous Don José Carvajal and his parricide child Catalina. Catalina is 'the very image of her father' (*Théâtre*, p. 492) and this resemblance seems to motivate his lust: 'we are two demons at war', he gloats (p. 496), 'if I win, we'll bring forth a race of demons' (p. 513). The affirmed parallel here serves to disguise (as an implicit one will in *Carmen*) how different the violence of father and daughter actually are. His is a gratuitous greed and sadism, hers is self-defence. The female is the murderer here, as later in *La Vénus d'Ille*, even though here as there a strongly sexualised violence is found emanating unexplained from the imagination of the male protagonists. In *Carmen*, though it is the woman who is stabbed, this exchange of properties has become so fixed a habit that the third Don José is, even by his most far-sighted and suspicious readers, judged innocent of the murder.

Don José is forgiven always at the price of a certain manly contempt on the part of the critics: he is 'one of the least convincing bandits of the period', 'a weak character with no will', 'manipulated by a woman despite the protests of his queasy conscience'; in short, 'Don José is not of equal stature to his misfortune'.[14] The combined argument that really he is the woman and she the man, and that he, in killing her, remains the victim rather than the perpetrator of violence, occurs so frequently that we can have no doubt of the link between gender and guilt in this powerful myth.

Carmen is made to concede that she is the devil. She even says it with a certain pride. How does this affirmation of herself as the 'dark side', the admitted inadmissible of Western religion, go together with the evidence that she is 'a total Self, complete, the image of the absolute subject' (Chabot, p. 201) against which the protagonist's weakness and dividedness become so unbearable that he kills her so that he might stop being what she is not? In order to put this problem in context before looking at details of the text, I want to begin by thinking about the connected questions of the frame-narrative and of 'local colour'.

Carmen is the most framed of any of my texts. Out of a total length of sixty-four pages, Don José's confession takes up only thirty-six, forming the third of four sections.[15] The rest of the time, the frame-narrator speaks, mediating between us and Don José and, more importantly, Carmen, through his mixture of erudition designed rather to bore than to impress and a self-directed irony typical of

Mérimée's self-portraiture as Inspector of historic monuments. The frame-narrator invites us to share his passion for dry facts; the author's irony ensures that we will not. Together they prepare us already to care for Don José's point of view.

A similar narrator appears in two other *nouvelles* by Mérimée: each time the central text is one concentrating on sexual violence. The unnamed frame-narrator of Carmen, like that of *La Vénus d'Ille* and Professor Wittembach of *Lokis*, is a bachelor, little used to the 'ways of women'. Let us look for a moment at these two doubles. Forced to leave his researches and witness a marriage, the first goes to bed in a bad mood, feeling left out – 'a bachelor plays a foolish role in a house where a wedding is taking place' (p. 113) – and imagining the most violent of primal scenes: 'I was thinking of that pure and beaut-iful young woman handed over to a brutal drunkard' (p. 112). Simil-arly, Professor Wittembach, who has left his fiancée in order to follow his researches to Lithuania, finds himself officiating at the wedding of ursine Michel and the 'frolicsome' Mademoiselle Ioulka. Both pedants observe with careful lack of interest a pent-up violence in the bridegroom which, sure enough, issues in bloody carnage on the wedding night.

In *La Vénus d'Ille*, Alphonse is hugged to death by the statue on whose finger he has unwisely placed a ring. The Venus is an object powerfully positioned at the tangent of the conscious obsession (archeology) and the unconscious one (sexuality), for it has recently been excavated, is of mysterious provenance and terrifying attractive to behold:

> one could imagine nothing more perfect than the body of this Venus, nothing more voluptuous or shapely than her form. . . As for the counte-nance. . . I observed with surprise that the artist had contrived to repro-duce a malice bordering on evil . . . Disdainful, ironic and cruel as it was, the face remained extraordinarily beautiful (p. 97)

Here, as we have had occasion to observe in *Manon Lescaut*, a quality that is normal and reasonable in a male – irony, the very property of the Mérimée's implied author – is, when allied to physical beauty in a woman, uncanny, enigmatic and dangerous. The malice of Venus has a double in the otherwise innocent eye of the fiancée whose twinkle suddenly recalls the look of the statue, though not its oddly animate power. On the wedding night an imagined intercourse be-tween the malicious innocent and the brutal drunkard gives way to the murderous embrace of her massive double, which leaves the husband dead and the wife irrevocably crazed.

A huge woman appears in *Lokis* too, already quite mad. She is the mother of Count Michel, and her insanity is explained by the nasty experience of being carried off by a bear not three days after her wedding. You and I know, but everyone in the story as well as Mérimée's implied reader fails to realise,[16] that the precipitating trauma was not an ordinary shock but a rape, and that her reaction to her son at his birth and again on his wedding day – "'Kill it! kill the beast!'" ... "stop the bear! ... he's got that woman, kill him!'" (pp. 451 and 486) – is just and reasonable. Michel's fiancée, like Carmen, is ironic, witty and impulsive: she tricks the professor where it hurts, by forging a traditional ballad in the rare local language of *jmoude*, and elicits his unadmitted sexual irritation by playing party games with blindfolds and pots of honey. In both these texts, then, we are invited to see the women, terrorised, violated and driven mad, as essentially out of line and deserving what they get,[17] all primeval Venuses who have called forth the animality in the men and the horrible fates they share in the marriage-bed. The narrating pedant, only (we are told) tangentially involved in all this, is perhaps the one who has, through his author, the most to lose by it – for his status depends on his celibacy, erudition and monopoly on irony: when the woman coopts these by her 'malice' and 'disdain' or her skill with tricks and foreign languages, she has to go.

The length and dominance of the frame in *Carmen* and the other two tales suggests, in contrast to the rest of my main texts (though it is true also of *Frankenstein* and *Le grand Meaulnes*) a certain problem of definition between the two narrators. Which is the central figure, after all? It might be argued, following Rank and Freud, that the creature who enters the deadly bedchamber fantasised by the pedant, and there kills or is killed, is the disruptor of erotic life, the double, not its dreamer, the protagonist. The frame-narrator, pedantic, voyeuristic and, as victim of authorial irony, safe from any but vicarious adventures, is perhaps the one in whom the author has the most psychologically invested and with whom he has the most ambivalent relationship.

For he is never ironic with Don José. Don José is truthful, noble and pitiable. The frame-narrator remembers without a flaw exactly what he is told because, reliably different, he is able to vouch for

Don José's fundamental goodness and his right to speak.

It is through the intermediary also that we experience the famous motif of local colour. The latter is one of Mérimée's emblems, not least because he was frequently enough sarcastic about it to give it a place inside the brackets of his well-known irony. What many commentators seem to ignore are the two key issues of local colour: its ambiguous status as a marker (like the 'uncanny') of the border between realism and the overtly fictitious, and its politics. Both these aspects will help us in our main task of contextualising and understanding *Carmen*.

Freud has shown how an effect of uncanniness is achieved in fiction only if the premises of realism are first established.[18] We could, this suggests, draw a fine line to show the precise point where reader-assent (which is the essence of realism) is likely to be refused and an event or motif is perceived as belonging to the uncanny, no longer to the 'real'. Thus one or even two repetitions might be called coincidence – they are surprising but somehow delightfully plausible – then the third repetition supervenes and we are in the presence of the overtly fictional, the Gidean angel on a park bench. Local colour stands on the same borderline between the realist touch that seasons the appetite for fiction and the marked pedantry that makes us over-aware this is 'just a story'. Mérimée's dull fourth chapter on the lifecycle of gypsies is clearly there to pull us out of the quicklime of fictional seduction by reminding us that the frame-narrator and his author-double are still in control. This is local colour at its most burdensome, artfully unintegrated into the pleasures of plot.

Local colour is the point of keenest authorial control over reader and characters alike. This surely explains Mérimée's ironic self-doubling in the pedantry of his frame-narrators: they are bad local colourists, therefore he is a good one. Carmen on stage, loaded down with the props of gypsyhood, is a siren because she looks like one and a devil because she acts and speaks as one. She is the demarcation between the credible and the wild mythology favoured by the Romantics under the epithets of 'typique' or 'pittoresque'.[19] It is true that *Carmen* is not one of Mérimée's *contes fantastiques*, but that is not because of a discreet use of local colour – rather, it is because, behind all the razmatazz, we realise that the problem Carmen poses for Don José has to do with her individuality as a real other, not to do with the colourful trappings of costumery.

This is because she is, as well as a woman, an individual who to an unusual degree 'assumes' her social position and the politics of her national group. She has a sharp and malicious eye and a quick, witty tongue because she has preempted local colour, chosen to be the 'dark woman' to the full, and to use the props and the script for her own ends.

Like Grillparzer's Medea, this dark woman opts (but without tragedy) to act upon the image they have given her. She agrees that she is the devil, because the devil is the name they – and this includes not just Don José and the frame-narrator but the implied author and implied reader – give to her kind: as a member of a despised race and sex, she focuses the negative anima that is the obverse of the soul.[20] This assumption is of course a political act, for it is done not, as critics seem perpetually to argue, in the name of pleasure, but in the name of work.

All Carmen's so-called wiles can be better understood as skills. She talks fast, fluently and in many tongues. She knows how to seduce and, more usefully, how to keep men interested. She enjoys eating sweets, dancing and making love – but these are clearly leisure activities, relaxation between jobs. All this is taken as such a scandal against nature that it is no surprise to find her labelled 'masculine' on the one hand and stabbed to death on the other. Her sexuality, to her a skill or refreshment, is alienated from her and designated her chief characteristic – she is both only-woman and not-properly-woman – because, like Manon, she is the object in which the man's desire has been invested.

Let us turn, then, to the text of *Carmen* and see where she is to be found. The frame-narrator hunting for an archeological site finds, like Narcissus, a beautiful shady resting-place with a view and a spring. Someone else has got there before him: 'a strapping young fellow, of average height but robust appearance, with a dark, proud look. His complexion, once fine, had been tanned by the sun till it was darker than his hair' (p. 346) – here the toughness, the ordinariness and the blondness of Don José (under his enigmatically darkened skin) are at once established. Like Des Grieux, he is immediately trusted, in spite of adverse circumstances – his muscular look, his hefty gun and the fact that the frame-narrator takes him for a certain terrifying bandit, José-Maria – and the laws of hospitality ensure that he will be no threat. José smokes his 'host's' cigar, eats his food and later is saved by him from police arrest. Through all this, he becomes, in the narrator's eyes, a 'poor devil' (p. 349), at once dangerous and deliciously tamed, local colour in person and provoking thoughts of Milton's Satan.

In the introduction to Don José, then, we find some of the elements of which Carmen will consist: he is dark of skin and of expression, a kind of devil, wild and dangerous; but these motifs are all tempered by qualifiers that show them to be temporary aberrations from a 'true self' which is blond, noble, pitiable. He resembles Tiresias in never really becoming what he may seem. Like the Man of Quality, this frame-narrator gets the protagonist in his debt, willingly and in advance of the story that will solve an unfrightening mystery. As José leaves he hints: 'there is that in me still which merits the pity of a gentleman' (p. 355); the good self is perceptible under the tanned skin, and will soon be on show.

The first sight of Carmen is rather different. She arrives in chapter two and, like Manon distinguished from a faceless group of prostitutes, emerges from the waters in which, almost visible, the naked girls of Cordova bathe at dusk. The frame-narrator takes pains to stress the local colour of this custom, that is, his personal lack of salacious interest in it. A woman sits down beside him; a bunch of jasmine in her hair gives forth 'an intoxicating scent. She was dressed simply, even poorly, all in black, the colour worn by most *grisettes* in the evening ... I observed that she was small, young, well-formed and had very large eyes' (p. 358). Nothing enigmatic yet about this Venus emerged from the waves, but already we know she is a *grisette* – what the Victorians used to call 'no better than she should be'. They talk and smoke. Then, guessing her origin by her accent, the frame-narrator slips in a bit more local colour:

'I believe you are from the country of Jesus, a stone's throw from Paradise'.

(I had learnt this metaphor, which refers to Andalusia, from my friend Francisco Sevilla, a famous picador.)

'Bah! Paradise ... Folk round here wouldn't let us in there.'

'Oh, then you must be Moorish, or – ' I hesitated, not daring to say 'Jewish'.

'Come on! Can't you see I'm a gypsy; would you like me to tell your *baji* [fortune]? Have you ever heard of "la Carmencita"? That's me.' (p. 359, ellipses Mérimée's)

Speech and sight are interestingly juxtaposed here. The narrator does not, as Carmen assumes he must, see that she is a gypsy: he learns it, not from her accent but from what she says. She refuses his unctious compliment, and the paradise that goes with it: she is a devil because that is what the 'folk round here' see when they look at her kind.

Here the difference between Carmen's view and that of the frame-narrator/implied author is precisely set up. The latter, with an autobiographical note about his past dabbling in things black magical, jumps right into the devil-mythology by adding: 'in those days, fifteen years ago now, I was so wicked that it did not shock or horrify me to find myself sitting beside a witch'. Carmen, on the other hand, proudly establishes her name upon the group-reputation. Let's contrast this also with what, later, Don José uses to make clear who he 'really' is: 'I'm Basque, of an old Christian family. I have every right to call myself *don;* if I were in Elizondo I'd show you my family-tree on a parchment' (p. 366). Two footnotes by Cégretin inform us that *don* is the title of a *hidalgo* and the latter term denotes 'Spanish nobles who claim descent from an ancient Christian race with no admixture of Jewish or Moorish blood ... Etymologically, *hijo de algo:* son of something'.[21] Don José is properly positioned under the 'name of the father' because his blood is unsoiled by any unspeakable elements; Carmen is no-one's daughter (we never learn for sure whether she is, as she sometimes says, a child adopted by gypsies, or a gypsy born) but cleaves to the ancient race by choice.

It is only in the *femme fatale* texts that the frame-narrator sees the woman – dead at the time of the narrative – within the opening frame. Obviously this is to show that the quality by which she has ensnared the hero is perceptible, though carefully less strongly felt, by other men than he. It is important, then, that the frame-narrator should see her both similarly and differently. The Man of Quality, in his middle-aged wisdom, finds Manon resistible but thought-provoking; this frame-narrator, worldly but unpassionate, enumerates her visibility in an almost mathematical manner, adding only that (like his predecessor) he finds it difficult to forget the face. In both cases, equivocality is the key characteristic and the crucial feature is her gaze.

The description of Carmen ends: 'her eyes above all had an expression at once sensual and fierce that I have never seen since on any human face. "Gypsy's eye, wolf's eye" is a Spanish saying that shows good observation. If you have not the time to go to the Zoo and look at the wolves, just watch your cat when he's eyeing [quand il guette] a sparrow' (pp. 360-1). Here the power of Carmen's gaze is tamed not simply by the chatty examples but by being made itself the object of a cunning and joint observation: the predatory animal is domestic or caged, the watcher watched. Further, she is desexualised: the cat is male (as animals always are generically) and thinks only of eating. Thus the woman's desire is known.

In an ice-cream parlour, Carmen is telling the frame-narrator's fortune, when Don José bursts in and greets her with abuse; she replies with a rapid-fire speech in Romany in which the only word the frame-narrator understands is *payllo* (someone not of the group). Here again the eye of Carmen is marked as uncanny. While José's death-threat is accompanied simply by 'a fierce look' (p. 362), her reaction is described thus: 'she grew more and more animated. Her eye filled with blood and grew terrible . . . her features were clenched'. Somewhat inexplicably, she turns out to have plotted the death of the frame-narrator, but he is rescued by José and escapes with only his watch stolen.[22]

Some months later, the frame-narrator returns to Cordova and learns that Don José is to be garotted. He immediately goes to visit him in prison, plies him with cigars and hears his sad tale.

Thus we enter Don José's narrative, and the first thing we see is what he was before he met Carmen, that residue of old self hidden beneath the tan. Like Des Grieux, he comes from an old, respected family; he too was a student of theology, but his vice was sport. After a game of *pelota*, he fought and killed another boy, and had to leave home. It is clear then that he has been impulsive and violent long before meeting Carmen. At the same time he is instinctively submissive: needing some institution to which to devote his aggressive instincts, he quickly joins the cavalry and is progressing well therein when, 'to my misfortune' (p. 366), he is posted as guard at a tobacco factory.

This factory is a women's workplace. To the men outside, it presents another version of the swimming scene of Cordova: indoors, where they cannot peer, women have stripped off, 'because they like to be comfortable, especially the young ones, when it gets hot' (p. 367). Women at work are imagined, then, as unconsciously stimulating to male desire. But not for young José. He thinks only of home and girls in blue skirts with plaits. When Carmen first appears, dressed to kill, he is disinclined to look.

Yet he does look, and judges as immediately as Des Grieux that here he has found a new deity; the difference between them is Don José's failure to admit desire and the consequent more extreme interpretation of the woman as a devil. 'I raised my eyes and saw her. It was a Friday, I shall never forget it . . . In my part of the world, the sight of a woman dressed like that would have made everyone cross themselves'. She is wearing red, one acacia flower in her corsage and another in her mouth; her skirt is short and a lowered mantilla reveals plenty of shoulder. It is her appearance first and then her speech that makes Carmen Don José's sorceress. He insists (despite this very full and partial description) that he has not really looked at her; so she comes and talks to him.

Carmen, like Venus before and Ioulka after, speaks to mock: she has the forbidden irony that most fascinates Mérimée in the 'bad' women he portrays. Her irony consists in playing Echo's game as an active ploy: picking up and tossing back the very prejudices that the other is thinking about her. Just as she preemptively accepted the appellation 'devil' from the frame-narrator, so now she anticipates José's thoughts about sexuality and accuses him of feminine bash-fulness: 'make me seven ells of black lace for a mantilla, my little pin-seller!' (p. 368). Tossing her flower between his eyes, she emblematically kills him (as he feels) with the male equivalent, a bullet; he is immobilised and struck dumb.

At their first meeting, then, we have in miniature the whole story of Don José's 'downfall': the woman as seen object, the man's failure to admit desire, her initiative anticipating his unadmitted response and inverting it into the language of mockery, and his suicidal re-action, typed as her aggression against him.

Two or three hours afterwards, José returns to the cigar-factory to arrest Carmen for attacking another woman who called her 'a gypsy, Satan's goddaughter'. As he leads her away to prison, she persuades him to let her go, first by offering him an aphrodisiac charm, second by claiming to be from his neighbourhood. The second approach, in which she reveals a sharp sense of his suscep-tibilities, works as an exact substitute for the first. Don José not only wants the charm, he clearly believes in it, but he dare not assent to it directly; instead, he responds to the charm of her voice:

She was lying, monsieur, she did nothing but lie . . . but when she spoke, I believed her, I just couldn't help it. She was mangling the Basque language, yet I believed she was from Navarra; her very eyes and mouth and colouring proved she was a gypsy. I was crazy, I didn't know what I was doing . . . it was like being drunk (p. 371)

The identification of Carmen as liar is as essential to Don José as the image of himself as bewitched, intoxicated and irresponsible. He ends up in the cells, while she escapes, unlike Manon, alone.

The next time they meet (for José has served his time, refusing to use the money and file she smuggles into his cell) he is standing guard outside the young colonel's house. The narrator marks this day as the moment he began to love Carmen 'in good earnest' (p. 375), when he watches her dance and hears officers saying things to her 'which brought a flush to my cheeks'. As José blushes in Carmen's stead, she becomes indispensible to him: the figure of other men's desire, taking risks for his own. In her, he embodies a sexual wish that appears to emanate from her; but the narrator forgets, as he now knows, that here once again she is working for her living, using others' desire, not hers.

When they meet up later and spend a night together, Carmen's mockery easily persuades José to waive the army curfew. In the morning, she explains herself. She has willingly repaid him although as a *payllo* he had no right to this, because 'you are a pretty boy and I liked you' (p. 379).

But it can't last. Dogs and wolves can't live together for long. Maybe, if you took the law of Egypt, I wouldn't mind being your *romi* [wife]. But that's just silly: it's not possible. Bah! my child, believe me, you're better off out of it. You have met the devil, yes, the devil; he isn't always black, and he didn't wring your neck. I may be dressed in wool but I'm no sheep. Go and light a candle to your *majari* [the Virgin Mary]; she's earned it. Come on now, goodbye once again. Don't think of Carmencita any more, or she'll see you married to the old widow with wooden legs.

In this patronising and lively speech, similar in some ways to Manon's first letter, Carmen gives him fair warning that he is out of his depth. What he cannot bear to hear is the brevity of her desire; in its place, the vocabulary of witchcraft becomes translated, in the structuring of the narrative, into an assumption of fatality: Carmen will indeed lead him to the gallows, the only marriage she can offer. Thus the unregenerate liar, here at least, 'was telling the truth'; soothsayer of her own doom, she is allowed to use those gypsy gifts in speech, for this makes sense of his story.

Some time later, José encounters Carmen with her troop of smugglers; she mocks him again, he lets them through. That evening she succumbs to his tears of frustration and they spend another night together. When she fails to appear the next day, José concludes that she is as changeable as a force of nature. But again he reads the uncanny into an impulsiveness no more elemental than his own.

Soon afterwards, José burns his bridges: he kills a lieutenant in a fit of jealousy. Carmen nurses him with gypsy remedies and offers him a job: 'you are too stupid to steal *à pastesas*;[23] but you are quick and strong: if you have the courage, go down to the coast and learn to be a smuggler. Didn't I promise I'd get you hanged?' (p. 383). Thus he replaces the army as pretext for his violence with the troops of Carmen, who implicitly promises not just exercise and a wage but herself as well. She will be available to him both sexually – 'I thought I was sure of her love from now on' (p. 384) – and also to serve as justification for whatever crimes he will commit. But both plans are flimsy: '"Oh you are jealous", she said, "more fool you. How can you be so stupid? Can't you see I love you, because I've never asked you for money?" When she talked like that, I felt like strangling her'.

It seems reasonable to infer that to Carmen, as to Manon, sex without asking money is pleasure because it is not work. Don José is appalled at the ease with which she adopts the discourse of what he regards (too awful, and not necessary, to say) as prostitution, but she is not intending what he understands. To her, sex for money is no aberration of the desire he thinks 'belongs' to him, but an act of no desire at all, a use of her skills to manipulate those outside her group, for the sake of the nurturance and maintenance of the group. This is made explicit several times later on. In joining the smugglers, José becomes an honorary gypsy, but he does not learn their attitudes, nor earn the right to attribute his crimes to their ideology: none of the murders he will commit is done for the sake of the group – all, like the first, are personal acts of jealousy. They express a violence that is not so much oedipal as anticipatory of the ultimate act of aggression against the mocking mother Carmen.

For a time, as in the army, Don José is happy. The smugglers are respected, he enjoys particular acclaim because he has killed a man, and Carmen is always around, treating him with warmth. 'I scarcely felt any remorse' (p. 385), he cheerfully admits. But the narrator is careful to note his subordination to Carmen, as he concedes to her request not to make their liaison known: 'I was so weak before this creature that I gave in to all her whims. Besides, this was the first time she had shown the reserve of an honest woman, and I was simple enough to believe she was genuinely cured of her old ways'. His own simplicity – singleness of desire, innocence of heart – is stressed at precisely the moment he has entered the outlaw's world, where the status he enjoys depends on the unatoned murder of a brother soldier.

Carmen's essential role in this otherwise all-male company is to spy out the land and prepare the ground for their smuggling; she is 'the providence of our troop' (p. 388). Then one day Don José learns that she has just brought off the coup of freeing her husband, 'one-eyed Garcia, a gypsy as wily as her' (p. 386). In presenting the repulsive Garcia, whose violence is an ugly double of his own, the narrator articulates the significance of the hero's brave new world. The husband finishes off a wounded friend in order to save their booty; afterwards, 'that infernal Garcia' (p. 387) sits down to play cards, while Carmen takes the opportunity to kiss José on the quiet: '"You are the devil", I said to her. "That's right", she replied'. Subject to these two Satans, any crime that Don José might commit will be an innocent, almost a redemptive act.

The brute ugliness of Garcia is a realistic unexplained of the text: it is hardly plausible that the gorgeous Carmen would have chosen as husband such a physical monstrosity. In one sense, he is marked with the oedipal loathsomeness of the legitimate rival; but there is more to this figure. Though it is never stated directly, his one-eyed look is an embodiment of the evil eye, seen here without seductiveness, as a sort of midway form between José and Carmen. Garcia serves (like Manon's brother) as a horrid double of the hero, but he also suggests the crippled status that the narrator wishes to assign to Carmen's potent gaze, itself most dangerous when single-eyed, as we see three times in the narrative:

> as José leads her off to prison:
> She slipped [her mantilla] over her head, leaving only one of her large eyes visible, and followed my men, quiet as a lamb (p. 369)

> when she is involving José in the deception of the Englishman:
> The blinds were half-open, and I could see her large black eye watching me [qui me guettait] (p. 392)

and immediately after he has killed her:
I can still see her large black eye staring at me; then it clouded over and
closed (p. 402)

Each of these scenes is a turning-point for Don José, in which a
criminal act, either just committed or about to take place, must
urgently be attributed to her as temptress or black magician. Just as
the survival of Colomba's homicidal energies is read, in that text, as
the pretty young lady's 'evil eye' (p. 275), so Carmen's survival in
this narrative must be marked out as devilry. One-eyed Garcia, a
gypsy like her and therefore her *rom*, is used to stand in for her
representation of José's worst impulses, so that she can be his mirror
and cited as the source of his violent acts. To go back to the analogy
of *Frankenstein*, Garcia plays the monster in order to mediate Carmen
as the protagonist's Justine.

But there is more, as we shall see in later chapters. The woman's
eye, both subject and object of an uncanny gaze, is single like the
'hole' of her genital. Where Garcia's gaze is castrated, Carmen's is
a black gulf to the tempted hero, the pool where Narcissus finds death.

Carmen is not just an uncanny eye. Her freedom is based in her
range of skills, her *disponibilité:* she can dress in any costume and
speak any language, unrecognised even by her own gang. A smart
lady with a parasol rides by on a mule: 'the woman, catching sight
of us, instead of showing terror (and our costume alone would have
justified that) bursts into loud laughter. "Oh, the *lillipendi* [idiots],
they think I'm an *erani* [fine lady]!" It was Carmen, so well disguised
that I would never have recognised her if she had been speaking
another language' (p. 388).

We see her at her brightest and most inventive in the scene with
the Englishman in Gibraltar. Don José has been sent by Garcia to
track her down. Dressed up as an orange-seller, he wanders the streets
of the town: 'it's packed with riffraff from every country in the world,
it's like the Tower of Babel: you can't go ten steps down a street
without hearing as many languages' (p. 390). Here, Carmen is in her
element; Don José, who has adopted foreign ways, language and
costume only, he claims, because of her, is alien where she is at home.
She appears at a window and calls to him in Basque to come up;
standing beside her is an English fop ('an officer in red uniform, gold
epaulettes, curled hair, with the posture of a smart gentleman'), the
picture of what Don José, in another life, might have become. Carmen

plays a trick very like that of Manon: to each man she mocks the other, understood only by the abused, silenced José. Her command of several languages is contrasted to the Englishman's mangled Spanish, but José's acquired skill in languages allows him only to hear himself and his nationality insulted. "'I told you'", she says to the Englishman, "'I could tell straight away he was a Basque; you'll hear him speak the funniest language. Doesn't he look stupid, eh? just like a cat caught in the pantry.'" To José's furious response, she mockingly replies that this is all "'gypsy affairs, and I'm handling them brilliantly'" (p. 391). Continuing to mistranslate their exchange for the benefit of the Englishman, she laughs aloud at both men at once, and both are seduced into laughing with her.

It is a hazardous game: Don José walks away plotting revolt. For Carmen, like Manon before her, has rejoiced once too often in her creativity and the stupidity of men. When she goes on to taunt his sexuality – "'you are even sillier [plus niais = more of a virgin] than before our nights in Candilejo street'" (p. 390) – and offers him the role of *minchorrô*, favoured lover, this is the last straw. In several ways, Carmen has proved too forceful a mirror. She has dressed José up in gypsy costume, taught him her language, brought him to the point where he laughs with her at men in general and himself in particular, and now she redefines desire in her terms. When she showers him with caresses, the next day, it seems merely a hollow copy of the first night: 'no monkey could have done more capers, grimaces and devilry' (p. 392). She suggests 'with a diabolical smile' that he is to let Garcia attack the Englishman first and therefore be killed, and suddenly Don José casts off his new skin and reasserts the solidarity of men. "'No . . . I hate Garcia, but he's my comrade. One day maybe I'll get rid of him for you, but we'll settle our accounts in the way of my country. I am only a gypsy by chance; in some things I'll always be a true Navarrese, as they say in the proverb'" (p. 393). Like Des Grieux endorsing the very fathers against whom he is in revolt, José will kill Garcia in comradeship, restoring the oedipal solidarity against the woman.

He lures Garcia into a duel and kills him; after the parricidal deed he feels 'stronger than a giant' (p. 394), but Carmen warns him that his time will come; he returns the prediction. By this point, José is chafing at Carmen's control: he needs to preempt her by taking back her use of the discourse of fatality; the only way to make this happen is to do away with her. All the murderous impulses of the past gather into an intention. But it is not so simple. It is at just this moment that the widowed Carmen declares him her *rom;* the term means not only 'legitimate husband', having total rights to his woman's devotion and even her life, but also 'gypsy'. If José is to be one, he becomes the other.

According to the frame-narrator's presentation of their language, the nation of gypsies refer to themselves as '*Romé* or *the married ones*' (p. 405): thus they define themselves by a strict endogamy which – 'there is no example of a Gitana falling for a man who is not of her race', (p. 404) – Carmen appears to transgress. Either Carmen has trangressed it or else Don José is a gypsy after all, not just by adoption or chance but right through to the bone. In the Gibraltar scene, Carmen offered him a way not to be a 'niais': to share her sexuality rather than her laughter; but to do this will make him no longer a 'true Navarrese'. Like Orso in *Colomba*, Don José cannot have it both ways: the choice is between exogamy or endogamy, and everything draws him to the side of endogamy. In *Colomba*, the cards are rather differently stacked: mother-tongue and the wild laws of the homeland belong to a sister who is ravishing but unmarryable; the temptation of incest is more direct, but less admitted. In *Carmen*, it is a question of self-definition by separation: to have Carmen is to lose the old self: the only safe way to 'possess' her is by murder.

Yet, like Des Grieux's, the murder will also be a suicide. To kill Carmen is to take back, like a host, the definition of devil onto his own tongue; in borrowing her apparent assent to justify his act, José will swallow for ever Carmen's proud inversion of the term used by the 'folk round here'. He changes from the hero to the narrator, and his narrative is full of Carmen; no Miltonic Satan, but a poor *payllo*, the narrator restores all the power to its source.

In the final dialogue, Carmen both is and is not the echo of José's desire. By assenting to the inevitability of her murder, she makes it possible, but she also allows it by her refusal to go away to America or compromise her freedom: '"what I want is to be free and do what I like"' (p. 395); '"I like it here"' (p. 398). Instead she provides the language of fatality that, we are to understand, forces the protagonist's hesitant hand. At the very last, Carmen does not even take the oppor-tunity to escape. Cleaving to him, she is making him her *rom*, the gypsy he does not wish to be. '"So, my Carmen" I said after we had gone a little way, "you are following me of your own accord, aren't you?" "I will follow you to my death, but I won't live with you any more"' (p. 400). And, when they arrive at the Narcissistic glade where she is to die: "'You want to kill me, I know it", she said; "it is written; but you will not make me yield"' (p. 401). Carmen's strength is, by definition, Don José's weakness. He cannot win. When she agrees to her murder, her very submissiveness affirms her freedom. But the opposite is also true. Carmen is the loser if she seems (as she does to most readers) so much the stronger that she ends up the perpetrator of the violence. And either way she dies.

She reiterates her terms: "'I loved [the picador] as I loved you, for a moment, less than I loved you perhaps. Now I love nothing, and I hate myself for ever having loved you"'. The brief affection for Don José was, she now admits, a transgression: it made her less a gypsy; now she is restored: "'Carmen will always be free . . . it's impossible for me to love you any more. As for living with you, I don't want to"'. It is this fixity in herself that José must destroy: 'I'd have like her to beg for mercy, but that woman was a demon'. As he strikes her, the evil eye outlives her: 'she fell at the second blow without crying out. I can still see her large black eye staring at me; then it clouded over and closed' (p. 402).

The eye has closed, but the narrator sees it still; thus Carmen survives him. Like Des Grieux, he collapses: 'I remained prostrate for a whole hour before the body'. The birth of the narrator is a kind of suicide. His last word is an attempt to prove her, as he was, a gypsy by nurture and not nature; this way, she can become the weaker, a 'poor child! The *Calé* [Gypsies] are to blame for bringing her up like that'. And the closing frame reiterates this: Carmen fits some of the definitions of gypsyhood, not others. To be the unique temptress, the frame-narrator agrees, she must be not quite herself.

The *femme fatale* narratives can serve as both an extreme case and a model for the confessional *récit*. In them, the power of the woman is evident, so far superior to that of the protagonist that she remains indicted of all his crimes. Killing her in order to speak to the fathers, he concedes that the pre-oedipal drama of separation is what gives him language, and that in her desire and her refusal of his desire, he will seek for a mirror-identity which is his version of narcissism. The text is both his revenge and the repetition of his defeat.

Chapter 3: *René* and *Adolphe*

'I cost my mother her life when I came into the world'
(Chateaubriand)

The grand-daddy of all nineteenth-century *récits* is, of course, Goethe's *Die Leiden des jungen Werthers* (1774). Its influence all over Europe was spectacular, leading to a plague of adaptations, parodies, suicides and the uniform of blue jacket and yellow trousers. I want briefly to see how it serves as a model for the oedipal themes of the récit, pointing to both similarities and differences in its French followers.

Werther falls in love with Lotte after he has heard that she is engaged to another man. In his first view of her – 'the most charming performance . . . I ever saw' (p. 21)[1] – she stands doling out slices of bread to her brood of brothers and sisters. Much is made, in sentimental conversations, of Lotte's resemblance to her dead mother; she became engaged to Albert at the latter's deathbed instigation, and at the same time was placed in the role of surviving surrogate: 'show . . . your father the loyalty and obedience of a wife' (p. 59). Werther is emotionally adopted into the family, even replacing Lotte in the children's eyes as worthy distributor of the evening bread. Albert is good but dull; Lotte herself expresses the wish that Werther could have been her brother, then searches her mind for a friend she might marry him to, and finds none quite right for him.

The theme of sibling-incest and its place in the oedipal structure is, thus, adumbrated here. We also recognise the theme – a staple in Romantic writings from here on – of blaming the young man's failure on the world which by horrid chance or simple human malevolence cannot provide the true fit for his large desires. Werther finds Nature and country life growing grim and unresponsive as he is overtaken by depression. He hangs onto his image of God but only via an identification with Jesus in which the cry 'my God, my God, why hast thou forsaken me?' justifies a suicide that will restore him to an understanding Father. He quarrels with the law and, earlier, with the snobs of a small principality. He confuses frustrated desire with the infinitely-stretched tension of sexless innocence. He 'is' a child. He and Lotte share tastes in literature and feeling: together, they read a long chunk of Ossian, reproduced for us in Goethe's translation. Moved by Lotte's passionate tears, Werther is convinced that she loves him in return (though at this stage, with the intervention of the frame-narrator, we have a good enough view of Lotte's perplexed feelings to see that this 'discovery' is reductive); he covers her face in kisses, is repulsed, climbs a mountain and then shoots himself.

The latter act is one of many elements in *Werther* that distinguish it from its French descendents. None of the French protagonists dies; even Adolphe, whose narrative is recovered in writing rather than speech, has simply disappeared from view; René's death is very much a postscript. In most German equivalents of the *récit*, as also in the English, the death of the male protagonist is a crucial event. Lotte, though not for long perhaps, survives Werther. Werther's mother, unlike those of most of our French heroes, is still alive, though kept at a distance. The text is in epistolary form, except for the closing section, in which an anonymous frame-narrator appears for the first time, curiously privy to all the correspondence and the characters' innermost feelings. This use of a closing frame only is strikingly effective in showing how far gone Werther now is; it carries the critique of the pitiable egotist which features also in all my texts.

Three other nineteenth-century *Novellen* would seem to belong to the genre: Stifter's 'Kalkstein' (first published as 'Der arme Wohltäter' in 1848), Grillparzer's *Der arme Spielmann* (1848) and Storm's *Immensee* (1851). In the first two, the protagonists are martyrs, who have only the briefest of encounters with beloved women commemorated ever after in the fetishes – dazzling linen, a curvaceous violin – which are all their saintly anorexia permits them;[2] in the third, an old man remembers with marked selectivity the student days in which his own neglect and a mother's influence lost him his girl-next-door to a friend who stayed in the provinces.

If we think of the English equivalent of the genre, we find almost all texts in the Gothic mode – Mary Shelley's *Frankenstein* (1818), James Hogg's *Confessions of a Justified Sinner* (1824), R. L. Stevenson's *Dr Jekyll and Mr Hyde* (1886), Wilde's *The Picture of Dorian Gray* (1891) or Fitzgerald's *The Great Gatsby* (1925) – in which interest is directed above all towards the doubling of the male characters, at times to the extent that it is difficult to decide who the protagonist actually is: Frankenstein or his monster? Gatsby or Nick Carraway? Doubling is the crucial issue: the picture, potion, monstrous twin or misshapen progeny suggest an anxiety about separating the self into dark and light, 'real' and shadow, the inadmissible of desire appearing as a problem of conscience, not relationship. In these and the German texts, it seems that the woman scarcely takes shape enough to die; she is not the matter.

Let us turn, then, to the nineteenth-century French texts, in which many of the oedipal themes of *Werther* are reproduced and developed. Chateaubriand also borrows elements of the colonial exotic from *Manon Lescaut* and from Bernardin de Saint-Pierre's massively popular *Paul et Virginie* (1787), a brother-and-sister idyll of noble children on a wild island. Hints of this poignant tale are evident especially in *Atala* (1801), which I want to take a look at before its mirror-piece, *René*.

Atala is most obviously a mirror for *René* in that it is the life-story Chactas tells to René, a narratorial relationship reversed in the later text. Far more deeply implicated in the myth of local colour, arguing more strongly and quite twistedly for the advantages of Christianity and civilisation over a savagery on which author and reader jointly feed, it also carries a blatant mystique of incest and an obsession with the mother-child relationship that reappear more carefully wound-about in *René*.[3]

Chactas (now blind and venerable) was adopted at the age of seventeen by a missionary, Lopez. After two or three years without converting, he chooses to go back to his people and is immediately captured and sentenced to a gruesome death. A beautiful girl – 'she had pure, regular features, and there was something virtuous and passionate about her face which made her irresistibly attractive' (p. 50) – takes pity on him, unties him and bids him escape.[4] He refuses to leave without her and together they flee into the wild. Madly in love, they are about to succumb to desire, but prayer (for Atala is a Christian) saves her from temptation, giving her a look of divinity and 'an immortal beauty' (p. 63). Recaptured, they escape for the second time, Atala swearing, like Manon, that 'the sacrifice will be reciprocal' (p. 77). They tend, groom and console each other. Then Atala grows sad: alternately ardent and withdrawn, she seems to be keeping a secret from her adorer. He comments, in a turn of phrase that could sum up the whole role of the woman in the confessional *récit*: 'Atala's power over a man could never be a feeble one: full of passion, she was full of potency [puissance]; one had either to adore her or hate her' (p. 82). Eventually, she reveals a part of her secret: she is not really the daughter of Simaghan, the chief of her tribe, but of the missionary Lopez. After the discovery of this quasi-fraternity they both find it much more difficult to resist desire. At the key moment, there is a thunder-clap from on high, and the priest Père Aubry rescues them from themselves, taking them to his colony of labouring converts, where desire fades away and Chactas learns the advantages of white civilisation.

When, that evening, Atala needs to talk Aubry, he has gone to pray and contemplate Nature. The next day he takes Chactas to see his Mission. They arrive back to find Atala dying; like Manon, 'her half-extinguished gaze still sought to express her love for me' (p. 115). She reveals the rest of her secret: after an agonising birth in which both nearly died, her Christian mother dedicated her to eternal virginity. Seeing no way out, even in Christian marriage, Atala has poisoned herself, innocently unaware that suicide too is condemned by the Church. Chactas's brief howl of rebellion is thundered down by the good Père, who goes on to assure Atala that the Bishop would probably have absolved her from such an injudicious vow; but the poison is irreversible. He makes a long speech about the frailty of human happiness and the superiority of going quickly to celestial bliss.

Atala dies and is lengthily buried, her alabaster hands and dazzling white cheeks making her the image of 'Virginity at rest' (p. 144).[5] This story is supposed to represent 'the triumph of Christianity over the most fiery sentiment and the most terrible fear, love and death' (p. 151), although of course Christianity only triumphs over them after having first provoked them. Chateaubriand guarantees a sandwich of the most delicious kind by placing, between two slices of local colour, thickly spread with Nature, torture and a glimpse of female wrestling, a solid wedge of Christianity to provide the mechanics of a tragic plot. In the *Génie*, we find a similarly paradoxical view of the link between the two: 'the Christian religion, properly understood, is nothing but primitive nature cleansed of original sin [la tache originelle]'.[6] Like poor Atala's problem, original sin is the invention of the very ideology that offers to take it away: the 'stain' washable only by a detergent made of the same dirt, a nice homeopathy. The intended reader joins the implied author in keening over a tragedy they have ideologically engineered. Who are the innocent savages thus condemned and enjoyed? Why, another Paul and Virginie, babes in the wood, above all brother and sister.

The theme of incest is not only everywhere dwelt on in epithets which stress the erotic power of the (after all only metaphorical) sibling-tie;[7] it is also extolled in a curious apologia of prelapsarian innocence by Père Aubry:

> No doubt, my daughter, the most beautiful love was that of the first man and the first woman, fashioned by the hand of the Creator. A paradise had been formed for them, they were innocent and immortal. Perfect in soul and body, they suited each other in every way: Eve was created for Adam and Adam for Eve. If even they were unable to maintain that state of bliss, what couple could do so after them? I shall not speak of the marriages of the firstborn of men, those ineffable unions, when sister was bride to brother, love and fraternal friendship mingled in the same heart and the purity of the one increased the delights of the other. (pp. 130-1)

What is perhaps oddest about this argument is that the bliss of total union is available after Eden just as much as in it: the children of Adam and Eve, because they too are inevitably incestuous, enjoy the same edenic bliss. This is, in fact, a fantasy of 'primitive nature' in which there is no such thing as original sin and no Christian ideology. The seductiveness of the Romantic myth of the exotic lies precisely in the stories of lost incest that it makes possible, just out of conscious view. The overlay of careful Christian moralism is like the *Avis* of *Manon Lescaut*, a way of making an example of the protagonists and disguising a more reprehensible thrill.

Local colour is always a form of colonialism. Here, it allows the critique to coexist with enjoyment of the spectacle of incest heroically resisted, and also with another fantasy, no less pervasive for being less explicitly stressed. This is the myth of maternity as observed with a certain envy and fascination by a son; it appears in many forms, but I have room only for brief examples. The captured Chactas muses: "'man comes forth from your bosom to hang upon your breast and your lips; you know the magic words that quiet all pain. This is what she told me who brought me into the world and will never see me again"!' (pp. 48-9). Atala appears as mother before she is sister: she calls him "'my young friend'" even though she is six years younger, causes him to forget 'my country and my mother' (p. 57) and to fall back 'suddenly into a kind of infancy'; later when she comes to release him, she appears like a mother to a woken child, as 'a great white figure bending over me' (p. 75). Motherhood is a frequent marker of local colour, generally linked to violence or death: the grave of a child placed as the border of two tribes; the female elder's argument against torture that '"the cries of the prisoner . . . trouble the mothers' breast"' (p. 68); the girl wrestlers, erotically described, who 'glance blushing towards their mothers' (p. 71). But it is above all associated with the mother's own failure, especially in the end-frame's lengthy description of the ceremonial and lamenting of René's granddaughter over her dead child. It is her fault the infant died: exile made her milk dry up. Most deadly of all is Atala's mother, noble but excessive, whose mental blackmail of her daughter threatens the eternal damnation of both, and survives even Atala's suicide: '"to die so young, all at once, with my heart so full of life! . . . Do you think my mother will be content?"' (p. 128). Here the mother devours both the child's life and her desire, having satisfied her own. Christianity, while deploring her ignorance, essentially endorses her view: life is a vale of sorrows, even in the valley that the local inhabitants 'call the new Eden' (p. 30).

Naomi Schor suggests that a future feminist criticism might begin by substituting 'Chateaubriand's *Atala* [for] his *René* as the founding text of nineteenth-century French literature, for it is in the former that the enchaining of the female protagonist is explicitly staged, as Atala is transformed from the mobile liberatrix of the male captive with whom she falls in love to a suicide who dies ruing the vow her mother made forbidding her daughter from ever knowing jouissance'.[8] This is perhaps an over-optimistic view, for Atala dies accepting the patriarchal consolations of her mother's religion and entombed in its mythology of female hatred, and I think one can use *René* as a continuation of Atala's story rather than a wrongful substitute for it. As Delécluze noted in 1862: 'the public's admiration for *Atala* had slowed down and was diverted to *René*. This little drama has a basis in truth, the characters belong to our time and the events take place in our country, all almost indispensible conditions for pleasing the new tastes of 1819' (quoted by Letessier, p. xlvi). In other words, in bringing the *récit* back home, cutting down the local colour to almost nothing and pushing the theme of deadly maternity underground, Chateaubriand was able to make incest and its discontents a safe subject.

René too appears as part of the argument of the *Génie du christ-*

ianisme, exemplifying the dangers of premature vicarious experience: this state

> comes before the development of the great passions, when all the faculties, young, active, complete, but turned inward, are exercised only upon themselves, with neither aim nor object. The more a people advances in civilisation, the more this *vagueness* of the passions is increased; for a very sad thing happens: the large number of examples the young have before them, the multitude of books that tell of man and his sentiments, give them knowledge without experience. They are enlightened without having known pleasure [sans avoir joui]; desires remain, but no illusions. The imagination is rich, abundant and wondrous, existence is poor, dry and disenchanted. With a full heart, they inhabit an empty world; despite having used nothing, they are disabused of everything. (p. 170)

Secondhand experience, this argues, makes direct experience impossible: the 'wise child' knows it all. This state has affinities with those invoked by the terms 'mal/maladie du siècle' or 'Weltschmerz', but more perhaps with Hofmannsthal's term 'Praeexistenz' (preexistence), which combines precocity with a suicidal sense of pastness.[9] Over-civilisation is stressed by both authors: the young mind is as far as possible from 'primitive nature', fallen into the opposite extreme to Atala, an inability to feel properly because knowledge has preempted desire. Don Quixote and Emma Bovary retain their belief in the object that fits the word – but they are mad or foolish. The wisdom of René is his doom.

René, as his author seems to conceive him, is *homo Derrideanus:* there is no place of originary presence. His quest is a futile search for a stable site of origin where he will not already find himself written and foreknown. He wants to be a chicken without an egg. But we all know that a chicken is an egg's way of making another egg. The infinite unstoppable regress of models is perhaps always a fantasy of total femaleness: for the only possible asexual transmission (in the perfect mirroring of the clone) is the chain of mothers and daughters of which a large proportion of living species consists.

It is not easy to be quite sure who the intended reader of *René* is: presumably not the dutiful pupil implied by the 'examples' of Des Grieux or Atala, since it is by being such a reader that René has come to suffer 'the vagueness of the passions'. The critique of his state of mind is certainly present in the text, though appended in the speech of Père Souël rather than integrated, a 'tacked-on morality'.[10] René is the first of many heroes who are presented as innocent victims of themselves. But the text does little to endorse the prefatory critique in the author's voice, and renders very weak the attack by Père Souël which follows the narrative, since both carefully step away from the crucial issues of incest, desire and longing for the mother.[11] In René's Narcissus, we find the first and most concise instance of the search for a reflected, lovable self in the lost mother's body.

The frame-narrative opens in the third person and *in medias res:* we are perhaps expected to be familiar with the massive *Les Natchez* (completed around 1798 but published only in 1826), in which René arrives in Louisiana, is adopted by Chactas, eventually hears *Atala* and later tells his own story. For long years, 'savage among the savages' (p. 181) he spends his time with the East-West patriarchate of gentle Chactas and the severe Père Souël, but is unwilling to talk about himself. Then he hears word of his sister's death, seats his audience comfortably and begins his 'deplorable confession' (*Natchez*, p. 400).[12]

'I cost my mother her life when I came into the world; I was pulled forth [tiré] from her bosom with iron. I had a brother whom my father favoured because he saw in him his elder son. As for me, handed over early to strangers, I was raised far away from my father's house' (p. 185). The relation to the father outlined here is one that recurs more or less exactly in all our texts. Romantic heroes, like those of many fairytales and other myths, are in the vulnerable position of the non-inheriting son who fails visibly to be the father's legitimate firstborn double, entitled to his name. This is never a disadvantage without being also a kind of election: Julien Sorel's brutish father and brothers render him a kind of changeling, Fabrice del Dongo and Bernard Profitendieu are the happy bastards of their unloveable and ridiculously-named fathers. The bastardy of the Romantic hero performs a kind of cuckoldry on patriarchy and guarantees his specialness – let's not forget that Jesus is the best-known and most-endorsed of such heroes. Essentially these texts reproduce the childhood fantasy that Freud calls the 'family romance', once and literally for the protagonist, doubly for the author who adopts the genre of fictional autobiography in order to make free with the same obsession.[13]

But while the *récit*'s rewriting of the father-child relation appears to be a casting-off of the patrilinear bond, it is of course nothing of the kind. It redoubles the significance of patriarchy, the rule of male authority, by coopting it; the narrator-son takes for himself the imaginative job of conjuring father- and brother-doubles, including and most importantly the fictional hearer/s and the implied reader. This use of doubles is, as I have argued elsewhere, not an instance of the Lacanian *imaginaire* but a direct engagement with the conditions of the *symbolique*. The confessional *récit* is situated at the point of transition between these two positions, where the boy-child is battling to get in to the order of the fathers on his own (creative) conditions, and – which is of more interest to my argument – battling with the mother, both to lose and to capture her for good.

'I cost my mother her life . . .I was pulled forth from her bosom with iron . . . handed over early to strangers': René's moment of origin is the mutual murder of birth. The torture implied by the caesarian or forceps delivery is clearly inflicted on both partners in the birth, though the mother alone dies; and her dying is a further offence to the child, for she abandons him just when he needs her for everything. The myth of maternity as failed nurturance reappears in these crucial opening lines. No amount of romantic bastardy will ever compensate the hero for the involuntary loss of the mother, in which his first outraged assumption of guilt resides – for he has killed her, and she has avenged herself by his unjustified life. Guilt and anger are forever inseparable and tied to the image of the mother.

We shall find that many (almost all) of the authors of these texts had mothers who survived their births; Chateaubriand's mother died when her son was thirty 'as a result of maltreatment in the dungeons [of the Terror]' (*Atala*, p. 4). The death of the mother becomes, in each of these writers' work, the injury for which there is no sufficient punishment, even if it has not in reality occurred; it must be repeated like a *fort-da* in which we site both the symptom of the death instinct and the origin of language.[14]

The author's utterance, then, is generated by a phantasy of the death of the mother. Let's reverse the Lacanian hierarchy by suggesting that, whereas doubling is a matter of the world of the father, language and its utterance of desire belong to the quarrel with the mother. We have seen this in the *femme fatale* narratives, where Manon and Carmen preside over language; in these more directly oedipal texts, the whole enterprise is born as language out of the need to re/enact a coincident moment of separation and origin. Origin as separation: 'the vagueness of the passions'? Not exactly –

for there *is* such a thing as the mother's body, if the male protagonist can find a way to admit it. This is his quest.

The boy René has a mixed, unstable character. He spends the autumns at the estate where, 'timid and constrained before my father' (p. 186), he is blissfully happy with his elder sister Amélie. They share tastes and interests, and wander freely around the edenic landscape, kicking leaves or repeating melancholic poetry. These 'innocent pastimes' (p. 187) belong to a rather more advanced age than one might expect: René is around sixteen years old when he indulges in them.[15] Thus already at 'the dawn of life' (p. 188), René is looking back to a recollection of 'my earliest infancy'. This is both an endorsement of the prefatory critique and also a clue that all his recollections will be screen memories, the displacement of something earlier.

As in many of my other texts, a second death serves the narrator as a screen for the mother's; when René's loveless father suddenly dies, we are told: 'I learned to know death upon the lips of him who had given me life. The impression it made on me was great: I feel it still' (p. 189). A nice ambivalence is given in the words 'in a state of sublime pain that approached joy, I longed for the day when I would go and join the spirit of my father', for 'pain' and 'joy' are the two terms used a moment earlier to describe the emotions of an imagined mother on giving birth; René disposes of his father and mother together under this myth of the power of the imagination to conjure other, surviving lives.

Amélie and René are forced to leave home by their brother's inheritance. René is *disponible* and cannot decide on a career; 'Amélie spoke often to me of the happiness of the religious life; she said I was the only tie that kept her in the secular world, her eyes gazing sadly upon me' (p. 191). Here begins the 'secret' of René's text, the enigmatic motive attributed to the sister, not so much through her speech as in the mirror she holds up to him. The sadness in her eyes is implicitly in excess of the reciprocal 'melancholy' they have hitherto shared: in the very expression of intense loyalty, she is transgressing the bounds of sisterhood.

René decides to travel. 'I bade my sister farewell; she clasped me in her arms with an impulse that resembled joy, as if she were glad to part from me; I could not help reflecting bitterly on the brevity of human friendship' (p. 193). Thus, like Des Grieux, he misreads her ambivalence as betrayal. His famous travels take him in six pages over the whole surface of the globe, reaping disillusion wherever he goes. Classical and modern worlds, politics and culture are all sewn up. Two moments stand out, apportioning the worldscape into images of the father's and mother's body; the first when 'occasionally a tall column stood alone in a desert, just as a great thought arises, now and again, in a soul wasted by time and misfortune' (p. 194); the second at the mouth of Mt. Etna where René stops and weeps. A volcano set in the middle of an island, it becomes the uncanny object of a half-unwilling gaze: 'while to one side my eye perceived [the landscape laid out like a map], to the other it plunged into the crater of Etna, and I discovered its blazing entrails amongst the gusts of a black vapour' (p. 200). Not until Sartre's description of opening the books in his grandfather's library do we have a more seething metaphor for the boy's traumatic view of the mother's genital. The narrator hastens to recall his interlocutors with a philosophical metaphor – 'a young man full of passion, seated on the mouth of a volcano . . . thus, all my life, I have had before my eyes a creation at once massive and imperceptible, and an abyss wide open at my side' (pp. 200-1) – but the harm is done. Able to look out with one eye and down with the other, he is also capable of sitting next to and on top of the volcano at the same time.[16] Unlike the dull admiration of the phallus in sublime isolation in a desert, this vision is full of the central ambiguity of the text: the horror and fascination of the Narcissistic search for self through maternal death.

René returns to France and discovers that his sister 'inexplicably' (p. 204) left Paris a few days before his arrival; she writes to dissuade him from joining her. Again he leaps to condemn her for a failure of friendship. He looks for an object of passion, but the city, religion and nature all prove empty. Asking himself what it is he desires, he perceives a kind of overweening and yet shapeless innocence of demand that refuses to phrase itself into a purpose: this is the self seen in the pool. Objectless desire is the 'disease' of Romanticism. Typically, René describes himself as the vague unslaked seeker in a world too narrow for him: he complains of 'this ardour of desire that follows me everywhere' and of being 'pursued' by the instinctive search for an unknown and infinite object. Desire thus stands metonymically displaced outside the self, as close as Etna but a pace behind. That is the position of the sister.

Sexuality however is shown as an arbitrary effect of solitude:

I was overwhelmed by a superabundance of life. Sometimes I would blush suddenly, feeling a substance flowing in/into my heart that was like the streams of a burning lava; sometimes I gave involuntary cries, and the night was as troubled by my dreams as by my wakefulness. I needed something to fill the abyss of my existence; I would go down into the valley, I would rise up into the mountain, calling with all the strength of my desires upon the ideal object of a future passion; I embraced her in the winds, I seemed to hear her in the groaning of the river; everything became this imaginary phantom, from the stars in the skies to the very principle of life in the universe. (pp. 209-10)

This passage is among the most symptomatic of the Narcissistic text. First, in its scale: the rhetorical embrace of valleys and mountains repeats the search 'through the whole world' for an impossible object of desire; secondly because the Romantic image of Nature as the ungraspable body of the mother is very visible here. Thirdly because the way desire is presented, with the stress on isolation and objectless-ness, evokes a masturbatory phantasy too picky to admit an act of touching: thus the senses are disincarnated, the cries just occur, like the blushes, in a world without situation. But fourthly (and I think there is no contradiction), the passage suggests that all these elements unite in a phantasy of *being* the mother's body: the desired embrace of the landscape is a deferred self-touching, in which the boy imagines himself as a hole to be filled and senses a hot lava not issuing from him (as the Etna image might have suggested) but flowing in/into him. The displaced blushes, cries and groans suggest nothing so much as a lady in a soft porn movie performing for the unseen audience of the male fantasy gaze. Everything follows from the crucial absence of object: as for Narcissus, there is no other and there is nothing but other.

'Possessed by the demon of my heart' (p. 214), René begins to fantasise a kind of gestation: 'it seemed as if life were being reduplicated deep inside my heart . . . O God! if you had given me a woman to answer my desires; if you had only brought me, as you brought our first father, an Eve drawn [tirée] out of myself' (p. 215). The edenic incest-image reappears here in similar terms to that of Aubry, but with an added component: René will give birth to his sibling wife in an unfatal repetition of his own drawing-forth which will allow him to replace, punish and embrace his mother all at the same time. The incest phantasy is a dream of repeating that mortal birth as, this time, the active (maternal) partner.

'A secret languor took hold of my body': what grows inside him is a secret. He resolves suicide and writes a letter to Amélie from which her sensitivity is certain to piece out what he carefully presents between the lines. She calls him home. Her maternal role is stressed in several ways: each swears to the other that therir unique affection has its roots in childhood; she chides him tenderly; like Atala's mother, she makes him swear that he will obey her and stay alive. Above all, it is her look that makes her the mother: 'Amélie gazed at me with compassion and love, and covered my brow with her kisses; she was almost a mother, she was something more tender . . . I yielded to her authority' (p. 218).

The hero is satisfied; only the narrator interposes premonitions here. But this is the point at which Amélie begins to die. The mirror is too good;[17] reciprocation is not allowed to be mutuality: 'Amélie was losing the calm and the health that she had begun to restore to me' (p. 219). For in this myth, the mother must die if the son lives; René's death-wish is transferred to his sister in the form of desire. She loses weight, is alarmed by everything, picking up his inconsistencies along with his involuntary sighs, his trails through nature, and above all his secret. She becomes enigmatic. 'In vain I tried to discover her secret. When I questioned her, clasping her in my arms, she told me with a smile that she was like me, she did not know what the matter was [elle ne savait pas ce qu'elle avait]' (p. 220). In becoming like him, she too does not know what she 'has', for she now has nothing, she has entered the objectless state.

It is quite clear here that Amélie has relieved René of his demon, taking the host into her body. In the end, she departs, leaving a note that he will fail to understand. She claims she is leaving to fulfil a longstanding wish to join a convent; he must learn to be happy without her, either by taking up the monastic life too or by marrying:

> And what woman would not long to make you happy? The ardour of your soul, the beauty of your genius, your noble, passionate manner, that proud and tender look, all these would combine to assure you of her love and fidelity. Ah, with what bliss would she not clasp you in her arms and press you to her heart! How all her looks, all her thoughts would hang upon you to preempt your least troubles! She would be nothing but love, nothing but innocence before you; you would feel you had recovered a sister.
> . . . Dearest companion of my childhood, shall I never see you again?

Scarcely older than you, I rocked you in your cradle; often we slept side by side. Ah, if only the same grave could hold us both one day! But no: I shall sleep alone beneath the icy marble of the resting-place of those girls who have never loved.

I do not know if you will be able to read these lines half-erased by my tears (pp. 222-3)

He cannot. These and other clues – 'I stole from your house like a guilty thing' (p. 221), 'beloved, too beloved René' (p. 224) – should make her 'secret' clear, but for René it is illegible; he simply registers abandonment and cries aloud like Des Grieux that she is ungrateful and he would never have treated her thus. In blaming the failure of mirroring on her, he misses not only her fantasy of incestuous wife-hood but also the more dangerous echoes of the mother's role: 'heaven is my witness . . . that I would give my life a thousand times to spare you an instant of suffering' (p. 221). As this acknowledges, the mother can neither live with him nor coexist with him in death.

The letter is what remains of the woman's direct voice, and the man uses it as a mirror in two main ways. First as offering him a multiple portrait: the happy adult who finds in marriage or the cloister a companionship Amélie's cold future must lack; the adorable brother/lover whose attributes are so flatteringly listed; the unique genius for whom the world is inadequate; or the youth who might try 'to resemble ordinary people a little more and suffer a little less' (p. 222). In each of these images, what Amélie is expressing above all is her own gaze, the direction of her desire (which at the same time she must disavow: 'those girls who have never loved'). It is a mirror in a second and more problematic way: Amélie's expression of passionate desire actually replicates his own: she has escaped 'like a guilty thing' because she knows he would have begged her to stay. His 'noble, passionate manner' and 'proud and tender look' are both manifestations of his desire for her, in which she has read the danger of mutuality. The repeated images of the sister/mother's embrace expect to be recognised: it is a seduction and an accusation as well as a farewell.

René goes to the convent to make a last attempt to penetrate her secret before she makes her vows. On the way, he pays a visit to the lost Eden of the family estate, and entering its halls from the long avenue is like a journey into the mother's body and the past; as he hovers at the threshold he learns that a few days before him Amélie came here and fainted away, unable to make the symbolic entry.

The scene at the convent is justly famous. It is full of scarcely disguised incestuous Romantic agony, much of which is provided by the Catholic ceremony, in which the girl is 'married' to her chastity, disrobed and her hair cut off. René is asked to act the role of father – she must be 'given away' – this, Amélie hopes, will bring her peace of mind. Her brother finds this cold and resolves to ruin the 'sacrifice', possibly by stabbing himself in the church. Again, her repose is seen as a closed whole that he must sado-masochistically invade. Amélie appears, dazzlingly costumed and shining with 'the glorious suffering of the saint' (p. 231). She nearly swoons as she hears his step; his fury arising again, she quells him with a glance; he holds out the scissors that cut off her superb hair. In her simple robe, veil symbolic of virginity and with her 'shorn head' (p. 232), the narrator declares: 'never had she seemed so lovely to me'.

After the marriage comes the funeral: to pronounce her vows, the girl first has to pass 'through the grave'. René, witness to this avatar of the mother's effigy as he was to the last, kneels by the coffin in which she is placed, and there he hears the fatal words: '"merciful God, grant that I may never rise up again out of this funerary bed, and heap your blessings upon a brother who has never shared [partagé] my criminal passion!"' (p. 233) For Amélie, this is the logical culmination of her assumption of the role of the mother: René's continued life depends on her death. But there is also a kind of threat. *Is* he 'a brother who never shared her criminal passion'? Surely she knows he is not. He can only be blessed if the mirror is broken, if at last Amélie becomes the mother's double only, and not his reflection.

In a sense he is right: Amélie is, like the mother, abandoning him as a punishment. He both has and has not shared her passion; above all, he has used her as a mirror but refused to be hers, just as he has failed to read her though she could always read him.

'At these words from the coffin', he flings himself on her for a last embrace, faints, is carried away and 'the sacrifice was consummated'. And then suddenly we find a new René; noting that it is easier to recover from a personal disaster than to know that one has been 'the involuntary cause of another's suffering' (p. 234), he skips the issue of guilt, both hers and his own, because all is wonderfully resolved. Everything Amélie ever did was caused by him. He weeps, relieved he says to be suffering from 'a pain that [is] not imaginary', but rather more perhaps because in the sister he now recognises, intention and significance are happily one: she *means* him. By her very withdrawal, her stability as mirror is now guaranteed; he has what he wants – a grief that exactly fits his desire, 'an occupation that filled all my moments' (p. 235). Aloud, he expresses this as the relief at finally finding an object of feeling – 'my passions, so long indeterminate, flung themselves violently at this prey' (p. 234) – but the sadism of the image is not fortuitous.

For, along with the gratification, the guilt remains, and perhaps it is rooted in the knowledge that, after all, her words in the coffin were ambiguous. Meaning him, she cannot at the same time mean the idealised brother who did not reciprocate and the desired brother who did. If he is to be mirrored, he must also admit he has 'partagé' that feeling: sharing, he will be split.

Amélie survives to suffer a while longer, and René, after prowling around her convent, sets sail for America. He leaves in rather good spirits: 'my very grief, by its extraordinary nature, brought with it its own remedy: one gets pleasure from something exceptional, even if it is a misfortune. I came *almost* to hope that my sister would in her turn become less unhappy' (p. 237, italics mine). He does not quite want her less miserable, because her misery supplies his guilt, and his guilt is the source of his pride.

The sea, on which he dwells lyrically at this point, suggests the sister/mother both metonymically (the convent is by the ocean, she must pray for sea-travellers like him) and metaphorically ('O Amélie, tempestuous as the ocean' (p. 239)); in embarking on it, he crosses beyond her to a world where, on arriving, he finds a father. The narrative ends with the narrator throwing himself into Chactas's arms, a sign of Amélie's replacement, the entry into the symbolic through language.

This is not quite so easy. In the closing frame, Chactas – for René is his double – returns his embrace. But Père Souël gives René the dressing-down that most readers feel he has long had coming, criticising his gratuitous self-centredness and vanity. In effect what René must do to enter the symbolic is what Des Grieux did before him: return to France and speak to its patriarchate. For all the comradeship and bravery in *Les Natchez*, this isn't really a man's world: local colour is never after all the real thing. René is berated by Souël in exactly the terms of the Preface: they are meant to be the true test that he must fail. For the implied author must retain his seriousness and go some length to counterbalance the monologic voice of the foregoing narrative, but the protagonist, to be a real Romantic hero, must be unable to learn from adult wisdom. Both Souël's and the author's words go past their goal, not least because René, though he has not got any wiser, is no longer an example of 'the vagueness of the passions': he has an object now, the incestuous passion of Amélie. This is the burden he carefully carries in his knapsack, wrapped up as another dreadful secret.

And what about Amélie? She has been his *femme fatale*, carrier of his badness, has suffered as she had to and died in her convent, so that he may tell his tale. But she is not quite buried; as Souël observes – 'your sister has expiated her sin; but, to be quite frank with you, I fear that, by a horrible justice, this confession from the grave may have troubled your soul in its turn' (p. 243) – her voice is still echoing.

Although *Adolphe* (1816) is one of the earlier confessional *récits* and has caused at least one critic to identify a Romantic 'type' with its protagonist, in certain fundamental ways it steps out of its moment and seems strikingly modern. Unlike René, d'Albert or Dominique, Adolphe does not see himself as suffering from an excess of desire without a fit object, but – since infancy apparently – from lack of desire, against which his impassioned quest for Ellénore is only a momentary respite. Separation ('freedom') is his problem. He is, in many ways, an existential rather than a Romantic hero.

In this he resembles Nietzsche's Hamlet, who fails to act not because there is no fit goal for his extraordinary powers, nor by 'that cheap wisdom of Jack the Dreamer who reflects too much and, as it were, from an excess of possibilities does not get around to action',[18] but because he has insight:

> the Dionysian man resembles Hamlet: both have once looked truly into the essence of things, they have *gained knowledge*, and nausea inhibits action; for their action could not change anything in the external nature of things . . . Knowledge kills action . . . Not reflection, no – true knowledge, an insight into the horrible truth, outweighs any motive for action, both in Hamlet and in the Dionysian man.
>
> Now no comfort avails any more . . . Conscious of the truth he has once seen, man now sees everywhere only the horror or absurdity of existence; now he understands what is symbolic in Ophelia's fate; now he understands the wisdom of the sylvan god, Silenus: he is nauseated.

'An insight into the horrible truth' which makes him 'understand what is symbolic in Ophelia's fate' is, surely, the glimpse of himself that Narcissus finds in the mirror of the mother's genital. The 'Dionysian man', like Faust, has been down to 'the mothers', and after that encounter no 'eternal feminine' will be able to draw him up to salvation.[19] He is, as Sartre will repeat about sixty years later, suffering from nausea.

The unspoken of this text in which 'I never acted out of calculation and . . . was always guided by true and natural feelings'[20] is not a lie but something the confessing narrator (like an analysand) genuinely seems to have forgotten: the death of the mother for which the whole struggle with Ellénore is a transferential screen. We learn little of Adolphe's infancy; he begins his narrative with the awkwardness of his relationship with his father. Only once do we glimpse a memory already tinged by the 'family romance'. Here the fantasy of an ideal fiancée is integrated into a purely paternal landscape, 'the ancient castle where I lived with my father, the surrounding woods, the river that flowed at the foot of its walls, the mountains that bordered its horizon' (p. 105). By disrupting this, Ellénore stands for the lost mother repressed from this Nature. This fiancée is the original Amélie, the Manon promised by Des Grieux's father, who will be just like her only faithful; it is left to Ellénore to represent the inadmissible 'horror' of incest and separation.

Of the books we have looked at so far, this is the most autobiographical – not in precise details, necessarily, (though this is the first of several whose authors avowed privately that they would tell 'our story')[21] but in the urgency of the author's irritation with strong and dominant mistresses, especially Madame de Staël. Ellénore is, of course, a composite, so designed that she brings together the incompatible social humiliations of one, fiery abuse of another, simple sweetness of a third; she is Everywoman, the maternal target impossible to miss. Constant's mother did die days after giving birth to him; Adolphe, it seems, never had one.[22]

In the author's Prefaces to the second and third editions, we already see the mirror in operation. In it, women's introspective existence is sympathetically described. But Constant himself (for whom 'order in his emotional life governed the order in his creative life' (p. xlvi)) and especially Adolphe have, precisely, no distraction or occupation other than their dependent relationship with a partner, no position at the centre of a patriarchal order like 'my father's ancient castle' in the carefully circumscribing landscape. Adolphe has that very confusion between 'the need for support and the need for love' (p. 6) that is defined as the prerogative of idle women. In other words, it is the failure of the symbolic order imperialistically to centre the world of this text, in which experience is male-dominated as far back as infancy, that makes Adolphe the lost soul he is, forever carrying the image of the mother around with him as a pretext for his own weaknesses.

The author takes the familiar position of wise father, berating both a society that corrupts its young men with false levity and (in the latter Preface) the male readers who have flattered themselves by identifying with Adolphe's position as victim of a woman's excessive love. This final denial is there, of course, to absolve Adolphe (and the author) from any possible charge of similar vanity. But how can we do this? What do we know of the real nature of Ellénore's dependence? Because of the image of her 'sacredness', very little.

It is a premise of *Adolphe* that Ellénore's behaviour might be wild and inconsistent but her feeling is something uncomplicated: she loves. The complexity of Adolphe depends on the simplicity of Ellénore. Bizarrely allied with actions and speech that show her to be tormented, humiliated and yet insurmountably powerful, her soul is defined as simple and pure.[23] She is holy because she devotes herself to an object that, if unwillingly, answers her desire exactly as it is conceived. She is unhappy but not *hingeworfen;* that is what he is. Whatever demands or insults she might throw at him, he will need her insatiably because of this image of himself that he sees in her mirror: a creature of infinite moral complexity.

The text proper begins with the account of the frame-narrator; he describes Adolphe as he met him in an Italian inn. His servant does not even know his name. When he falls ill (and is devotedly nursed by the frame-narrator) he chooses the doctor he thinks the least likely to cure him. Thus we meet a protagonist who is drained, hopeless, a zombie, like the Des Grieux or the Don José who 'died' with their mistresses. The manuscript that follows is found in a box; addressed to no-one, it is reproduced by the 'editor' when he is confident it can no longer do any harm.

Adolphe begins the tale of his life at the age of twenty-two, encouraged by his father to travel around Europe before settling down to replace his father as 'minister to the Elector of ***' (p. 19). Like Des Grieux, he has always been accounted a boy of promise: 'I had lived a very dissolute life but by dint of bouts of fairly diligent work, I had obtained successes that distinguished me from my fellow students and made me the object of my father's probably much exaggerated hopes'. Adolphe's father treats him both indulgently and with apparently coldness: 'his behaviour was noble and generous rather than affectionate' (p. 20). They cannot talk to each other, both too shy (as the narrator now understands) to express their mutual feelings. The boy is full of youthful passion, the father is ironic, 'a cold, caustic observer, who would begin a conversation with a pitying smile but soon lose patience and bring it to a premature end'.

Adolphe's father is, with the difference of age, an exact double. Only the son's 'agitation' divides them, and that is simply an effect of his youth. Irony, coldness *and pity* are features that will characterise the young man's future behaviour. The narrator insists on the profound sensitivity they share but cannot express to each other. Unable to converse, they communicate mediately, by letter. Adolphe thinks of himself as a closed, independent unit, making decisions on his own for 'when I have to choose between two alternatives the human face disturbs me and my instinctive reaction is to run away and deliberate in peace' (p. 22). Yet even alone, he is not whole: 'although I was interested in nothing but myself, I found myself very uninteresting' – at the centre of the fruit, there is nothing. He is, in other words, a motherless child. Thrown straight into a ternary relationship with a double so close as to seem the exact opposite, he has no experience of duality, still less of partnership. He does not even talk to himself. Like the René of 'the vagueness of the passions', he has known writing but no speech.

The experience of death appears as a screen-memory, the death of an elderly woman friend when Adolphe is seventeen. This woman (the likely model for whom, Madame de Charrière, died when Constant was in his late thirties) is most specifically neither an Ellénore nor a mother: her influence consists in the power of her mind which, stifled by a frustrating society, is her only resource and consolation. They talk about everything, especially the omnipresence of mortality, and then 'I saw death strike her down before my eyes' (p. 23). To this shock is attributed 'a feeling of the uncertainty of fate and a vague pensiveness which never left me'. An echo of the suppressed death of the mother and an anticipation of the death of Ellénore, it convinces the boy 'that no aim was worth taking any real trouble over'; disabling the very independence of action that he attributes to his father's influence, it reveals its hollow interior.[24]

In the small town of D***, Adolphe joins court society and gains a reputation for sarcasm and aloofness. An object of scrutiny, he is either taciturn or speaks for no reason: 'I spoke because I felt like talking, not out of an impulse to confide' (p. 25). Other people judge him harshly, but no more harshly than he judges them. Adolphe is negatively *disponible:* 'distracted, indifferent, bored, . . . I divided my time between studies I never kept up for long, plans I did not carry out and pleasures in which I had no real interest' (p. 29). It is important to note here, just before he meets Ellénore, that his later view of life without her as being full, positive and potential is a piece of self-deception: even in boyhood Adolphe has never had the Baudelairean confidence that 'l'univers est égal à son vaste appétit';[25] rather, his inner emptiness before he loves anticipates his final state after the beloved's death. His existence is already posthumous. Being with Ellénore is, as she rightly perceives, the only way for Adolphe to live.

He decides to break the boredom by falling in love as he has seen a friend do. In a sense, there is a genuine desire – 'a fresh need stirred in the depths of my heart' (p. 30) – but it is indeterminate and conceived in terms inherited from his cynical father, who has handed down the men's-talk of '"*It does them so little harm and gives us so much pleasure!*"' (p. 31). It is the purpose of the narrative to prove father and his sources wrong: Ellénore will suffer unto death and Adolphe will find everything except pleasure.

The quest for a love-object worthy of him is soon answered in the person of the mistress of Count P*** and mother of his two children. Like Lotte, Madeleine or Alissa, Ellénore is first glimpsed in a coherent familial context; indeed it is in preferring Adolphe to her children, rather than simply her lover or father, that Ellénore shows the extent of her attachment.[26] Though wellborn, she is now, like Manon and Carmen, declassed by sex; the protagonist, we are expected to understand, can no more marry her than René could marry Amélie. But she is a pattern of feminine qualities: 'beauty . . . a distinguished character . . . pride . . . devotion . . . zeal . . . purity . . . disinterestedness . . . activity . . . courage . . . reason . . . sacrifices of every kind' (pp. 32-3). These have added up to ten years of wifely

loyalty to her 'protector' who, like her own father, has suffered pros-
cription and temporary bankruptcy; she in fact has been largely
instrumental in restoring his fortunes.

Ellénore is a moral paragon, but strangely torn: society damns her
and she rebels against its fixity: 'perpetually at war with her destiny'
(p. 34), she is the hysteric refusing to concede to the consequences
of anatomy. A hysteric rather than a regular rebel – 'Ellénore was
not especially intelligent' (p. 33) – for she cannot help reproducing
the social estimate of her worthlessness; thus 'all her prejudices were
contrary to her own interests' (p. 34). By an understandable attachment to the conventions that exclude her, no wife could be more
devoted, no prude more critical of loose morals, no martinet more
strict with her children. It is perhaps this alienation that provokes
Adolphe's initial desire: her struggle gives her a certain tragedy, she
knows what she is fighting against. While he has no self to oppose
or contort, she is nothing but her situation.

Adolphe is already empty before he meets Ellénore, and Ellénore
is unhappy and frustrated before she meets Adolphe, but in each
other they find the perpetuation and confirmation of what they are,
briefly hidden beneath a veil of mutual desire. In Ellénore we see a
rudimentary protest, 'a secret revolt' (p. 35), and an excess of feeling
that is expressed in contradictory moods. 'Often she was *pensive* and
taciturn; sometimes she *could not stop talking* . . . even in the midst of
the most general conversation she was never entirely calm. But by
that very token, something *passionate* [fougueux] in her manner made
her more exciting than she probably would have been naturally'
(italics mine). All the terms I have italicised here are ones applied
earlier by the narrator to the young hero: the 'vague pensiveness'
(p. 23), 'profound taciturnity' (p. 25) followed by impetuous speech,
and the agitation, tendency towards the 'fougueux' which distinguished him from his father (pp. 20-1). Thus he finds in Ellénore,
that 'magnificent tempest . . . offered to my gaze' (p. 36) a justified
and aestheticised image of what he thinks himself – captive, however,
in the socially circumscribed situation of her womanhood. The differences and similarities in what the narrator claims is an entirely
arbitrary choice are very exactly ranged to attract Adolphe to Ellénore
as a mirror.[27]

She is not merely the object of his gaze; Ellénore is, like Manon
and Carmen before her, multilingual. For all his patronising estimate

– 'she spoke several languages, imperfectly it is true but always with vivacity and sometimes with grace' (p. 36) – she is offering him a wholly new dyad: unlike the double he has in his father, she seems a mirror he can talk to.

This is never a true possibility. Speech in *Adolphe* is everywhere blighted; there is no duality. In his first attempts to communicate, he is silenced by shyness. Their earliest encounters are conducted entirely through the eyes, in a gaze that seems encouragingly mutual. In her salon, he watches her from a corner, observing her paleness, interpreting it as a confusion he is excited to share. At this stage, Adolphe is gratified to assume a reciprocation of signs. His obsession focuses (as will so many other protagonists' later) on a will to make her look at no one but him: 'I tried . . . every way to fix her attention upon me' (p. 45).

All Ellénore's often desperate attempts to escape this pursuit are in vain: gradually, by promises, a shared secret and finally a bout of childish jealousy, Adolphe forces her to admit that she loves him. Immediately he feels the sense of familiarity which will predominate in their relationship, especially long after he feels no further affection: 'love creates, as if by magic, a past in which it embeds us. Somehow it gives us the feeling that we have lived for years with a person who, just a while ago, was a complete stranger' (pp. 51-2). At last, the return of the repressed. In a second way we see here how little his choice was really arbitrary; the pair-bond that seems always to have been there is the one which, on birth, replaces the inside-outside of gestation: the neonate indeed sees this stranger's face for the first time but it has always known her. During a brief interim Adolphe plays the role that will later fall to Ellénore: shy, demanding, irritable, 'I complained, stormed, heaped reproaches on her' (p. 52), until she agrees to sleep with him. In the next sentence, the narrator warns: 'woe to the man who, in the first moments of a love-affair, does not believe this affair will last for ever!' (p. 56). Does this malediction fall on Adolphe? we are not told. All we learn is that he feels 'the charm of love' (p. 57) because it has given him a sense of power over other men, conceived as a dominating gaze. And she has acquired that 'element of sacredness' which will be her doom.

'Sacred' is extrapolated into 'sacrifice'. The sexual act between them is described nowhere in terms of pleasure or desire (so Proustian is this text) but is, immediately, the 'sacrifice she had made for my sake' (p. 58). Ellénore at once becomes demanding; Adolphe feels psychologically pursued. There is no space in nature but her need for him fills it. He is now the centre of the world. As for him, he is already chafing to rejoin the triadic system: 'Ellénore . . . was no longer an aim; she had become a tie' (p. 59). This pattern is set for the rest of their lives together: she is importunate, he is paranoiac; her death alone will release her from the definition of the hero's view of her, and then only to deliver her into the hands of the narrator. One loves, the other doesn't. There is nothing very unusual in this plot, except that the story is normally told from the point of view of the unrequited one, not the undesiring. What is extraordinary is the fact that Adolphe, who does not love Ellénore, is as tied to her as if he did. The rest of the text consists of his apparent wish to break free; by a series of twists and motives, he never succeeds. Separation is only consummated when Ellénore pines away and dies, by a kind of suicide that we will come to read as murder. It seems that he must manoeuvre her into leaving him because he cannot act upon his avowed wish to leave her.

The dyadic structure is a knot of mutually inflicted pain. Much is done to stop us allocating guilt; there seems no first cause. Each suffers by the other's fault – but who can blame Adolphe's coldness (which he fights so valiantly to suppress) or Ellénore's dependence (explained by her social maltreatment and her pure, devoted heart)? Nor is it seemingly the fault of the pair-bond itself that it brings no happiness and often little solidarity. The displacement of blame is a key issue, as it will be in *La Confession d'un enfant du siècle*, though in a different way. Musset's text lays blame centrifugally on everyone but the central couple; Constant's is based on a moral *perpetuum mobile* in which guilt is omnipresent but nowhere stable. Above all, Adolphe, who dutifully berates himself for Ellénore's suffering, is using guilt as a justifying principle – insofar as he is correct in blaming himself, he has a duty to expiate, insofar as he is zealously excessive in his scruples, he is a good and selfless chap. Excluded by this justificatory transaction (which is shared by hero and narrator), Ellénore is left out in the cold. Not until we see her letter – another undirected document, for she makes Adolphe swear he will burn it unread – do we understand how complex and selfconscious her feelings are.

Just as guilt has no place of stable origin here, so freedom (separation) has no instigator. Adolphe cannot leave the couple he claims so reluctantly to form; Ellénore apparently does not wish to separate, though it is she who makes all the moves, down to the 'ultimate sacrifice' of opting to die. This structure is modelled on the childbed death. Here the mother abandons the child to an unnurtured life; the child, in leaving her body, destroys her. This originary separation is rehearsed over and over in the confessional *récit*'s version of the *fort-da*. That Adolphe, after Ellénore's death, is a zombie testifies to this: like Des Grieux or Don José, he is as much murdered as murdering. Every mother is a *femme fatale*.

All this is already implicit at the point where Adolphe and Ellénore have just become lovers. The benignity of the desiring gaze is all gone; now already their mutuality is a visual sado-masochism. For what else is the famous 'pity' (shared, we are commonly assured, by the author) if not a version of sadism? Blanchot refers to the 'fascination' that the sight of suffering had for Constant;[28] one is reminded of Freud's insistence that he became a doctor for the sake of research and not to help people, since his sadistic impulse was not developed enough for that motive.[29]

The Count returns, Adolphe begs Ellénore to be more circumspect: she has so much to lose. She speaks directly for more or less the first time: "'one way or another ... you will leave soon enough; let us not preempt that moment; don't worry about me. Let's save a few days, a few hours; hours and days are all I ask. Some presentiment tells me, Adolphe, that I shall die in your arms'" (p. 61). This is Echo speaking: like Carmen she predicts what the narrator knows has happened. We know that death as separation permeates Adolphe's whole cast of mind. Now Ellénore, who has taken over the role of filling his mental universe, coopts this motif also. But whose volition will bring about her premature death – she is only thirty-two – she does not say.

Ellénore decides to leave the Count, annoyed at his strictures; Adolphe cannot dissuade her without insult. Two days later she has installed herself in rented rooms. "'I have broken off", she said; "I am entirely free'" (p. 68). But in interpreting her declaration as a brave and pathetic lie, the narrator strips her action and discourse of all autonomy:

> She tried every way to convince me that she would be happy, that she had made no sacrifice for my sake, that the decision she had taken suited her quite irrespective of me. She was visibly making a great effort and

did not believe half of what she was saying. So afraid was she of hearing me speak, her words were running away with her; she spun out her speech to put off the moment when my objections would plunge her back into despair. I could not find it in my heart to make any. I accepted her sacrifice, thanked her for it; told her it had made me happy; more, I assured her that I had always hoped an irrevocable decision would make it my duty to stay with her for ever; I attributed my own indecisiveness to a delicacy about consenting to a change that would ruin her. I had, in a word, no other thought than to dispel from her mind all trouble, all fear and regret, all uncertainty as to my feelings. As long as I was speaking, I had no motive beyond this and I was sincere in my promises (pp. 68-9)

Both their speeches are presented indirectly, but we see far more of his than hers: merely a nervous babble, her assertion of independence is predicated as untrustworthy. A careful reading shows that it is his facial expression that inhibits and confuses her: his visibility makes her 'visible'. In the narrator's hands her language becomes simply an effort to avoid hearing his. Like the traditional loquacious woman, however little she speaks it is too much, an irruption into the language space of men. When Adolphe replies, he tells soothing lies that, in one sense, serve him better than they do Ellénore: his indecision, her determination, gell into an act of kindness on his part. He removes from her all initiative and responsibility; like Amélie, who likewise made all the moves, she finds her intention proceeding from him. As her speech is coopted, made rhetoric, his intentionally rhetorical language becomes 'sincerity'. But this 'sincerity' ensures that we will see his utterance as something above accuracy and will miss the point that, precisely, she has given him what he craved.

Adolphe goes off to see his father, and he and Ellénore correspond; aware of his own battles with sincerity, he presumes her pathetic and deceived. One day, planning out loud a letter to break off with her, he finds the image of her reaction paralysing his 'dominated hand' (p. 78). Here the mediate paternal structure of writing is disrupted by the image of Ellénore as pitiful present reader; what 'dominates' his hand is the compulsion to speech, stronger than that to writing. In the image of Ellénore despairing there is something he undoubtedly wants. He sends an awkward plea for postponement and Ellénore arrives, angry and insulting. Her presence is not what he anticipated. 'She slandered my character. She drew such a picture of my despicable weakness that she made me even more disgusted with her than with myself' (pp. 79-80). His pity, that comfortable reaction formation, is slipping. Ellénore's anger here preempts Adolphe's guilt-mongering, showing him a reflection he does not want to see.

Then the patriarchy begins its end-game, moving familiarly in mysterious ways. His father announces that he has arranged for Ellénore to be thrown out of town. Adolphe immediately resolves to stand by her, pausing to blame his father for strengthening the tie. In restoring the poignant image of 'Ellénore persecuted', his father permits the interim of revolt that precedes the oedipal defeat, and at the same time, Adolphe's attachment to his mistress can seem noble, even gratifying: 'proud to defend her . . . if at this moment Ellénore had wanted to part from me, I should have died at her feet rather than let her go' (p. 82). Into this ternary idyll, the woman's truthful speech makes an ugly disruption: as he begs her to marry him, Ellénore accuses him of the pity he thinks he has surpassed. In thus speaking aloud 'these fateful words . . . a secret I wanted to forget' (p. 83), she restores the vicious circle wherein Adolphe's 'pity' and her unloveability are fixed and enclosed.

They run off and set up temporary home in Bohemia. Here the fathers urge on Adolphe the flattering image of a young man of talent and future whose place in the symbolic order awaits him. '"You are using up the best years of your youth to no purpose, and this loss can never be made good"' (p. 85), his father writes. Compared to Ellénore's face-to-face authority, patriarchy has the resources and confidence to use a long rein: 'the freedom he gave me served only to make me more impatient of the yoke I appeared to have taken up by choice'. Two further opportunities follow. First her former lover P*** offers her a regular income if she will leave 'the ungrateful, perfidious man who had come between them' (p. 87). She refuses, but Adolphe decides to force her hand by declaring he no longer loves her. He speaks without looking up; when he does he sees an automaton, immobile, expressionless, her skin cold, swaying on her feet. '"Leave me alone, go away, isn't that what you want?"' (p. 89) she cries, and faints. Appalled to see his conscious motive echoed, he revives her, swears eternal loyalty, and as (so he thinks) she is taken in by his lie and the balance restored, 'she was intoxicated by her own love, which she took to be ours . . . I found myself more committed than ever'. Once again, the failure to part is typed as Ellénore's fault: as directly as she offers him the truth, his lie is seen as her initiative. For deeper than the wish to leave her is the unconscious wish to see her love stand for theirs, and to site the mutual murder precisely in her maternal dominance.

The second offer comes from Ellénore's aged father in Poland; she refuses to go, even though both filial and maternal duties urge it, on the grounds that the sufferings inflicted on her by Adolphe are preoccupation enough. A bad daughter and a bad mother, she is assuring Adolphe (as Dominique will later long to be assured) that he is all the family she needs. He reads this as 'another sacrifice' (p. 93), a further burden on him; yet at the same time the familial bond justifies itself: 'the lengthy habit of being together, the many experiences we had shared . . . We were living, so to speak, on a sort of memory of the heart, strong enough to make the idea of separation painful, but too weak to make us happy together' (p. 94). At home Darby to her Joan, out of doors he is the rising young exec., if only he can cast her off. Ellénore is growing old alone, like the portrait of Dorian Gray.

The patriarchate has not abandoned the direct tack. In Poland, Adolphe's father has a surrogate, the baron de T***, whose task it is to seduce Adolphe away from his lady. Adolphe's status is embarrassing: now Ellénore is rich, as his father points out, he is her protégé, not she his.[30] To be a man, he must leave her. When he visits T***, the latter adopts the father's voice, uttering the sanctioned misogyny that a part of Adolphe longs to hear. He presents Ellénore as an ageing nag, Adolphe as brilliant, his present life as vegetation. Just one thing stands between the young man and success, 'and that obstacle is Ellénore' (p. 100).

This is a familiar view of Ellénore, but we must remember that Adolphe has never yet heard it reproduced in another's voice. It is combined with an image of himself that is not just flattering but specifically opens up all possibilities without demanding any choice. In this seductive image, he is invited to take all, step into the ternary structure by denying it, by-passing the 'not-all' of the obstacle-woman. A new pairing seems to be offered, at the simple oedipal price of abjuring the feminine.

Adolphe demurs by retorting that just to care for Ellénore, after all she has suffered at the hands of cruel society, would be career enough for him; in saying this he reveals how far he has gone in feminisation. But such an admission is intolerable, in balance with the seductive image offered him by T***: as soon as he is out of the house, he comes back to the vision of a future without Ellénore. In it he will enjoy both the dignity of patriarchy and its fatherly approval; the fantasy fiancée replaces the importunate mother within a landscape that is suddenly masculine, his 'fatherland' (p. 103), full of the creativity of memory, imagination, even abstract ideas. It is with reluctance and irritation that finally he goes home to Ellénore's house with the servant she has sent out after him: the men's-world of the mind is invaded by her.

At this point, Ellénore counteracts the father's double with one of her own and, like Manon, she loses more in the use of a surrogate than she could have hoped to gain. For just as, from T***, Adolphe heard his desired portrait spoken, so it is to this woman that he utters aloud the truth that he does not love Ellénore. Moved, she translates Adolphe's repetition of Ellénore's critical terms 'weakness' and 'hardness' into 'generosity' and 'misfortune', and holds up to him the most flattering mirror of all: like the idealised fiancée of his imagination, she belongs to the admiring men's world while retaining the female sex that makes Ellénore replaceable.

Ellénore makes another move: she tries to escape her isolation by starting a social life. She is, after all, only doing what he wants to do – and why not: she is beautiful, rich, an object of social interest. What success she gains is, however, difficult to perceive through Adolphe's grudging narrative. According to him she is embarrassing, humiliated, precipitous. 'How many mortifications she swallowed without revealing them to me!' (p. 115), he exclaims with remarkable second sight, 'how many times I blushed for her without finding the strength to tell her!' Here more than anywhere else we are given the image of Ellénore as 'pathetic old bag' which the whole text conspires to create. But Adolphe's is not the only view available to us: we also have that of the letter reproduced by the editor at the end of the text. While Adolphe tries to preempt it by showing how her friends misread their couple, seeing him as the interloper and her as the victim, the writer of this letter describes how he 'tried by my counsels to wrest the charming Ellénore, who deserved a gentler fate and a more faithful heart, away from the mischievous creature who, no less miserable than herself, dominated her by some sort of spell [charme], and was tearing her apart with his weakness' (p. 146). Here the mirroring of Adolphe – his sinister 'charme' overcoming her 'charming' character – is diagnosed without sympathy, and 'generosity' and 'misfortune' turn back into 'hardness' and 'weakness'.

Adolphe attributes Ellénore's supposedly clumsy socialising to his own power: 'in picking out these faults of Ellénore's, it is myself I accuse and condemn. One word from me would have calmed her; why did I not say that word?' (p. 115). However successful – she attracts friends, admirers, even suitors – her behaviour is deemed 'a false and deplorable strategy' (p. 118) to make him jealous, not worth getting angry about because it is really 'of my own making' (p. 119). There is, thus, nothing Ellénore can ever do that will constitute an act of her own, and no way that she can stop casting back a flattering image – except by stepping out of the looking-glass into death.

Stung at her friends' condemnation of him, Adolphe has words with Ellénore; the friends disappear and, isolated together, their sado-masochistic relationship becomes ever more defined:

> we no longer had even those brief moments of respite that seem to heal incurable wounds. The truth showed through everywhere; to make myself understood, I adopted the hardest, most pitiless terms. I would stop only when I saw Ellénore in tears, but her very tears as they fell like molten lava drop by drop upon my heart, making me scream with pain, could not induce me to recant. At such moments I saw her, more than once, rise up pale and prophetic, crying: 'Adolphe, you do not know the harm you are doing; one day you will realise it, you'll learn it from me, when you have driven me into the grave'. Wretched creature that I am! when she spoke like this why did I not fling myself into the grave before her? (p. 121)

Here, the narrator has reached the point of coopting her suffering into his own. Her disadvantage is weirdly turned about, so that her tears torture him yet cannot wring a lie from his lips. Ellénore's strength and autonomy, always bitterly opposed as female power, are here focused into the ultimate offence of her knowledge. The curious parenthesis 'to make myself understood' implies that he will not believe in Ellénore's knowledge of him; this justifies repeated verbal humiliations that are never enough. In return, with her version of 'they know not what they do', Ellénore effectively offers to call her murder suicide, as by her act she will. But she also warns that, like Echo, Amélie and Marceline, her death will let her finally speak and be heard. The narrator turns the prediction back to himself: why did he not preempt this, making himself the murdered one, the one with the last word? That both must perish he does not doubt – if he leaps to the grave it will be not 'instead of' her, but only 'before': the question is who will get there first.

In between these storms, Adolphe finds himself cosseted and admired at T***'s and it is not long before he has agreed that the latter shall write to his father saying he is breaking off with Ellénore. This again is the woman's fault: the last straw is a letter from her that arrives invading this patriarchal space, her writing irrupting incongruously into the place where she is spoken of. As soon as he has made his promise to T***, Adolphe, feeling free in advance, puts off the day of telling her. An insurmountable obstacle from without is, it seems, gently making a wedge between them. But he is wrong. The patriarchy has already specified the triad it requires: the dispensable third party is Ellénore. One night he hears an odd noise in the castle; in the morning he is told Ellénore has taken to her bed, gravely ill. A letter arrived, he learns, she read it and threw herself on her bed 'without uttering a word' (p. 132). She refuses to see him, 'with a kind of terror so violent that no-one dared disobey her', and appears to be dying: 'she could make out nothing around her. Every so often she cried out, repeated my name; then, appalled, she would make a movement with her hand as if to make them take away some object that was hateful to her' (pp. 132-3).

Ellénore cannot push Adolphe away. He goes straight into her room and reads two letters: one from T***, the other the one he sent T*** swearing he was about to leave her. She looks at him apparently without recognition, shudders at his voice – '"that is the voice that has hurt me"' (p. 133)[31] – and forbids him to say another '"cruel word"' (p. 134). With this scene, Ellénore emancipates herself at last from her role as Adolphe's mirror: both the looking and the speaking are now dictated by her. The double price is, first, her conceding to the only image she has left, that of purity – '"love was all my life; it could not be yours"' (p. 135) – and second, that she must quickly die. Like Manon and Carmen, she ends up speaking the language he desires from her; in return he perceives anew, as she leans like an old woman on his arm, her qualities of pride, energy, nobility and expressiveness that he has long since ignored. Her gaze appears to demand 'the life that I could no longer [?] give her' (p. 138) – the dying mother asking for birth?

Adolphe anticipates what will happen now: 'I had crushed the one who loved me . . . already I felt my isolation . . . I no longer lived in that atmosphere of love that she had spread around me . . . all nature seemed to be telling me that soon, for ever, I would cease to be loved' (p. 139). In this famous speech the narrator summarises in advance the grim pessimism of Sartre's being-for-others. Human bonds are based in bad faith; to be is to be seen; if my 'gaze gazed on' is imposs- ible to bear, yet without the other's look I may have no face at all; relationships are battles over who objectifies whom, and for how long. What Sartre does not say, but what the *récit* illustrates amply, is that the gaze we seek is always the effigy of the mother's earliest look which confirmed and created our separate, mirrored existence. Adolphe knows that the universe which has been overfilled with his paranoia will be emptied out completely – as it almost is now he can no longer speak to her – from the moment that he is no longer seen.

In her dying moments, Ellénore 'tried to weep, there were no tears left; she tried to speak, there was no more voice' (p. 142): as she no longer gives these forth, they cease to exist. After her death, exactly like Des Grieux and Don José, 'I remained for a long time motionless beside the lifeless Ellénore'.

Now that she has gone, the triadic structure is not waived but, on the contrary, is omnipresent. 'I felt the last link fall away, and a horrible reality interpose itself forever between her and me. How burdensome this freedom, once so ardently missed, now felt to me! ... Once all my actions had the aim of sparing pain or causing pleasure ... now no-one observed me ... no voice called me back when I went out ... I was a stranger to all the world' (pp. 142-3). Loss of the other makes every action insignificant. Nothing in the mediate world replaces what now seems a lost immediacy of meaning, a pre- sent speech. But this is the worst of Adolphe's delusions.

It is not by chance that the climactic end of *Adolphe* revolves entirely around letters, both as anchors of plot and as closing the central and frame-narratives. These mediate structures stress the impossibility of the dyad not only after Ellénore's death but also before it. The pair-bond of woman and man is blighted from the start by the forms of mediation that permeate this patriarchal universe. The unspoken of *Adolphe* – that the child is born of the mother – makes every encounter into mutual murder. Repressed out of discourse, the child- bed death is a phantasy whose logic marks every page.

In Ellénore's letter, written earlier but functioning as the narra- tive's last words, her voice echoes loud and clear. Nothing in the narrator's writing has expressed so acutely the effects of the paranoia whereby Adolphe has chased Ellénore out of the world. Here, Ellénore replaces the original 'prophecy' of '"I shall die in your arms"' (p. 61) with the recognition that she dies 'at your feet' (p. 144), abandoned and attacked. She diagnoses the cruelty disguised under his '"bizarre pity"'. But we also see how hopelessly she is trapped by the mirror: for all her insight, internalising the man's view of her, she reiterates the paranoid image of a world in which there is no space her desire has not filled: her negative reflection meets her everywhere. And if to Adolphe her gaze pursues him, for her his voice is omnipresent: the only way to obtain his silence and her invisibility is through suicide. Ellénore's death is a kind of anorexia: she takes in less and less of a nature filled with abhorrence of her. At the end of her letter, she fantasises her own absence in a displaced third-person: '"she will die, this Ellénore whom you cannot bear around you, whom you regard as an obstacle, for whose sake there is nowhere on earth you do not find tiresome"' (p. 145). But in doing this she is also arranging to outlive herself in an unseen but still perceived negative, against which his survival will be an undeath. Her prediction is also a curse.

That it comes true we know by the opening frame. In the closing pages, familiarly, the frame-narrator and his correspondent dispute over the nature of Adolphe's error. Was he pitiable or self-indulgent?[32] They end up agreeing that 'Adolphe was punished for his character by his character itself' (p. 150). We can leave others, but we cannot leave ourselves.

Whether by intentional irony or not, this misses the point. Adolphe has no self other than the image he invested in Ellénore, who died of it. His text reiterates the slow murder by which he forced a substitute mother to abandon him. Undirected, it makes no restored contract with the world of men; Adolphe has no occupation. The blighted dialogue goes on.

Chapter 4: *Mademoiselle de Maupin* and *La Confession d'un enfant du siècle*

'My soul is the enemy-sister of my body'
(Gautier)

Neither of the two texts analysed in this chapter exactly fits the formal definition of the *récit* and in neither does the female protagonist die. Both, published by their young authors in the 1830s, the heyday of French Romanticism, exemplify the male voice of that moment: a kind of innocence claiming both the blaséness of early corruption and the vulnerability of the child. The deformation of desire still brands the man but burns the woman. What they also share is a preoccupation with the surface, with masks and costumes, Gautier with the stress on what I shall call a 'horizontal' aesthetic, Musset with a moral obsession that both wants and fears to remove the outer veil.

In Gautier's major collection of poems, *Emaux et Camées*, we can find many of the motifs that inform *Mademoiselle de Maupin* (1835-6). In particular, it is full of the cultivation of the superficial,[1] of logical relationships that move horizontally, not vertically, from art to art, or among variations on a theme, or with tantalising instability between two poles: male and female, living and dead, flesh and fabric. The visible alone counts as beautiful. But what the visible signifies is – for all the invocation of the solidity of sculpture, the impalpable 'resistant block'[2] – something equivocal, maddeningly imprecise. D'Albert, in this as in much else, contradicts himself as to whether he likes the bold colour and strong form or rather the vagueness and uncertainty of the girlish boy or boyish girl he finds in Théodore/ Madeleine. Nervous where his author is (in verse at any rate) assertive, d'Albert becomes unhappy when the object of his desire proves of dubious gender. The poem 'Contralto' is much more positive; here a classical statue fascinates by its 'disquieting... accursed... multiple beauty' (pp. 30-31) because it is impossible to see whether it represents a man or a woman. The poem goes on to pour forth, verse by verse, a stream of comparisons: the voice of the contralto, the chatelaine and the page, two fluttering butterflies, Cinderella and the cricket, and a host of figures from Shakespeare, Rossini, Tasso,

Mozart and Byron – all variations on the theme of sexual ambiguity as the defining base of beauty.[3]

Desire is the leaven of poetry for Gautier, and it is no coincidence that Baudelaire dedicated *Les Fleurs du mal* to him, for the fetishistic, the scopophilic and the necrophiliac are just some of his own brilliantly-wrought 'flowers'. In 'le Poème de la femme' the woman takes up a series of poses; an image of the female body as text is exchanged first for 'this hymn of beauty' (p. 8), then for the sculpture and paintings that the woman mimes. The man who writes is 'the mirror that admires her'. The woman ends by mimicking the ecstasies of orgasm and dying; she leaves the humble poet, made apparently superfluous by this televisual narcissism, to pray on his knees by the tomb of her bed. In this poem the third-person voice attributes the will to be visible, the production of the text to the woman who is reading her body aloud; there is a reading, no avowed writing. Like much soft porn, this sets the terms of its genre as the woman's provocation by visibility: she is the speaking cunt which its owner cannot control. In 'Coquetterie posthume' the attribution of speech goes a step further into perversity: here the female speaker asks to be made up and dressed in her coffin in such a way as to provoke desire and remorse – is she pining away, or intending suicide? – in the unnamed 'him' who has abandoned her. We have to remind ourselves (as less necessarily in the earlier poem) that the text is written by a man: the male poet is imagining a woman so amorous that she will prepare a feast for the necrophiliac out of a mixture of vanity and wounded desire. The poem is brilliant in its symmetry and the seeming artlessness of its form; in each pair of stanzas, a fetish of Catholic ritual is replaced by an erotic bauble; by the end, the two have combined in the opal rosary blessed by the Pope in Rome. The speaker imagines herself, still active after death, telling this rosary:

> Je l'égrènerai dans la couche
> D'où nul encor ne s'est levé;
> Sa bouche en a dit sur ma bouche
> Chaque *Pater* et chaque *Ave* (p. 25)

> [I'll tell these beads in the bed
> From which no one has risen yet;
> His mouth has whispered on my mouth
> Every *Pater* and each *Ave*]

With the repetition of 'mouth', the opal beads become teeth, the prayer a kiss, and the sly union of patriarchal and matriarchal prayers an invitation to repeat past nights of passion with the overdressed corpse. Female narcissism is set up, in these poems, as a spectacle. The poet is not so much a voyeur as a scopophilic: he is not watching but looking, the aim is a *tableau vivant* just distinguishable from the real, dead thing.

In these erotic poems the females are both alive and sculpted. Women are posing even, or precisely, in their speech. The speaking of the woman is an assent to her display as aesthetic dish, she offers herself – or rather, the man conjures her as offered – as an exhibitionist. She poses as the generator of a poetry which immobilises her. Art is translated to a still of the 'little death'.

Many of the other poems recreate with the delicacy of the horizontal aesthetic the state between two things: 'A une Robe rose' is positioned at the meeting-point of skin and material, where visually the two are indistinguishable.[4] In 'Contralto' mystery and ambiguity is the very theme. The poetic gaze is set up as a kind of penetration – 'Beneath the solid drapery . . . My eyes have plunged so many times' (p. 31) – but it is not meant seriously. The eye that looks does not 'plunge' anywhere, for the mind does not want to know: uncertainty is the turn-on, and the turn-on is art. The woman described may die of 'volupté', but the poet does not. In *Mademoiselle de Maupin*, the key difference between d'Albert and Madeleine is her wish to know and his fundamental desire to remain ignorant. At the end, she both is and has everything, and he, all spent, has nothing.

Mademoiselle de Maupin is preceded by a long Preface which, unlike those of my other texts, is attached to the fiction only by the vaguest of tangents. It is celebrated in its own right as a polemic against utilitarian criticism. Such critics, the narrator declares, are envious eunuchs and journalism ought to be banned. As for moral effect, 'books follow social custom, social custom does not follow books . . . It's as if you were to say: the peas produce the springtime'.[5] He goes on to embrace a satirical utilitarianism: 'you are a cobbler, I am a poet . . . I would rather have my shoe come unsewn than my lines misrhymed, and . . . I can more easily do without boots than poems' (p. 52). The beautiful is always superfluous and 'everything useful is ugly, for it is the expression of some need and the needs of man are base and disgusting, like his pathetic, infirm nature' (p. 54).

It is perhaps not surprising that critics, seduced by the similarity of the name d'Albert and Gautier's earlier pseudonym Albertus, have identified author and protagonist in *Mademoiselle de Maupin*. They are, of course, both right and wrong. The tone of the Preface and much of the book is too ironic to detect a stable identification; but it is also, for the same reason, no guarantor of a position of critique. I want to argue first, that the critique, where it comes, is embodied in the subjectivity of the two female characters, and secondly that it is undermined, particularly in the character of Madeleine de Maupin, by the mixed function of her voice.

The text begins as an epistolary novel and *in medias res:* 'you complain, my dear friend, of the rarity of my letters' (p. 71). The writer suffers from ennui: each day is exactly like yesterday. Between plains of melancholic resignation, however, he is agitated: he describes himself rushing out of doors in a state of objectless desire, 'an undefined urge . . . a feverish irritation' (pp. 74-5). 'Is my existence trying to complete itself? am I trying to escape from my house or from myself . . . ?' (p. 74), he demands. In both these images d'Albert is already anticipating his *hantise* of femaleness: in his phantasy he is either a castrated body or one immobilized into passivity; the outward expression of phallic motion speaks of an inner sense of womanhood. This is objectless desire taken to a feminine extreme: 'I desire nothing, for I desire everything . . . I am waiting – for what? I do not know, but I am waiting . . . Nothing comes' (p. 75). In this fantasy, the self is a magnet, the tool of a powerful incorporation. We shall see further developments of this motif later. But when we meet Madeleine de Maupin we shall find her trying the opposite mode of desire: an active search for an object to whom she can play, physically at least, the passive role.[6]

D'Albert goes on to define his objectless desire as not so very vague after all: he wishes for 'a mistress of my very own' (p. 78). Possession is here fancied as an end in itself, even though, as he already knows, it will not bring pleasure: it is a habit of his to wish so intensely and so passively for a thing that if he gets it, 'my forces suddenly fail me and I no longer have the strength to enjoy it [pour en jouir]'.

The myth of sexual ambiguity that informs this book is based on a perpetual slide between *being* and *having*. D'Albert insists 'I have never had a mistress, and all my desire is to have one . . . I do not want 'any woman' but a woman, a mistress . . . what I ask is only just, nature owes it to every man' (p. 79). But, as he quickly finds confirmed in the first weeks with Rosette, the fact of sleeping regularly with the same woman (other people's definition of having a mistress) is not really what he means. His wish is not to have but to be something: 'until I have achieved my aim, I will regard myself as a child and I will not have the self-confidence I need. – A mistress, for me, is like the grown man's toga [la robe virile] for a young Roman'. Two images appear here: that the woman is a mirror in which he will see himself reflected as a man, and that she is a garment, the nicely ambiguous 'robe' that confers virility.[7]

To wear womanhood or to gaze into it, is to be a man. In both images, the narrator is 'seeing himself in' the woman. Implicit here is an image of gestation that is nowhere acknowledged explicitly. It might seem more apt to say – as in the early theories of the apparent transsexuality of 'uranism' – that d'Albert has a woman inside him, as it is said that the soul 'inhabits' the body.[8] Outer and inner would then correspond to a biological, male body housing an unconscious, female phantasy. But this is not what he says: it is the external existence of the phantasy of being a woman that haunts him, something that can be found and put on. For this is above all an aesthetic desire, in which the beauty of form is all visibility, even touch is secondary, and penetration is impossible. We shall see something similar in Musset's *Lorenzaccio* where a new self 'is stuck to my skin'.[9] Where then to find the sister soul? Uniquely, of course, in the woman who wears men's clothing. With her it would be impossible to know the meaning of appearance: what is inside what is inside the clothes? Has such a woman any mode of entry? Is she a woman at all? Like the poet of 'Contralto', d'Albert will only pretend to want to penetrate, for this 'completion' would also be a loss of himself.

D'Albert has a very precise set of negatives in his requirement, and no woman imaginable is likely to qualify. Despite the mystique of objectless passion, he specifies every material detail, down to her colouring (blonde with black eyes).[10] She will wear velvet and be extremely rich, for wealth and beauty go together. Only the rich and beautiful can be in love without looking ridiculous; and d'Albert frankly adds: 'by that account, few people would have the right to fall in love – I least of all; yet that is what I believe' (p. 85). This is no mere flippancy. It follows from the aestheticising of women that men cannot be beautiful. Desire cannot by this definition be directed towards men, for they can only be subjects. Women can thus want sex only out of curiosity, not desire. If a person is desired s/he must be female; this is the principle that makes it inevitable that d'Albert, after a suicidal few days, will 'recognise' Madeleine as a woman; indeed, it makes it impossible for her, since she is desirable, not to be a woman: Rosette too can only truly love her because of the beauty that makes her female. This means that lesbianism, though hushed up, is necessary and logical; and that male homosexuality simply does not exist.

D'Albert is taken by his cynical friend C*** (a double for all those urbane fathers and for Musset's Desgenais) to a house that seems midway between a brothel and a salon. There he catches the eye of a beauty in pink. As C*** describes her, she is ideal for him: 'in a week she'll get rid of all your scruples . . . On every matter she has inexpressibly positive ideas; she gets to the heart of everything with astonishing speed and certainty. That little woman is algebra incarnate: just what a dreamy enthusiast needs. She'll soon cure you of your vaporous idealism' (p. 104). This phallic woman (whom he casually nicknames Rosette after his dog) will both undress and penetrate the hero: her positiveness is described throughout in 'masculine' terms. Rosette stimulates him by mocking all the women in the room. This wit meets with his approval, combined as it is with a Circean corruption of the body: 'she is . . . sparkling with wit; and yet when one is with her one thinks of nothing but base and vulgar things . . . she aroused the animal, the brute in me' (p. 110). Rosette's very qualification as sex-object is her failure to be the desired ideal. With her he will, paradoxically, never lose his innocence.

One reason d'Albert decides to give her a try is to distract himself from his narcissism; he understands that gazing outward at the invisible ideal is the same as looking in at himself: 'perhaps, finding nothing in this world that is worthy of my love, I will end up adoring myself, like the late Narcissus of egoistic memory. – To keep myself from this disaster, I look at myself in all the mirrors and streams/gutters [ruisseaux] I meet' (p. 113). If the ideal woman is impossible to meet, Rosette is precisely the mirror/gutter whom he can meet: he will try looking at himself in her.

Becoming Rosette's lover seems to give d'Albert a certain 'consistency' that endorses rather than evades narcissism. He no longer feels like a boy and his appearance – long, lustrous curls, finely chosen clothes – no longer seems effeminate, unreal. Briefly (and probably deludedly) d'Albert imagines himself desirable exactly as he is. But he himself feels no desire. Full of life and amusement, Rosette is never boring, but by the same token she is no longer really a woman: 'she's a delicious companion [compagnon], a pretty comrade that one sleeps with, not a mistress' (p. 119). She consents to his most crazy fantasies, dresses up in finery while he, clad in a bear-costume, tears her garments off and devoutly admires the 'heroism quite above her sex' (p. 122) with which she joins in trampling them underfoot.[11] Rosette's involvement in this sacrilege as a 'disinterested witness' suggests nothing to her lover other than sublime self-sacrifice; it does not occur to him that she too might be participating in a desperate and ridiculous bit of theatre. No, like Ellénore, she is understood merely as loving more than she is loved. And when d'Albert suffers a momentary impotence after the over-stimulation of the bear-costume, she becomes another Amélie, gorgeous in a sudden nun-like inaccessibility: 'she had never seemed so lovely to me as in that moment.[12] There was something so chaste, so maternal in her gaze' (p. 123).

Nevertheless, none of these experiences seems real. However much he longs to 'live through the life of others' (p. 124), he has no true sense of their existence: 'whatever I do, other people are scarcely more than phantoms to me . . . I could easily believe that they are just the fleeting appearances that pass through me, their objective mirror'. Having no self, immobile recipient of others' unrealities, he mimics the role of the woman in the *récit*:

> If someone calls me *monsieur* or refers to me as 'this man', it feels very strange to me. My very name seems a name plucked out of the air, not my real name; and yet, however softly it might be uttered in the midst of the loudest noise, I turn around at once with a convulsive, feverish suddenness that I have never been able to understand. – Is it the fear of finding, in this man who knows my name, and for whom I am no longer one of the crowd, an antagonist or an enemy? (p. 125)

'This man' who calls him by his father's name (we only ever learn this protagonist's surname) is a ghost-double: we recall the primitive fear that if one's name is spoken it is stolen from one. It is also believed, according to Rank, that children named after dead parents are supposed to revive the latter's soul. D'Albert's father, whom we must presume dead, haunts him here as the older Hamlet the younger, claiming a possession of the inheriting body that carries the name. He haunts him especially through his feminisation. In sexual relations above all, the narrator notes, he feels alien, like a drop of oil in a glass of water. He is always faking it. 'Pleasure itself . . . as potent as it is, has never been able to conquer or touch me . . . my soul is the enemy-sister of my body'. The body is haunted both by the separation of its male doubles and by the feminine self, the soul, the mirror, that undermines from within.

If pleasure is never more than a '*jouissance* of the skin' (p. 126) in which the soul has no part, and at the same time d'Albert cannot get other people 'to enter my brain', he is like a closed body, a female virgin to whom there is no entry. The key problem is his simultaneous longing and inability to imagine himself as an object, for this (grammatically and aesthetically) is what a woman is to him.

It is at this point that the narrator declares his wish to be a woman, and the conscious reasons for it:

> I have never wished for anything so much as to be like the seer Tiresias and meet those serpents on the mountain that cause a change of sex . . .
>
> At first I wanted to change into another man; then, realising that in that state I would still be feeling things I could already predict, and not the surprise and change I wanted, I began to prefer the idea of becoming a woman; that idea always came to me when I had a mistress who was not too ugly – for an ugly woman is a man to me: at the moment of pleasure I would have loved to change roles, for it is very annoying not to be aware of the effect one is having and only to be able to judge the ecstasy [jouissance] of the other by one's own (p. 127)

There are a lot of mixed phantasies in this passage. First, like Tiresias, the wish to be a woman whilst safely remaining a man: man's consciousness with woman's appearance, the promise always of being able to change oneself back. Second, the substitution of the desire of the mirror for that of the double: to be another man would be more of what is known, nothing new. The adequate response to Romantic ennui is to reverse oneself: living to dead (as Baudelaire insists) or, here, man to woman, ugly to beautiful, subject to object. He wants both to see how it feels to be felt by him and also to discover the quite unknown *jouissance* of women. In this wish, D'Albert is seeking the woman who will hold up to him the mirror in which he can see his own superfluity.

That woman is not Rosette, he is certain, for he sees her as utterly different from himself; he cannot 'descend into her heart' (p. 128) and her 'young, smiling head' contains no ideas like his. He is wrong, of course: Rosette is not so much different as several months ahead of him. But what he sees is someone who cannot, as he wishes, make him a woman: with Rosette he is unable to penetrate to a self reflected 'in' her. She is, in the end, too complete: 'Rosette's qualities are all in her, I have given her nothing' (p. 135). Their affair continues because Rosette has infinite sexual tricks to keep him interested, but cast also in the pathetic role of Ellénore, she seems destined to remain nothing more significant than 'my thing, my property' (pp. 149-50).

Rosette takes him to her chateau; she showers him with adoring attentions; mistress of the house, she plays his slave. But he has thoughts only for Miss Right. Again the slide between being and having is expressed the narrator's aestheticising sexism. 'I have never asked anything of women except beauty . . . the one thing that cannot be acquired' (pp. 167-8), he avows, yet 'the only thing in the world I have envied with any consistency is the gift of being beautiful' (p. 170). Gazing in mirrors for hours for a sign of progress towards this aim, he has forgotten perhaps that for him beauty must be both innate and female, and he would have to be not 'a snake shedding its old skin' (p. 171) but rather the voyeur of the snakes, Tiresias.

In a brief glimpse of his infancy, the narrator pauses to conjure up a revealingly matriarchal world – 'I spent years in the shadow of my mother's chair, with my little sisters and the family dog' (p. 176) – in which he played the typical outsider of the family romance. 'In the midst of this honest, pious, saintly family, I had reached a horrible level of depravity . . . I do not belong to my family; I am not a branch of that noble tree but a poisonous fungus that grew [poussa] one wild and stormy night between its mossy roots' (p. 177). The fantasy of the primal scene in which he was nastily engendered shows how d'Albert's medusan attitude towards women is tied to a murderous imagination of his own birth: 'when I think that I was born of such a sweet and gentle mother, so resigned, so simple in her tastes and ways, I am amazed that I did not burst open her womb when she was carrying me' (p. 176). Hidden behind the surface rhetoric of self-love there is the same *hantise* of matricide – here mythicised variously as childbed death, rape and spontaneous abortion – as we find in my earlier texts: the prison of the impenetrable self, the obsession with surface are a dazzling elaboration of separation as murder.

A young man has come to stay in Rosette's chateau; 'his only fault is that he is too beautiful . . . for a man' (p. 178). D'Albert's Waterloo has arrived.

Mademoiselle de Maupin is exceptional among the *récits* for a number of reasons; the most important perhaps is that at the same time as it sets forth with unusual frankness the man's desire to be a woman, this text also offers the positive corollary: a woman in whom desire is superseded by the intelligent will to know. Madeleine de Maupin's knowledge is, by the end, the mirroring measure of d'Albert's ignorance. Even before the climactic conclusion, Madeleine and Rosette have joined in dialogue to cut the hero down to size. It is always difficult to attribute irony, since the attempt inevitably begs the question of authorial intention; but it is clear that here (as later in *Sylvie*) we find the women at their most free: female voices speak the critical truth which is sharply audible across the sound of the protagonist's vanity.

At this point in the story, the narrative changes to two chapters in the third person. They are both concerned with Madeleine/Théodore but retain a measure of suspense by taking a viewpoint position outside her. In the first chapter, two female pairs are presented: first Madeleine and her cross-dressed page 'Isnabel' and then Rosette and Madeleine, whom the former loves as the loveliest of men. Each of these pairs is exclusively female, but the male element is nevertheless obliquely present in the motifs of travesty and language. While Madeleine gazes with as much maternal as sensual affection on her blonde young friend, her thoughts are reproduced using masculine adjectives: 'truly I am jealous [jaloux] of your mother, I wish I were the one to have made you [t'avoir fait]' (p. 184). Though 'the master was as beautiful as a woman, the page as beautiful as a young girl' (p. 182), the narrator avoids a mother-daughter pairing: 'they seemed united by a greater affection than is usual between master and servant – could they have been two friends, or two brothers?' (p. 184). In the couple Rosette-Madeleine, Rosette's delusion that she loves a man lends a flavour of both perversity and suspense to the encounter; it also makes us read Madeleine's speech (which at this point is heavily rhetorical in the Romantic mode, reminiscent of d'Albert's worst *longueurs*) as an echo of men's language, patronising, 'protective', reducing Rosette to the clever sprite that d'Albert thinks her. Rosette alone comes out of this scene impressively for it is in her voice that we first see d'Albert cut down to size.

Rosette's heroism is to combine as neither of the others does the qualities of desire and knowledge. Except for the deferred recognition of Madeleine's sex, she has entire and depressing insight, and at the same time, in the generosity of her love, 'her soul is as fine as her body' (p. 348). While presented as something of a misogynist, at least in her wit, Rosette is 'all woman', with no conflict of inner and outer self. This is perhaps why she is vouchsafed at the end the secret *jouissance* of the lesbian embrace. But it also seems to be a reason why we never directly read her voice. The clearest and least narcissistic subjectivity of the text is without language, and thus is in many senses always 'jouée' (acted/manipulated/duped).

We discover from the women's conversation that d'Albert is a poet; he is not a good one. Like Wilde, his genius is in his life: 'he puts into his verse only [those ideas] he is not really interested in or which repel him; it is the door he throws them out by, and the public gets what he no longer wants' (p. 197): in other words, his writing is shit. Madeleine recognises a similar failure of creativity: everyone's 'most beautiful poem is the one they have not written' (pp. 188-9). Sterility is the rule: Rosette, despite her ten lovers, is and will die a virgin; Madeleine, we learn, can never even undress; d'Albert is no creator. There is no direct fantasy of maternity in this text, for production is part of the 'base and disgusting' human nature which the aesthetic of surface evades.

Soon after this d'Albert writes a longwinded letter to Silvio to admit, after many pages, the 'monstrous thought' (p. 218) that he has fallen in love with a man. And here we find what I suggested some pages ago: however deeply corrupt the heart of the Romantic hero, who could watch the most fiendish inventions of sadism, he claims, without turning a hair, however proudly he has avowed 'a liking for the impossible' (p. 174), there is no such 'perversion' as male homosexuality; it is simply unthinkable. Already 'Théodore' must be a woman in disguise: 'the thing is impossible otherwise' (p. 223). Extraordinary is, as for René, the found object of desire: 'what I feel for this young man is truly incredible; no woman has ever excited me so strangely' (p. 222). D'Albert could only love someone whose body is female and whose appearance is male. This is his 'soul as enemy-sister' in the flesh.

A double is not what d'Albert wants: a young man he once saw who had exactly his looks but better – this, one might expect, being what he had searched for in those looking-glasses interrogated for 'some improvement in my countenance' (p. 171) – seemed to him just a vulgar plagiarist of his features. 'Théodore' is, on the contrary, entirely other, a true mirror: 'although Théodore is very handsome, I do not desire his beauty, I prefer that he should have it than I' (p. 225). What 'he' inspires is the desire to look. The hero can conceive the fantasy 'that a very young, very handsome, completely smooth-cheeked knight should dress up as a woman' (p. 238), but the reverse, what Madeleine actually is, baffles and threatens him: 'everything in me is upset and upside down; I no longer know who I am or what other people are, I don't know if I am a man or a woman, I loathe myself' (p. 220).

Here we leave him, and the text is handed over to Madeleine. 'My beautiful friend, you were quite right to try to discourage me from my plan to see men – to study them in depth, before giving my heart to any one of them. What I have done has forever extinguished love in me, even the possibility of loving' (p. 243), thus her letter begins. Though most of what she writes is a light and self-deprecating picaresque of her adventures in men's clothing, we see from this opening that Madeleine too feels ennuyée and trapped. The mask is sticking to the skin. As mirror of d'Albert, her role in this rich, confused text is awkwardly double. She is forbidden desire since, appearing as a man and with now the habits and speech of a man, she wants both a male lover – out of the original wish to know that drove her out of doors – and the female other whose proffered sensuality is all she has seen of love. Perfectly *disponible*, she cannot act, for to undress, it seems, is to lose her duality. Yet she is very different from d'Albert, and the difference resides in her conscious choice of being both sexes; whereas he is empty, bereft, neither this nor that, prey to an inimical fantasy-world, she is by her will a uniquely, impossibly full self. As she writes just before the double loss of her virginity:

> My dream would be to have both sexes by turns, in order to satisfy this double nature: today a man, tomorrow a woman, I would save for my lovers my languorous tendernesses, my submissive, devoted gestures, my most abandoned caresses, my melancholy little sighs, everything woman-like, cat-like in my character; and with my mistresses I would be enterprising, bold, passionate, with a triumphant air, my hat over one ear, and the swagger of a swashbuckler or an adventurer. Thus my whole nature would come forth [se produirait] and be visible, and I would be perfectly happy,

for it is true happiness to be able to develop oneself in every direction and to be all that one can be (p. 394)

This is the reverse of ennui, an assumption of righteous freedom. Could it work? who cares – this Madeleine de Maupin, like her historical predecessor (1673-1707?) will ride off into the sunset and never be seen to die. We must not forget that it is the writing and the fantasy of a man; thus the female self evoked is all bedroom affectations and presumably naked, while the male is fully dressed, out of doors and ready to go; but unlike 'Coquetterie posthume', this is couched in genuinely subjective terms. Madeleine is not concerned with being looked at and desired but with her own pleasure and creativity: her nature will 'produce' itself. The decadent premises of this text have come full circle to a surprising acknowledgement of a woman's autonomy.

Madeleine left home because, despite sharp senses – 'I listened, I watched; . . . like the fabled eyes of the lynx, my eyes pierced through walls' (p. 245)[13] – she is incarcerated in the luxurious prison of repressive convention. Above all, girls are not supposed to know: 'the years of our upbringing are spent not in teaching us things but in preventing us from learning anything' (p. 249). What language do men speak when women are not there? their faces give no clue, clothed in 'a mask of convention . . . when they are in women's company' (p. 245). Women are excluded from discourse: 'they were uttering words in a language I did not know'. To acquire this knowledge she is prepared to relinquish desire, at least until she knows 'the way in which he [her potential lover] would have spoken of me to another man' (p. 246). The dangers inherent in this male author's fantasy are shown in a violently penetrative image: 'I wanted to study man in depth, to explore his anatomy fibre by fibre with an inexorable scalpel, and to have him alive and quivering on my dissecting table' (p. 247).[14] But for Madeleine, there is less interest in a covert phantasy than in action. A wealthy orphan, she can act upon her wish: she trains at all the male sports, changes her clothes and, after some moments of nostalgia, departs, 'courageous girl, all alone, to seek all over the world the great knowledge of life' (p. 255).

Though Madeleine's mother died when she was young, she like d'Albert describes the childhood home as matriarchal: 'we are well and truly tied to our mother's skirt, just as convention demands . . . our life is no life, it's a kind of vegetation, like that of mosses or flowers; the icy shadow of the mother's stem floats all around us' (p. 248). For both, the mossy world of the mother's body is the prison that precedes separation. But while d'Albert phantasises himself as always alien, a murderous poison within the maternal body, Madeleine's analysis recognises that the mother is only the appointed warder of her cell. The oppressive 'they' in her youth are not so much the mothers as the men whose speeches keep her immobile as a doll, in a vulgar version of d'Albert's own medusan aesthetic. Separation for Madeleine is a kind of suicide – 'the girl was dead' (p. 250) – but also a project of adventure. No childbed death for this infant: in an optimistic assumption of the split, she tells her new self: 'men are keeping some extraordinary secrets from us, Théodore!' (p. 252), and gallops away.

The first night, spent at an inn in the company of a crowd of vulgar aristocrats, teaches her the rudiments of male discourse. She spends a sleepless night beside a handsome deadweight, tempted to wake him up and say what she is. Desire seems very simple: curiosity and the mere fact that this creature is not a woman overcome her disgust at men's low minds; thus 'the body is an anchor that keeps the soul down on earth' (p. 265). We leave her thus weighted and return to d'Albert for an elegant disquisition on theatre.

For they are to play *As you like it*, he as Orlando, 'Théodore' as Rosalind, Rosette as Phoebe. Weeks of twittery preparation lead very slowly to the almost casual announcement that 'Théodore' has appeared at rehearsal dressed as a stunning woman. The men cheer, the woman blush scarlet, Rosette goes white as a sheet. With no further thought to her, d'Albert crows with relief: everything is simplified, he can love himself after all. 'I felt an enormous sense of well-being, as if a mountain or two [ie. breasts?] had been lifted from my chest' (p. 294). No longer a freak, he immediately restores the medusan gaze, imagining Madeleine the perfect work of art and himself a sculptor. Petrification, not self-production, is d'Albert's narrow desire. Thinking, nevertheless, that he wants to know the woman, he writes her an impassioned note and waits.

In the meantime we continue Madeleine's adventures and come on to the poignant meeting with Rosette, sister of the handsome drunkard at the inn. Rosette's desire arouses something in Madeleine, 'more than a woman's ordinary love for a woman' (p. 349). In the narrative of Rosette's attempts to seduce the frustrating but stimulated 'Théodore', we have bedroom farce with a dash of tragedy – the author perhaps highly amused at this subversion of women's desire as he watches Rosette try to get the trousers off and Madeleine to hide her blushes. Rosette's role is simply to suffer rejection; for Madeleine the apprenticeship of sexuality is a potential change of self.

Rosette unknowingly but with determination and Madeleine with a chaste awareness are, in the terms of Gautier's system, experiencing male desire. They are both turned on by a woman. Now at this point we find (as far as it can be quantified) the most obtrusive irruption of authorial motive into Madeleine's voice. Her lack of sympathy with other women, her repulsion from the old age of Rosette's aunt, the glib erotic terms she uses to describe Rosette and the thoughtlessness with which she adopts precisely the male strategy she most resented when a girl – 'so as to play my role as a man perfectly and also to amuse myself a little, I found nothing better to do than pay court to my friend's sister' (p. 324) – all these things make her less a counterpart than a double to d'Albert. To be prepared to undress for him, she must be made too much a man, stifled by the costume which is described as invading her very consciousness. 'Plenty of men are more women than I am. – All that is womanly in me are my breasts, my somewhat more rounded form, my more delicate hands; the skirt is on my hips, not in my mind . . . the thing I like least in the world is to obey, and my most frequent phrase is: "I want". Under my smooth brow and my silken hair run strong, virile thoughts' (p. 327). What we see here is a crucial twist: it is suddenly not possible for a woman to be 'enterprising, bold, passionate [entreprenant, hardi, passionné]' (p. 394), these are masculine adjectives in more than just grammar. Freedom, will and knowledge can be possessed by a woman only if she is not a woman. However foolish and self-regarding she has proved him to be, Madeleine is being groomed for d'Albert.

In several ways Madeleine seems here, compliantly in her independent voice, to be becoming him. What she lacks that he has – 'my virility, which is indeed rather slim' – it will shortly be his job to show her. As for Rosette, Madeleine longs to be able to play the man for her; and after the input from d'Albert, she will be able to fulfil this fantasy too. What seems to be suggested here is that he is as much for her as she has been for him in fantasy, a function of 'my existence trying to complete itself' (p. 74); if she is his lost phallus, he will equally be hers.

The virgin wants a man. Oddly, after all the definition of beauty and desire, she still wishes for something he alone possesses, for her knowledge must produce itself as the knowledge of the phallus. The text is twisting over onto itself here, in order to prove that after all masculinity is not just a costume but the only Real. Even so Madeleine, at the end, is the one with power. She ignores d'Albert's wordy letter and diverts us by a bitter-sweet recollection in which Rosette almost succeeds in seducing her and she ends up wounding the latter's irate brother. Even here we find echoes of d'Albert's misogyny: Rosette's clear expression of desire and maturity – '"I am not a foolish, giddy woman, nor a romantic little girl that falls for the first sword she sees. I have seen the world and I know about life"' (p. 364) – does not prevent Madeleine typing her 'the darling child' (p. 365) as soon as she gets into bed. In the fight where, turning from skilful defence to angry attack, Madeleine finds herself penetrating and drawing blood, she has (even in her thought, it seems) qualified as a man: 'the most extraordinary thing. . . was that this wound had been opened by me, and that a girl of my age (I almost wrote, a young man of my age, see how far I have entered into the spirit of my role) could have knocked a vigorous captain out cold on the floor' (p. 372). Here again, precisely as she disproves the weakness of women, she is forced to speak as a man.

Yet to be a man is to relinquish pleasure; the adventures have left her 'blasé . . . but without having enjoyed [joui]' (p. 381). She is suffering, in other words, from the supposed problem of René and Adolphe, desire preempted by knowledge. There is no logical place for Madeleine in the world of this text: if only women can be beautiful and desired, yet only men can know, then where is she to go? In the climactic night she organises for herself, she triumphantly exceeds the terms of the system, finally tiring the indefatigable phallus of d'Albert and then moving on to an embrace with Rosette that remains forever secret.

She is prepared to sleep with d'Albert because he has had the wit to recognise her and because there is something in him that aspires, if only towards material beauty. But Rosette alone can offer her the 'beauty of the soul' (p. 380). To complete herself, Madeleine needs to lose the last vestige of unknowledge, 'this ignorance of the body which, without the ignorance of the mind, is the most miserable thing in the world' (p. 398): the only cure will be, in tandem, the knowledge of the phallus and the sensuality of the woman's embrace.

The hero waits by his melancholic window in exactly the pose he fancied for his dream-woman,[15] when suddenly he is tapped on the shoulder by lovely Madeleine, her breasts bared to prove her sex (a hilarious touch of Page Three that we can perhaps best attribute to the repression of oedipal desire everywhere else in the text). We are back in the third person, and the implicit viewpoint is the man's. Madeleine available becomes 'the lovely infanta' (p. 404), but she sets the conditions: one night only, and no strings. She has a moment of seriousness, not out of virginal terror but because this is a major change, 'a metamorphosis, a transformation' (p. 406). Then with the temporary courtesy of the mirror – 'in her boundless generosity Rosalind let him do everything he wished, and contrived to return his caresses as exactly as possible' (pp. 406-7) – she undresses for d'Albert, satisfies his scopophilia, and lets him carry her to the bed.

Intentionally or not (and the tone is, as often, carefully ironic) this scene ends with the comedy of a braggart's total of orgasms: they come together once, then the rest, it seems, are all d'Albert's. 'Our charming reader would certainly refuse to have anything more to do with her lover if we revealed to her the formidable total that d'Albert's love reached, aided by Rosalind's curiosity' (p. 409): we are referred to our best night of love, to count on our pretty fingers. Let us say, then, that d'Albert is here briefly vouchsafed what is henceforth Madeleine's doubleness: the phallic potency prized by men along with women's prerogative of multiple orgasm. But he ends up spent, and when he falls asleep she moves on. At the door of Rosette's room the modest male narrator stops: 'what she said there, what she did there, I have never been able to find out, though I have made the most conscientious researches' (p. 410). Knowledge is, finally, the secret of women.

The triumph of women at the end of this text is markedly overt. The men – protagonist, third-person narrator – go hungry both epistemologically and sexually. Madeleine and Rosette, it is hinted, are satisfied. Most unusually for such a text, there has appeared a female implied reader, that creature who perhaps knows not just how potent men can be but a bit more of what went on in Rosette's bed than the writer does. Madeleine of course departs in self-possession. And what d'Albert stands to gain now that she has gone will have to be the trace of her transferred to Rosette and available only in sex and speech with the latter, a knowledge that is not phallic.

Musset's tragedy *Lorenzaccio* was written during the liaison with George Sand that provided the model for *La Confession d'un enfant du siècle*, and published in 1834, two years before the novel; but it was not staged until Sarah Bernhardt at fifty-two took the name-part in an adaptation in December 1896. It is an interesting curiosity that the hero was first played by a woman: aspects of the character lend justification to this transvestism. Lorenzo is a Madeleine de Maupin as well as an Octave or a d'Albert.

He lives in disguise, a mask of clothing, acts and words. 'Within' is (or rather, once was) an ardent boy planning the great oedipal act, the murder of the corrupt duke his uncle for the sake of the mother-city Florence. But to win his way into the duke's confidence, he has had to become his bosom friend, his accomplice in debauchery and even his pimp. Not until halfway through the play do we hear Lorenzo speak 'from the inside', frankly divulging his motive and sense of self. In earlier scenes, he is presented as an enigma. Like a woman, his appearance speaks for him, but may not be reliably interpreted. His feminisation is often stressed: he is glimpsed at a party dressed as a nun; described as 'a little woman' (p. 52), with sickly [fluettes] weak hands scarcely fit to hold a fan; addressed by the duke as 'Loren-zetta' (p. 55); and forgiven by his young aunt Catherine for fainting at the sight of a sword with the words: 'why shouldn't that child have the same right as all us women?' (p. 60). In his supposed camaraderie with the duke Alexandre, he is much to blame for corrupting Flor-ence, already 'a sterile mother'(p. 63) and 'a whore' (p. 71). Lorenzo's own mother remembers him as a scholarly, attractive boy; now the evil in his heart has permeated to his face. In an image of what might have been, she has a fantasy that the maternal role is inverted and she is rocked to sleep by her son; instead she now wakes in a bloody hovel among the debris of orgies and human remains, 'in the arms of a hideous spectre that kills as it calls me by the name of the mother' (p. 61). We have in the figure of Lorenzo, then, a son who both saves and kills his mother, who should have been a double for her, an unnatural daughter dressed mockingly in the costume of the nun. In his mother's words again, 'the smile, that sweet blossoming that makes youth like a flower, has fled from his sulphurous cheeks, giving place to an ignoble irony, a contempt for everything' (p. 61). This corruption of smile into grin is a repeated motif of the *Confession*.

In this play costume has first of all a political sigificance: the artist Tebaldeo refuses Lorenzo's offer of a new livery with the declaration, 'I belong to no one. If the mind is to be free, the body must be so too' (p. 72). Lorenzo turns this all about when his mother's relatives come to ask him if he is on their side: 'I am with you, my uncle. Can you not see by my hairstyle that I have the soul of a republican? See how my beard is cut. Do not doubt it an instant: the love of fatherland breathes in my most hidden garments' (p. 83). Deeply republican in his own style, Lorenzo is mocking the overt signals of clubs and conspiracies; no more than the early Madeleine de Maupin does he believe the costume tells the story; but if we cannot tell the soul from the garments, how can we know it? This is the question Octave demands of Brigitte, not so much because he wants to know the answer as because he wants, like Des Grieux, to hear a speech he can believe: there must be no difference between surface and depth. In the other, sight and speech should concur. But the self is much more complicated. For the hero is the site of motive, while the woman is perceived. The woman is required to reflect a pure self back to the hero repining in his garments of corruption; as mirror she will vouch for his internal, hidden innocence.

In his confession to Philippe Strozzi, Lorenzo stresses the split between motive and action. Youthful exaltation 'gave birth [enfanta] within me' (p. 113) to an isolated self: 'my pride remained alone among my philanthropic dreams'. This phallic self, pure as a lily, sought to penetrate to the duke and now the goal has been reached, Lorenzo himself has been destroyed. While the virtuous father Philippe has stood 'immobile on the shore of the human ocean . . . I have dived in' and seen, like Octave after him, the wrecks and drowned bodies under the surface. He now knows the truth, like Nietzsche's Hamlet; but the effort still to separate his self from his acts is illustrated by the genders in the following speech:

> Am I a Devil? Light of Heaven! I still remember: I would have wept with the first girl/prostitute [fille] I seduced, if she had not burst out laughing. When I took on the role of the modern Brutus, I strode in these new garments of the brotherhood [confrérie] of vice like a child of ten in the armour of a fairytale giant. I believed corruption was a stigma and only monsters wore it on their brow . . . – O Philippe! I was just entering life,

and I saw that as I approached everyone was doing the same as me; all
their masks fell away before my gaze; Humanity lifted her dress and
displayed to me, worthy follower, her monstrous nudity (p. 117)

That first girl/prostitute, the nicely-punning 'confrérie' and humanity in general are female bodies in which the pure phallic boy is soiled.
What we find in this passage is an inverse description of the experience of Madeleine de Maupin: Lorenzo, like her, enters the taboo
world and finds it speaking directly to him because he is clothed in
its garments and wearing its mask. But now, unlike her, he has no
way to divest himself. Vice has become a garment 'stuck to my skin'
(p. 118). By the end, like an existential hero, Lorenzo has resolved
to perform his act knowing it is gratuitous, for 'it is all that remains
of my virtue . . . my whole life is at the tip of my dagger' (pp. 119-20).
By the very pointlessness of the act he expresses a deathwish for all
of humanity. Lorenzo has assumed his pejorative nickname Lorenzaccio, the phallic self crowns murder with suicide, and the 'wedding-
day' (as he terms the day of the murder) will end in a bitter *Liebestod*.

If the difference between Lorenzaccio and Madeleine is that she
can remove the costume and he cannot, this must be because he feels
himself dangerously implicated by the 'feminine' element he has
entered. Madeleine is a whole body, clothing herself as she chooses.
The Lorenzo that moves in the taboo world is a part-object, a self
'enfanté' by the ego, separated from it by castration. The detachable
phallic self, entrapped, cannot come out again. In *Mademoiselle de
Maupin*, d'Albert's phantasy of 'putting on' womanhood is a desire
for a narcissism of surface, the être-en-soi that men have made
women. Lorenzo wants, like Madeleine, to go forth, but finds himself
a whore; corruption is the female element in which the innocent boy
drowns. When he recognises with horror that 'I would debauch [cor-
romprais] my mother' (p. 146) he is seeing himself not as her lover
– that is her fantasy – but as her pimping daughter. In carrying out
his assassination, he enacts his plea to enter the symbolic, but his
suicide proves that it is too late. The quarrel is not with the man but
with the loss of self into the woman. Symptomatically, the mother-
daughter pair haunts Lorenzaccio as it does *La Confession d'un enfant
du siècle*.

The novel has no first-person frame; it opens with an enigmatic
disclaimer: 'to write the story of one's life, one must first have lived;
therefore I am not writing my own story' (p. 19).[16] Thus the author

universalises a particular case – for he had started by writing to George Sand on 30 April 1834: 'I really feel like writing our story' – and distorts experience into a lesson. The whole impulse of this text is to cast away blame. Corruption is merely the garment that sticks to the skin, it is never the 'inner man'. Yet where, in this centrifugal gesture, can badness become stable? For the confession depends on the avowal *mea culpa* which indicts as it exculpates: to show how good he is, he must swear how bad he has been. But it must never really be his fault.

In the prefatory second chapter, the author's voice describes the general 'sickness of the century [maladie du siècle]'. During the wars of the Empire, fathers were absent, their sons – no daughters seem to have been born in this period – 'conceived between battles' (p. 20), occasionally glimpsing their 'bloodied fathers' who then rode off again to the front. Now this, logically, is the image of a matriarchal childhood; but the mother does not appear here or, directly, later. The mood is overwhelmingly patriarchal: the absent father is everywhere visible. 'One man alone was alive in Europe; the rest of the people contrived to fill their lungs with the air he had breathed': Napoleon is here, in the voice of the ambivalent son, both the sole supplier of air and the stale stifler of others' breathing. He is a Minotaur: tribute in young flesh is paid and consumed. But he is all man too – 'never were there suns as pure as those that dried all this blood . . . he made them himself of course with his ever-thundering cannons' (p. 21).

Death, meanwhile, is a lady: so fine and magnificent, sated on young flesh, that she looks young; 'all the cradles in France were shields, so were the coffins . . . there was nothing but corpses and demi-gods'. If the last image is the double face of the hero of the text, the image that births him is a coffin-cradle, an erotic couch in which desire is a deadly return of the repressed. From the impossible adoration of the sun-father comes the seduction of the deathly mother, mutton dressed up as lamb that will eat you.

When Napoleon is defeated, 'France, Caesar's widow, suddenly felt her wound' (p. 22). The wound is a castration, the god is gone. Again, the fantasy of massive living maleness is supplanted by an image of the female as [seemingly] dead: France is deeply asleep, wrapped in a shroud. The young men are a lost generation, born for the drama of war, finding an empty place. In this cold world reminiscent of René's, they share the latter's symptoms – old-youngness, objectless desire, fullness within versus emptiness without; but who is to take the place of Amélie? Where will they direct their desire? Blighted, without past or future, they see the present shivering, 'half mummy and half foetus ... like the daughter of the old count of Sarverden, in Strasbourg, embalmed in her betrothal finery. This childish skeleton makes you shudder, for on her slender [fluettes], livid fingers is an engagement ring and her head is crumbling into dust amidst a heap of orange-blossom' (p. 25). The self as 'corpse/demi-god' has been exchanged for the other as 'mummy/foetus', embalmed in her posthumous coquetry. But her 'mains fluettes' are those of Lorenzaccio. If the past is a lost father and the future a stone woman, the present is a narcissism of the dead, a necrophilia.

The young men of whom the hero is typical, then, are pitiable even or precisely in their hypocrisy, self-indulgence, debauchery and contempt. The harm they will do to others and themselves is someone else's fault, for they are always suffering children, sad Peter Pans of history.

And then, somewhat surprisingly, the story opens 'I must tell you of the occasion on which I was first overtaken by the sickness of the century' (p. 38), and we learn of the moment when the hero, not a newborn child but an infant of nineteen, discovers that his adored mistress is being unfaithful to him. We see nothing of his childhood; his mother is never mentioned and his father is introduced only a hundred pages later. A Parisian sophisticate who frequents fashionable dinner parties, he catches the 'maladie du siècle' one evening by dropping his fork and seeing that his mistress is playing footsie under the table while her face betrays nothing of it above.

'Under the table' is the first deadly place where the diver plunges. He learns there that the face's surface can lie. His own reaction is immediately to make his do the same – 'I sat up again with perfect calm' (p. 39) – but beneath the skin he is 'dazed, reduced to an idiot' by this unsuspected infidelity. Familiarly, he has been too simple to mistrust. But while this first mistress performs all the gestures of the *femme fatale*, we are never shown (only told) how he loves her. By contrast with the hard-done-by figures of Des Grieux and Don José, we are shown no innocent Octave; we have only his retrospective word for it. So the smiling infant, like the dead mother, is something we must infer from the grinning adult, his soul preserved within.

Only over-determination, it seems, can affirm this innocence: what the times have begun, everyone except Brigitte will build upon until, when he finds her, no harm he can do her will be his own.

Agonising over his experience, Octave recognises that he is shocked by the possibility not so much that she no longer loves him as that she can have deceived him; what matters is not how the woman feels but what she says. Against advice, he rushes to his mistress's house: she is all alone, distraught and repentant and throws herself at his feet, her hair wild, her clothes half off. 'Never had I seen her looking so lovely' (p. 43), he comments, like René and d'Albert on two other occasions of feminine humiliation. Rebuffing her, he returns a quarter of an hour later to find her seated in front of her mirror, loaded with jewellery, waiting for his rival, who is to take her to a ball. This Cinderella-like transformation is too much: he hits her violently on her 'impudent' (p. 44) neck, and (silent as Carmen) she falls without a cry. Octave goes home and collapses in a fever.

Octave has studied but has no career: love has been his sole occupation. Like Adolphe's, his father has left him free to waste his youth in procrastination. But, as we shall see, this does not mean moral neglect, for the role of paternal corruptor is entirely displaced onto his friend Desgenais. Paris is curiously both maternal and 'sedentary' (p. 49) and love inseparable from nature, for often he dragged his unwilling mistress out to the country, 'the sight of nature in her splendour having always been for me the most powerful of aphrodisiacs'. Like René, he has read and learned a lot, and this has made him old before his time; at the same time, his heart is that of a child, a motherless child now that he is alone and 'nature, my darling mother' (p. 51) instead of an aphrodisiac is 'more vast and empty than ever'. For if she is not a madame, there is no mother nature at all.

Desgenais is the dominant figure in the rest of the first section: he talks and Octave listens. This double is hard, dry, prematurely bald and has solidified youthful sorrows into a sort of armour: in other words he is skeletal through and through, the image of what Octave may become. He preaches the imperfection of life and love: women are only the fragile vessel of pleasure. To support his argument, he offers two extended portraits of womanhood that stress the effect of maternity as disfigurement. In the first, nature (pimping again) 'formed the virgin to be man's lover; but, at the birth of her first child, her hair falls out, her breast is deformed, her body carries a scar; woman is formed to be a mother . . . The virtue of the peasants is that their women are machines for birth and lactation, just as they themselves are machines for ploughing . . . Entirely lacking in sensuality, their wives are healthy; their hands are calloused, so their hearts are not' (p. 60). This charming unlogic is juxtaposed with a second, grimmer picture of the destiny of the middle-class female. Her arranged marriage to an old man is a kind of rape; she gives birth and, ugly now, has still not loved. The baby is brought to her but, dry-breasted, she sends it out to nurse; her husband agrees that her child would make her repulsive to him. Once recovered from the birth, with her child in Chaillot and her husband at the brothel, she starts to flirt, is abandoned by her first lover, takes more, and so on until she is thirty. Then, 'blasé et decayed [gangrenée], with no human qualities left, not even disgust, one evening she meets a charming boy with black hair, ardent eyes, his heart beating with hope; she recognises her youth, she recalls what she has suffered and, giving back to him the lessons that life has taught her, she teaches him never to love' (p. 61). Now this, apart from the colour of the boy's hair, would seem to be a portrait of Brigitte and Octave, uttered between the parentheses of Desgenais's discredited voice. The woman is pitiable but also inhuman, 'gangrenée', ancient at thirty and, above all, an appalling mother. The hot-eyed youth is surely her neglected son come back to haunt her, and she not only commits incest with him but a second time refuses him the sustenance of human kindness, feeding him instead with her cynicism.

The abandoning mother as object of both loathing and desire reappears like the uncanny here. The Brigitte of the text is on the face of it nothing like this, but the image, and her own lack of background, are sufficient suggestion; like Adolphe, Octave will be unable to love and his woman will be punished for it. Today's women, Desgenais insists, cannot be a true double for the heart and minds of men; the 'skeleton of all that God has made' (p. 63), they radiate a deadness contagious to necrophilia (which is all desire can now be), and in their mirror men will find only the distorting reflection of irony and mockery.

Octave, a good pupil, endorses the lecture: 'truly, a woman does not know what she is doing when she deceives a young man who has never before been deceived . . . if she thought about it, if she saw the dreadful wound she would make and the stream of blood that would pour out, then, sooner than open the door, she would wall it up' (p. 65). In this image the woman is rapist of the man: the flowing of blood as in menstruation, parturition or loss of virginity suggests that fear of castration is more exactly a horror of feminisation, of the woman making the man into her mirror. Seeking the preferable oblivion of alcohol, Octave goes one evening into a bar and espies 'a very young and pretty girl' (p. 81), who comes and sits at his table.

She is a prostitute. He has never met one before. She smiles all the time. He weeps. She asks him nothing but, while continuing to swallow a healthy supper, pauses every now and then to wipe away his tears with her handkerchief. He is shocked to find in her 'some strange quality that was so horrible and so gentle, an *impudence* bizarrely combined with *pity*' – as the terms I have italicised show, she stands at a midpoint between the first mistress and Brigitte, and his response to her is premonitory. When he hurls abuse at her, she smiles and offers to take him home to his mother 'since you find me ugly' (p. 82); but this good-humour cuts no ice with Octave. To him she is the poisoned sister-soul, incarnation of 'the sickness of the century' (p. 83) which, detached from himself in the figure of the whore, he can take home to pose as his lost mistress. Reminded suddenly of the castrated Abelard, Octave sleeps with this girl 'like my own statue on my tomb' (p. 86).

For the next while Octave joins Desgenais in the grim world of debauchery. Not just the retrospective narrator but also the hero, so we are told, is always distanced from what he is doing. Because he always remains 'a child', he is never more than clothed in vice; the mask does not stick to his face, a double is acting for him when he misbehaves. And just as Octave's fundamental goodness can be read forth from his superficial badness, so the departure of Brigitte with the equally unblamed Smith is, in a sense, always implicit in her seemingly unending patience. Female virtue is a mere garment: underneath they are all liars sooner or later. If they are not, then you must make them so. For it also follows from the bad behaviour of Octave that whatever Brigitte does – in this she is exactly like Amélie and Ellénore, and the obverse of Manon and Carmen – she is never seen as acting by her own will: both her long-suffering and her final 'betrayal' are Octave's doing not hers. If the proud and famous Staël and Sand reappear in fiction as figures of pure and agonised passion, it is to prove them mere females. Badness is strength, goodness is weakness; thus the power of the woman (which in the *Confession* is, after all, the first cause of the degeneration of the boy) is appropriated and her *mana* stolen once again.

The world into which Desgenais introduces Octave, in which fatherless sons sleep with ghostlike females, is crucially typified by a denaturing of the mother-daughter bond. Three examples are offered. In the first, Desgenais chooses to 'prove his friendship' by sending his mistress to Octave's bed. She enters pale as death, trying to hide her distress; she dare not go back until dawn because her mother is poor and Desgenais has threatened to turn her out. Octave, who finds her beautiful, reflects: 'a sublime, divine mystery was accomplished in the entrails that conceived her. Such a creature is made at the cost of nature's most patient and vigilant maternal care [regards]' (p. 107). Something poignant in this mother-daughter pair tied together by the economics of prostitution momentarily reflects against the dry Desgenais for, by contrast, 'his entrails are like those of sterile women' (p. 109).

The second prostitute-daughter is a humble seamstress who has observed how much the women she makes dresses for can earn on the streets; her mother is sick, she needs the money; the result is 'one girl I had' (p. 118). The third is the sensuous Marco, smiling and reptilian, who awakes in Octave a desiring self he acknowledges with distaste. 'She set a cord vibrating within me that was alien to my heart. The sight of this beautiful animal set another animal roaring in my vitals [entrailles]' (p. 121) – his entrails, at least, are not quite sterile. All evening he stares at her and she laughs. But after the 'beautiful animal' has taken him home, translated into a statue couchant, she seems to give forth 'the chill of death' (p. 126). A kind of spiritual impotence overtakes him. Looking out of her window, he recalls the long-lost days of childhood with his brother in the Bois de Boulogne. By now, Marco has fallen asleep. He reads a letter notifying her of someone's death; she wakes and tells him it is her mother; he leaves.

Debauchery is blamed for a corruption of the mother-son relation. Octave harangues Desgenais: 'nature herself feels her divine entrails withdrawing around you . . . you have played false with your mother's laws, you are no longer the brother of nurselings . . . every woman you embrace takes a spark of your strength without giving you any of hers . . . where a drop of your sweat falls there grows a sinister graveyard plant' (pp. 133-4). He has, as it were by contagion, become one of those unnatural daughters, fertile and deadly. But before this feminisation can be fully consummated, a *deus ex machina* calls him home to the bedside of his dying father.

Here, in the country home where his father died just before he arrived, Octave mourns in passionate obscurity, watched only by the silent double of his father's favourite servant. All we have heard of this parent before is that he gave Octave free rein; now stress is laid on his wasted role as 'a model of virtue, calm and kindness' (p. 138). His last words lie conveniently visible in an open diary: 'farewell, my son; I love you and I die'; his son feels 'a physical pain caused by his death' (p. 139). In this book, the childbed death is given to the father-son pair: paternity is a more developed transferential screen than elsewhere, carrying the loss and guilt of the original dyad.

Octave puts on his father's clothes and sits in his armchair. Like René, he finds a certain refreshment in suffering: 'whatever people may say, a great sorrow brings great repose' (p. 141). He weeps, walks and meditates. One day he sees a young woman, veiled and modestly dressed, emerge from an avenue of lindens with a pet goat; later the same day, taking shelter from a storm (shades of *Werther*) he watches her tend and save a dying peasant woman. His contempt for the vulgarity of the suffering family is matched by his admiration for Madame Pierson's nursing. He learns she is a widow living in extreme retirement with an elderly aunt. This first meeting is suffused with an aura of nurturance, 'charity' (p. 147) and 'sanctity'. The peasants call her Brigitte-la-Rose; she has been crowned 'rosière', a title given to the village girl most acclaimed for her chastity and virtue.

Once she sleeps with Octave, Brigitte will turn from a sister of charity to a cross between an over-eager schoolgirl and an abused mother. But the violence of the hero's jealousy is always strangely unfounded: we never know enough of Brigitte to be able to guess if he has any rival. This text is empty of narrative's usual hermeneutic code: there is no mystery to be solved.[17] The enigma is intrinsic: Octave demands proof that women are false. If she confesses perhaps he can paradoxically find truth confirmed, believe that the inside conforms to the face. But he poses no real question; he spends himself on the surface. What he really wants is, like d'Albert, not to know, not to enter the body he desires, for if he did he might find out what *he* is 'inside'.

Brigitte is required to serve as Octave's passive mirror. He is bad because abused and she is the body on which his badness is inscribed. Through him, the absent father, the non-existent mother, the *femme fatale*, Desgenais, Marco and the crew of prostitute-daughters all exercise their corruption on her. She ends by proving them right and, defiled by his cruelty, failing the test to remain patient forever. At this point, in her, the abandoning mother will be properly punished and left.

When they first meet, however, she is whole, private, 'this obscure woman whom nobody talks about' (p. 148). She smiles constantly, even when they speak of his bereavement, but never threateningly: 'I felt the piety of her smile' (p. 151). Created by God 'to heal those who suffer', she provides a precise replacement for the Desgenais who claimed he would 'cure' Octave of his first trauma. She herself has suffered but learned serenity. Obscurity and enclosure are her trademarks; this is how the narrator celebrates her metonymic greenhouse:

> Madame Pierson treated her flowers just like her birds and her peasants; she insisted that everything around her must thrive, every one must have its drop of water and its ray of sun, so that she could be bright and happy as a good angel; and so nothing could be better cared-for or more charming than her little greenhouse. When we had taken a turn around it, she said to me: 'There, M. de T***, this is my little world; you have seen all I possess, my whole domain' (p. 156)

Everything here is hers, including the peasants, just as later the village girls she likes to dance with are called 'her girls'; but she is dependent on them for her own peace of mind, possessed as well as possessing. Circumscription is the price of wholeness: if she is no more than what she seems, she is not free. It is the narrator's hyperbole only that extends her enclosure to the whole living world, she stresses the smallness of simplicity. In his phantasy – 'her presence filled my heart' (p. 158), her enclosure is enclosed within him – he is inevitably plotting her imprisonment.

Octave is straight away in love. Their relationship consists in speech felt as mutual but actually originating in him: she provides 'an echo' (p. 160). But what she says is always inessential. Whenever he broaches the subject of love, he is stopped; its taboo is written in her expression, in 'a slight hint of severity, even of suffering'. How to make her speak of love?

Like Adolphe and Ellénore, he pursues while she acts out a ritual retreat, he swears to obey and she is made to command what, perhaps, she only partly desires. A woman who appears to change her mind is, in this convention, not unreliable or ambivalent but an appearance forced finally to express an essence it belies. Their relationship is less between two bodies than two organs of speech. Thus when Octave (wordlessly, as it happens) has revealed his desire, he waits for Brigitte's response swearing that 'all the strength of my life was hanging on her lips' (p. 169). He suckles, she must nourish. But when, finally, she takes the initiative of inviting him to accompany her on an errand, he is suspicious of what has become an ambiguous surface, a conflict of behaviours: 'if I have touched her heart . . . why is she being so reserved? If she is just a coquette, why is she behaving so freely?' (p. 178). Any display of motive on the woman's part, however ardently wooed by the man, turns out to be not what he has been asking her.

Brigitte admits she loves him, and after a brief interval in which she demonstrates alternately 'a crazy joy' (p. 181) and maternal pensiveness, his irritation wins the day and they become lovers.

In an apostrophe to the silent 'eternal angel of blissful nights' (p. 184), the narrator represents mutual love as the child of a father God and a mother 'pleasure [volupté]' (p. 185). A momentary balance is struck, then, but the terms of the parental pair are menacing. It takes only two days for the mother to be vilified: a frenetically happy Brigitte indulges in a petty lie, playing as a piece by Stradella a composition of her own, and Octave begins to mistrust her. Let us look for a moment at this apparently casual occasion: the offence is somehow that Brigitte has hidden unsuspected artistic creativity under the name of a male composer. Like her pseudonymous original George Sand, she has thus exposed too much strength. The name, however feminised (Sand →Stra[n]d+ella), as is the character of Brigitte, expresses an assumption of power that cannot be tolerated. Octave feels 'a cloud', (p. 189), then 'a fog', finally 'thick darkness' enter his head; the malady has returned to 'pour its drop of poison into my veins' (p. 191).[18]

He is invaded: this suspicion is not natural to him, he feels inside himself 'a new being, a kind of stranger' (pp. 193). And if he has been impregnated with a new bad self it can only be by her. The strength of the woman is making him a woman, his jealousy is fathered by her. At no point in the course of his questioning does Octave show any interest in Brigitte's first marriage: the husband, like the father in this text, is intact and unimpeachable, well dead; for, like my other heroes, he is no parricide but rather a matricide. The passion to know is a destruction of the beloved; with an unhealthy version of Maupin's scientific quest, he begins to 'dissect the thing I loved' (p. 197).

The jealous self, separated from the ego, enters the secret, female world. A visit to Brigitte's kitchen to interrogate her servant turns into nightmare: the haggard cook, the stinking pots of his imagination, are 'my jealousy personified . . . sprung from my own heart' (p. 198). For this too is a mirroring: the badness he seeks in her is his own. Verbal and mental abuse replace the benign conversations of before; like the kindly prostitute in the bar, Brigitte replies: 'my friend, how I pity you' (p. 200) but her patience merely incites him to further sarcasms. When she tries to play the courtesan to please him, her success irritates, reminding him of a past he thought he had cast off. He flirts outrageously with a neighbour; when Brigitte gives way to anger, he throws himself at her feet. She forgives him again, and so it goes on.

Sometimes they go out for walks, Brigitte dressed up in men's clothing. At these times, he delights to watch her marching 'before me through the sand, with her steadfast tread and such a charming mixture of feminine delicacy and childlike boldness . . . her little velvet cap set upon her mass of blond hair made her look so much like a determined little boy that I would quite forget she was a woman' (p. 214), or speaking in her 'woman's voice, half joyous half plaintive, coming from this little schoolboy's body' (p. 215). Maurras points out with justification that there is little congruence between the character of the 'rosière' and this 'little man in the blue smock' (p. 234), but this figure is surely not there simply to make sure we all recognise George Sand. In appearance Brigitte provides Octave with the image of himself before the age of puberty, a reflection of his innocent boyhood. She has nothing of a man but no longer resembles a woman, not Stradella but a schoolboy. They frolic like children – like the brothers in the Bois de Boulogne. But when she speaks, it is to reiterate the message of motherly sacrifice: having restored him to life, she will die by his love if she must. He embraces her as 'my mistress, my mother and my sister' (p. 219).[19]

For six months, Brigitte suffers gossip abroad and his insults at home, no longer the obscure woman 'whom nobody talks about'. In between quarrels, the hero avows passionate remorse, swearing to blow his brains out rather than mistreat her again. Their relationship moves towards a sado-masochism both mental and physical to which she seems suicidally to assent: 'in these nights filled with terrible passion, Brigitte seemed to have forgotten that there was ever another man in me than the one she saw now before her . . . she knew she would die of this but hoped I would die also; she accepted everything, blessed whatever I might do . . . these pleasures were her tomb' (p. 232). They dress up in masks and costumes. He reads her diary: in her will, she vows 'to bear everything as long as I loved her, and to die [by her own hand] when I left her' (p. 234). Even in what is ostensibly addressed to herself (but which, like his father's diary, he takes as written for his eyes) she makes not a single complaint; she will go so far as to pretend that her death is her fault rather than his. So the childbed death is raised to a further power: give him life and, when he leaves, take your own life. Though it is understood that her suicide will be motivated solely by his effect on her, she will, like the *femme fatale*, take responsibility for her death as if it were a choice.

They go to Paris, determined to travel on together when they have found somewhere to go. They pore over maps like children. And suddenly he is changed: in total trustfulness, he trembles worshipfully at the sound of her voice and 'I wished there were somewhere a temple consecrated to Love, in which I could be baptised clean and cover myself in a fresh garment that nothing henceforth could tear off me' (p. 239). The roles are ready to be exchanged. It is he now who is precisely what he seems, ready to be robed in the purity he feels within. Aptly, though he poses as the adorer and likens himself to St. Thomas, the Christ-image can be seen here passing from one to the other: 'you alone in the world can kill me or save me; for my heart is marked with the wound of all the hurt I have done you' (p. 241).[20] All this self-castigation is reestablishing his innocence; he will now not suspect her when he has every obvious reason to.

A young man brings her some letters from her relatives; one day she suddenly seems less enthusiastic about the journey and complains she is unwell. Baffled, Octave tries to speak to Smith, the bearer of the letters, but is avoided. Far from suspicion, he merely notes a certain irritation: 'the disappearance of this young man was invincibly linked in my mind with the obstinate silence of Brigitte' (p. 245). He decides to visit Smith's apartment; going in to ask Brigitte the address, he finds her in bed, apparently having wept; she holds out her hands with the words '"What do you want from me?"' (p. 248). When he arrives at Smith's, he finds him also in bed and is greeted with the identical words. This twinned gesture bespeaks a desire that excludes him – but still he does not think of putting two and two together.

Smith, whom Brigitte has known since childhood, is the model son and brother: a portrait of his mother stands on his mantelpiece; he has given up the chance of marrying in order to preserve his sister's dowry, and still sends every spare penny home. He is exactly the same age as Octave, who likes and trusts him absolutely. The intermediary between Brigitte and her family, he also forms a salutory link between our couple, for by now 'our intimacy had become a burden to both of us' (p. 253). Thus he plays the idealised double. The disingenuousness of this stage of the narrative is, again, a problem to read. In the protagonist we must accept a transformation so total that he never dreams of mistrust: when he implores Brigitte to speak, it is out of puzzlement, not suspicion. Though the plea for her to release her 'secret' is as hyperbolic as ever – 'a dozen times a day, I was ready to throw myself at her feet, imploring her to take pity on me and strike me to death' – but their companionship has reformed into a triangle less deathly and more everyday. 'It was up to me . . . to set myself between them, to reassure them and help them believe in me' (p. 255); 'in front of Smith, Brigitte showed me more warmth than when we were alone' (p. 261); 'in the evenings, after Smith had left, we would sit in silence, or else talk of him' (p. 255). The third party binds rather than divides; he alone makes speech possible. At the same time, it is an oedipal triad – we see clearly how each man intervenes on a couple: Octave interrupts a piano performance à deux; Smith arrives to find them scratching the faces out of two figures in a brochure and drawing in their own; Smith and Brigitte are inexplicably sad, Octave stands 'immobile, like a statue, looking at them' (p. 261). Even thus, however, the triangle has its advantages, for it will make it possible for him to extricate himself with dignity. The oedipal child, he will be able to find a mature role for the first time, as grown-up son, the statue that immobilises the paired other with his gaze.

Merlant points out that Octave takes a certain delight in bringing the other two together; he terms it 'curiosity' (*Le Moment de 'Loren-zaccio'*, p. 38) but we could use the less charitable term voyeurism. The imaginative gaze here, precisely because the narrator makes it innocent of all aggressive suspicion, takes on the atmosphere of the child's compulsive creation of the primal scene, the image of fathers against mothers. In taking up the position of the outsider, Octave is condemning the others to replace his bitter couple while he leaves, his hands sacrificially clean.

Though jealousy is never explicit, these pages return to the more fevered tone of the early rhetoric, with imagery of penetration and death. The narrator describes how once, diving into the river to try to rescue a drowning man, he explored the half-lit amniotic world below the surface. Or, in a more familiar series, the truth is an eternal skeleton that every man must one day touch at the depths of a momentary wound; a debauchee is accustomed to the horror of the depths; has he not lifted the garment of chastity and seen death inside? his very sister is a whore. Like Nietzsche's Hamlet, the face he has seen under the skirt is the horror that nothing can make him forget. What Octave must do is divest himself of Brigitte.

In a particularly revealing simile, the narrator evokes the obsessive nature of his thoughts:

> When the mind, like those mad dervishes who find ecstasy in vertigo, grows weary at last of turning round upon itself, endlessly hollowing itself out, it stops short in terror. Man seems to be empty: he has descended so deep into himself that he finds himself standing on the last rung of the spiral. Here, as at the summit of a mountain or the depths of a mine, there is no air and God will not allow anyone to go further. Then the heart, struck by a mortal chill, thirsting for oblivion, wants to leap out and be reborn; it demands new life from everything surrounding it, it tries ardently to breathe, but can find nothing around it except its own illusions [chimères], which its now exhausted strength has been animating and which, created by it, stand about it like pitiless spectres (p. 271)

This is an exact representation of the situation of Narcissus: he plunges into himself and finds himself unborn inside the mother. The vortic in-turning of the spiral has carved him a cavern, in which he asphyxiates. Is this emptiness or an over-peopled cell? Is it the mountain-top or the bosom of the earth? The phallus/heart asks to be reborn but finds itself stuck for ever in this 'inside' which is, perhaps, after all, only in the mind. The image of the mother is inverted into both the massive 'everything surrounding it' and the

feminine 'chimères' which stand about pitilessly and are its own children. A Lorenzaccio unable to emerge, Octave determines a last
attempt to 'be reborn'.

He orders coach and horses, but tells neither of the others; they
pass a delightful evening together; Brigitte confirms that she is happy
to leave, he alone has been procrastinating. Let's leave now, then,
he proposes. The other two consent and make their farewells. Neither
reveals any 'secret'; even through the keyhole, Octave only hears his
mistress say that Smith will never see her again. Alone with her, he
begs her once again to tell him the truth, or he will die. There follows
a long scene in which Brigitte does nothing to provide the confession
he craves: the more she repeats she loves him, the less he is satisfied.
What Octave is demanding is an enactment of the childbed separation: as he dismisses the coachmen and bolts the door, he vows to
himself: 'here you stand face to face with the one who must give you
life or death' (p. 281). Like self and reflection, they must play out
the end-game of his birth.

No furniture is described in the room except a mirror. In the scene
that follows we will find a version of the familiar struggle in which
the woman echoes the man's discourse and is killed, while he survives
only in a living death. But in this text, everyone must end up walking
away to a fresh start; and what makes this outcome possible is the
paradox in Brigitte's character that makes her both *femme fatale* and
self-sacrificing martyr. She has resolved, we must understand, out of
sheer love of the boy, to stay with him to the end although she does
not desire him.

In order to cohere these contradictory motives we have to see
Brigitte as sacrificing a lesser, sexual love to a greater maternal one.
This in turn depends on the fulfilment of the whole text's argument:
that Octave is so prenatally vulnerable that she must and will set
aside everything she desires so that he may live. In this logic, giving
birth is inevitably a kind of maternal death: her body is not hers but
his. Brigitte can only be good under these extreme conditions. The
burden of motive is here placed so twistedly onto the woman that
her character seems to sprain under its weight. The man is left,
justified as ever, playing games at the feet of her monumental nobility.

To seduce her into speech, he tries on a few costumes and masks.
He tries to trick her by pretending to be calm. He offers her the
image of them both as children, ready to love again: she laughs at

him. He tells her to be brave and honest like a man: she keeps silent. He swears that the only man who can get the truth out of a woman is 'one ... who turns himself into a woman, and whose baseness reveals to him everything stirring in the dark shadows' (p. 285). Finally, in an image of himself as prisoner and her as the door to freedom, Octave declares brutally: 'to smash the seal on her lips and force her to speak, I would have exposed my life and hers' (p. 286).

It has taken a very long time for Brigitte to lose patience, but this is finally it – in obstetrical terms, she has reached transition. She expels Octave by a speech in which, in similar terms to those of Ellénore's letter, she complains of his cruelty, insisting that her only secret has been to love him. At the same time, it grows obvious that she is speaking less to him than to herself: the violence that is to give birth to his new self is directed towards her mirror-image, which she addresses in a bitter harangue. Like the poets Mary Elizabeth Coleridge and Annette von Droste-Hülshoff, she accosts her reflection as a ghost of herself, the image of the uncanny.[21] Echo lives as the voice that survives her body: the strength of Manon and Carmen, the words of Amélie from her coffin, the letter that outlasts Ellénore's death and, as we shall later see, the remembrance of Marceline or the diary of Alissa; here, Brigitte's speech is that of a ghost, accusing Octave of her martyrdom even as she reiterates her loyalty. Finally, she collapses and 'instead of an outraged mistress, there was suddenly nothing but a plaintive child [un enfant] in pain' (p. 290). The gender of 'enfant' is not fortuitous: Brigitte is now for Octave without sex. He carries her to bed, and while she sleeps, he meditates.

'Just as the ploughman after a storm counts the remaining ears of a field laid waste, so I began to plumb within myself to sound the harm I had done' (p. 291). Refreshed again by another's effigy-death, he feels a new man. For the first time, he considers living without Brigitte: she has got him born. Now he has to emancipate himself from the kind of undeath that remained to Adolphe. Thinking of all those who live 'without a mother, without family, without a dog' (p. 295) – exactly like himself – he pities them, reflecting that by contrast he and Brigitte have been in their time bound together 'like a single being by the blood-ties of sexual pleasure' (p. 296). With these words, he defines them as the primary couple of mother-child incest. From here he can cast her off, choosing instead to be mother to himself. The harm he has done is that of a double whom he has fostered, 'my evil genius, some creature inhabiting me that was not born there! . . . was it he whom my mother called Octave?' (pp. 296-7). He recalls his childhood, but the memory is interrupted by the image of Nero 'when he killed his mother' (p. 298). In all these rehearsals of the dyadic relation, he evacuates what is left of the old passion.

Close to suicide, he turns instead to look again at the woman. She has turned over in her sleep and exposed her breast. A comical part-object both good and bad – 'if she wanted to die, this beautiful breast would tell her she had to go on living' (p. 302) – it provokes him into deciding to murder her. Only the crucifix she wears saves her life, sending Octave into a meditation on the merits of Christianity. Jesus saves: 'how could you dare raise your hand to God?' (p. 307). Thus the patriarchy, in the nick of time, is restored. Addressing Jesus, Octave ends: 'your suffering draws us to you as it brought you to your father' (p. 309); he too can aspire once more to the father who makes him good. A new Messiah, he has recognised his double, born and reposing on the mother's breast. Her suffering is now dispensable. And as if in reward, the truth is indirectly revealed after all. Opening a letter, Octave finds it dated Christmas Day and addressed to Smith, bidding him an eternal farewell: 'my destiny is tied to that of a man for whose sake I have sacrificed everything; he cannot live without me, I must try to die for him. Farewell, pity us.' (pp. 309-10).

In the short third-person chapter that closes the text, Octave proves her wrong: he can live without her, and he will not make her die after all. Paternally giving Brigitte away to Smith, he makes himself interpreter of the ambiguous 'us' of her letter. She will never forget him of course. As the woman goes off to her new life, 'the young man remained alone; he took a last look at his native city . . . and thanked God that, out of three people who had suffered by his fault, only one was left unhappy' (p. 315). With these closing words, the family structure is restored: he is no longer an orphan, for God has shown him the way, and as for the mother, here she is all around him – à nous deux maintenant! – the Paris of corruption cleansed now as he is.

Chapter 5: *Sylvie* and *Dominique*

'It is your fate always to regret and never to desire'
(Fromentin)

If the fundamental structure in *René* and *Adolphe* is a pair, and that of *Mademoiselle de Maupin* and *La Confession d'un enfant du siècle* a pattern of three, the two texts which form the subject of this chapter are both based on a pattern of four. But in neither case are the four figures related in the way we might expect, as they are in, say, such a classic of symmetrical adultery as Goethe's *Die Wahlverwandtschaften* (1809). There the married couple Eduard and Charlotte each fall in love (in rather different ways) with one of their house-guests, her niece Ottilie and his friend the Captain. Symmetry is stressed by the near-identity of their names: the palindrome 'Otto' is the Captain's first name and Eduard's second, and its root forms the first and last syllable of the two women's names. When Eduard and Charlotte make love, both fantasising the presence of the one they really desire, they have a baby who exactly resembles Ottilie and the Captain. The poor little freak is quickly drowned in an accident by Ottilie, who declines into an anorexia of speech neither taken nor given forth. Like her almost-homonym Ophelia, she continues after her death to be saddled with significances upon which other people act.

Neither *Sylvie* (1853) nor *Dominique* (1863) reproduces this murderous balancing act. On the contrary, their asymmetry is the crux of their problem: from the protagonist, in each case, proceeds a small, unbalanced community of others in which he can neither direct and control desire nor see himself reflected as he wishes. While the central woman dies in neither of these texts, the death or near-death of others variously reflect the violence of the protagonist's self.

Nerval is one of those Romantic figures whose own life and death seem to preempt fictionalisation. In his writings, especially his poetry, the personal 'family romance' is recast as cosmic myth; it is not surprising that Jungian rather than Freudian criticism has made much of him. I want to look briefly at some motifs from *Les Chimères* and other fictions before turning to *Sylvie*.

Rather than die in childbirth, Nerval's mother sent him to a wet-nurse in the country, then left France to go with her doctor husband to the army on the Rhine. In a parenthetic page of 'Angélique', the narrating heroine, who has followed her lover to the army, is quoted as observing how Frenchwomen dislike war and its honours, and the frame-narrator concurs: it is 'because of the love they bear their children' (p. 556).[1] He continues incongruously: 'warlike women belong to the Frankish race . . . Their courage and even their frequent cruelty led to the adoption of the Salic Law. And yet women, warlike or not, never lost their powerful position in France, either as queens or as favourites' (pp. 556-7). This stress on children, female cruelty and female power – all irrelevant to the story of Angélique – is symptomatic of the oedipal inspiration in Nerval's writing which shows itself most strikingly in a pervasive matriolatry. Just as the woman-garden in *Aurélia*, in dying, takes the whole world with her, so the goddess Isis stands for all matriarchal deities: 'the original identity of that queen of heaven with her diverse attributes and ever-changing mask!' (p. 657). In *Sylvie* the three others of the central configuration of four are women among whom the reflection of the mother is distributed and sought.

We have already seen several times how dangerous doubling can be for the woman in the *récit*. Manon breaks her power by sending her lover a surrogate, for her status depends on a uniqueness that makes her the first and only substitute for the lost mother; her replica-bility is a threat to the preserved/repressed image of the mother, for it exposes and makes it mutable. If Manon is a whore (in Des Grieux's eyes, that is), then his mother too is 'merely' sexual. A similar sense of the transferance of sexuality to an implied original produces the mothers inferred through prostitute-daughters in *La Confession d'un enfant du siècle*. Menace is felt when women form a group amongst themselves: thus, even in *Mademoiselle de Maupin* the clever Rosette and Madeleine form the briefest of couples, and express contempt for their sex. In *Sylvie*, as also in 'Octavie', three women appear but never form a group.

We shall see more presently of how this is done. Let us first briefly trace some avatars of the mother-goddess in Nerval's poetry. In the sonnet 'Horus', Isis acts out the oedipal parricide on behalf of her offspring who as 'the new spirit' (p. 698) will become her new consort. But by the end of the poem she has abruptly disappeared, leaving only the reflection of a rainbow for 'us' (presumably the father and son) to gaze at. In 'Antéros', the son is his own avenger and the unique protector of the mother in homage to whom he sows 'the teeth of the ancient dragon' (p. 699). But there is no harvest: in 'Delfica', despite the opening promise that the old deities will return, 'the antique seed of the conquered dragon is sleeping still' (p. 700) and the arch of Constantine stands firm over the slumbering latin sibyl. The mother goddess, identified with pre-Biblical religions, seems always on the point of returning, but never quite arrives. In parallel, the father-god whom only she and the son together could overcome, is never as dead as he is wished; even in 'Le Christ aux Oliviers', the revelation changes in a line from 'God does not exist!' (p. 705) to 'God no longer exists!' and by the end of the poem the *deus absconditus* seems altogether restored. Thus the cult of Isis is made precarious by what also makes it necessary: the adored mother has died because she preferred the father to the child, and abandoned them both to a posthumous rivalry.

The family romance appears all over Nerval's writing in the form of myth, and *Sylvie* is no more directly autobiographical than my other *récits*. The protagonist is never named and this lack of appellation helps to make the central 'I' as undefined as possible so that, as in the writing of Proust who much admired Nerval, we can neither affirm nor deny the personal reference. For most of the text we dwell in the dreamland of his memory; but the hazy atmosphere undermines itself. In *Aurélia*, the coherent narrative of two experiences of prolonged hallucination is designed to 'fix' (p. 822) dream into articulation in order to make others understand: 'the experience of each one is the treasure of all' (p. 463). Thus here again we are referred to a general truth behind the fictionalised confession of the author. But the critique of *Sylvie* is more embedded than that of any other of my texts so far: it is the first to be perceptibly ironic; and the ironic standpoint is that of the eponymous heroine. Where the protagonist tries to make her his mirror, she evades and surpasses him. Work and laughter are her main counterweights to his self-indulgence.

The structure of four in *Sylvie* is non-oedipal. There are no heterosexual couples. Or rather – and this is one source of the irony – the narrative proposes, and then rigorously excludes, the three possible couples of the hero and Adrienne, Aurélie and Sylvie. In each case, an acceptable rival takes his place. The possibility of a self-other pairing is, in *Sylvie*, systematically and preemptively refuted; in this sense it is a narrative of undesire.

As the heterosexual couple self-woman is rendered impossible, the possibility of pair bonds amongst the women is proposed instead, not as a choice amongst them (each of the women is as carefully isolated from her sex as Manon or Carmen) but as a compulsion in the mind of the man. There are two kinds of pairing: the uncanny (mythical, psychotic) between Aurélie and Adrienne, and the complementary (if one not the other, day/night, pink/blue) between Sylvie and Adrienne, or Aurélie as Adrienne's surrogate.[2] The complementary relationship, which has realistic roots in an event of the story, is the one the protagonist works on so as to exorcise the other. The value of the pairings among the three is not so much, as Kofman suggests, to evade the hint of death, as to keep the group of women unstable. The protagonist is a juggler. Isolated but sole motivator, he ensures the separation of the women by continually making one of them a third, so that a woman is always in circulation, his thing, the detached signifier kept in the air. Flying helplessly, she is in no danger of seeming that inadmissible absence of the text, the betraying mother.[3]

Sylvie is the key third figure and it is with her that the protagonist comes nearest to proposing a couple. But as Sylvie acquires a voice (she sings, she laughs), the protagonist is left with the mediate form of writing.[4] The power of the narrator as writer is merely to recreate the fluid dream-world which he has seen discredited. What Sylvie has laughed at is exactly what the narrator, half-sheepish, half ecstatic, works to reinstate. The famous 'charm' of *Sylvie* derives from this. Like that of Proust's 'Combray' or *Le grand Meaulnes*, we read it with the special shamefaced pleasure reserved for outgrown vices like nostalgia.

The *récit* has no frame, though the final chapter forms a free-standing conclusion in the present tense. It begins in an unspecified past, throwing us straight into the looking-glass world: 'I was coming out of a theatre in which I *appeared nightly* at the front of the house in the full *costume* of the *suitor* [soupirant]' (p. 589, my italics). The terms I have italicised show how the hero has coopted the actress's role, so that he rather than she is the performer. Already we can see how the hero makes a mirror of his beloved 'apparition' (p. 590). This actress is so fixed by the gaze of protagonist that (even though, as we learn, she is unaware of his existence) in his own mind he possesses her. 'I felt myself living in her, and she lived for me alone'. Here we have a primary image of pregnancy – the self inside the woman, her life dedicated to its nurturance – but also an inversion of that bond: his obsession with her means that, however passively or unknowingly, she has meaning only through him, he makes her live, he is her mother.

'In all that year, I had not thought of enquiring what she might be; I was afraid I might cloud the magic mirror that cast me back her image'. With these words, the narrator makes explicit the theme of mirroring and its significance. The woman here, as Woolf notes in the formula I quoted earlier, serves as a mirror 'possessing the magic and delicious power of reflecting the figure of man at twice its natural size'; and the irony of *Sylvie* comes from the fact that the protagonist is aware of this. He admits without shame that his desire for her mirror is based not so much in vanity as in fear.[5]

One way of covering up this fear is offered by the discourse of the fathers. The protagonist's uncle has offered him a men-of-the-world misogyny to assure him that actresses have no hearts. He was a man of the last century, but the influence lingers on, both in his ideas and in the portraits and keepsakes he has preserved. This generation is, like Octave's, living out of time:

> We were living in a strange era, like those that usually follow a revolution or the collapse of a great reign . . . the eternally young, pure [Isis] appeared to us by night and made us ashamed of our wasted daytime hours. But ambition did not belong to our age, the greedy scramble for position and honours drove us far from all spheres of activity. The only refuge left to us was the poets' ivory tower; there we ascended ever higher in order to isolate ourselves from the mob. In these elevated places, guided by our masters, we breathed at last the pure air of solitude, we drank oblivion from the golden chalices of legend, we were intoxicated with poetry and love. The love, alas, of vague forms, shades of pink and blue, metaphysical phantoms! Seen from close up, the real woman outraged our naivety [révoltait notre ingénuité]; she must appear as queen or goddess, and above all never be approached (p. 591)

Rich enough to spurn the vulgarity of work, this all-male community sees the goddess in dreams, but she is always reproaching them; and Nerval's analysis (markedly cooler than Musset's) goes straight to the reason: their sense of youthful ingenuousness depends on a horror of the female body and of women as real. The poetic reveries are born of a deferred sexuality, and their mythological nostalgia is grounded in repressed terror.

This critique is focused on two female figures. The 'alas' is the narrator's, but his too are the rosy terms; only the clear figure of Isis disperses the pinks and blues with her reproach. In *Sylvie* where the actress (as well as generic 'easy lay') is cast as the queen, and the sainted Adrienne plays the goddess, Sylvie is 'the real woman' – rather more than the hero bargains for – she incarnates the nocturnal figure of the maternal superego simply by continuing to live while he is not dreaming of her.

One of the hero's friends points out the actress's lover, a loyal member of their group who waits till morning to join his mistress. This rival, not surprisingly, provokes little emotion and provides a reassuring double: well-dressed, melancholic, indifferently losing at whist. The hero is not jealous because 'it's just an image I am pursuing, nothing more' (p. 592). From the lack of desire we can easily infer that the image he is chasing is his own reflection mirrored by the woman.

This text is Proustian, among other things, because of its use of involuntary memory: when the hero recalls a key scene of his child-hood it is because of a chance snippet in a banal newspaper. But since Freud we know that nothing is really arbitrary or incidental, and the most symptomatic adverbs are those that try to minimise an act of real significance. 'On my way out I passed through the reading-room and glanced *mechanically* at a paper, *I think* to see how the stock-market was getting on' (my italics): with this throwaway phrasing we discover that the head-in-air poet has a well invested inheritance. Sure enough, he finds he has recovered his fortune overnight. His immediate reaction is to conclude 'that my beloved . . . was mine if I wanted' (p. 593): thus she is assumed to be for sale because he has the impulse to buy her. 'I was near enough to touch my ideal', he comically exults. But the next thought restores undesire, ostensibly for the sake of the rival; to go to the woman now would be to fill his place: 'I shuddered at that thought, and my pride rebelled [se révolta]'.

The protagonist is far from admitting either that his impulse to buy the actress is a political one or that his thoughts of the rival are a function of undesire; instead, he invokes the innocence of both the century and his own youth: 'no! . . . at my age one does not destroy love with gold; I will not be a corruptor. Besides, that idea belongs to a different age. And who has told me the woman is venal?' The last question remains rhetorical, because he would have to point at himself, and the very asking suggests the possibility that the actress could refuse him. Another change of subject hurriedly supervenes, as he turns away from what does not bear thinking of. Carelessly glancing down the page, he sees the announcement of a traditional celebration in the Valois region where he grew up; his mind's eye fills with garlands, archers and young girls, and himself as one of the children dressed up as knights in a druidic ritual.

At home, he relives in half-slumber an incident from his childhood. On a lawn outside an old chateau, young girls dance and sing 'old airs they had learned from their mothers' (p. 594). In this matriarchal circle he is the only boy, but during the course of the memory he is responsible for isolating and dividing the group of girls. With him is 'Sylvie, a little girl from the neighbouring village, so lively and fresh, with her black eyes, regular profile and slightly tanned skin! . . . I loved no one but her – till then!' (pp. 594-5, ellipses Nerval's). Then he notices another girl in the circle, 'tall, beautiful and blonde, they called her Adrienne' (p. 595). The latter is the same height as he; when the two find themselves in the centre, he kisses her and squeezes her hand; the two are momentarily one as her golden curls 'brushed against my cheeks. From that moment I was gripped by an unknown excitement'. Adrienne is everything Sylvie is not: older, blonde, distinguished; as forfeit she sings an old romance, and her 'fresh, penetrating voice' accompanies nightfall and the rise of a moon which picks her out like a spotlight. When she stops no-one speaks, for it is like being in heaven; the young protagonist runs to crown her with laurels. We learn that she is of royal descent; dedicated by her family to the monastic life, she is already not of their world, but carries the regional name in her Valois blood, a myth by birth. Sylvie weeps with jealousy and will not speak to him. He returns to Paris carrying 'this double image of a tender friendship sadly torn apart – and of an impossible, vague love which gave rise to painful thoughts that school philosophy was impotent to calm' (p. 596). Again, the final phrase offers an older-brotherly irony, but the impossible complementarity set up here is an obsession that will persist to the end of the text, despite being discredited.

This memory wakens the protagonist (now back in the time of the first chapter) and makes everything suddenly explicable. His passion for the actress is a double for the similarly distanced and impossible love of Adrienne. They even look alike. But, 'to love a nun in the form of an actress! . . . and what if they were the same person! – That way lies madness, a fatal pursuit of the unknown that flees like a will-o'-the-wisp across the rushes of a stagnant lake ... Let's take a foothold again on the real' (p. 597, ellipses Nerval's). Madness lies here because if two women are the same woman the world is uncanny: either his hallucinating imagination has created the double and it is unreal, or else the return of the repressed hints at the terrible coexistence of nun and whore, saint and siren, in the body of the mother. To find his feet again, he turns instead to the canny complementarity of blonde and dark, related by the everyday divisions of class and jealousy, Adrienne and Sylvie.

Sylvie herself is made to embody the real, here reassuring precisely because it breaks up the imagination's deadly doubling. To be real is to be conserved. How could he have forgotten her for three years, 'Sylvie, whom I loved so much ... She exists, of course, good and pure of heart'. He pictures her window encircled with vine and roses, a comfortably unintoxicating entrance; she is good 'of course' because she is *there*: 'she will still be waiting for me ... Who would have married her? she is so poor!' (ellipses Nerval's). For a second time, we see him identify money with possession, the only mode of access to women and a gauge of their immobility. If money is 'the male instrument',[6] poverty and venality are women's place.

There are dangers even in the figure of Sylvie, however. For if she truly becomes real, and thus evades him, she will leave the circuit of three and throw him back upon the uncanny couple Adrienne-Aurélie. Sylvie must submit to a safe mirroring, supporting the protagonist's sense of existing in the real world, she must not exist in her own right. This is what he expects when he resolves to go and see her. What he will find is that she has grown too much like him to serve him as a looking-glass.

In his imagination, Sylvie is the practical peasant girl who could have helped him economise: spendthrift Parisian, he would have been domesticated. And in her image also, time becomes not that starlight of the poet's world, but something you must keep if you want to catch buses. 'There is still time' (p. 598), he promises himself, and fantasises what she might be doing 'at this hour'. But he does not know the hour because he has no watch, only an elaborate renaissance clock, left unwound for two hundred years; he has to go down and consult the vulgar face of the concierge's cuckoo-clock. Psychological time is the fluid in which the text amniotically bathes, and it is central to the narrator's art, as I mentioned before, that we drift where he takes us and do not ask too many questions. But it is this luxury that marks out the occasional use of exact numbers as significant and ironic. The cuckoo-clock, like the monetarist assumptions of Aurélie's venality and Sylvie's unmarriagable conservation, argues a political critique as loud as Sylvie's laughter. The coach has to be caught, the journey takes just four hours, he will arrive at four exactly; the last word of the text is a date.

In between these punctuations, memory travels like the hero, and we are taken back to the group boat-outing (he must have been about sixteen) where he first observed Sylvie's maturing 'Athenian' (p. 601) beauty. He spends the following night prowling around the convent where he thinks Adrienne is incarcerated – but to gaze over that wall would be profanity; in the morning he decides to go and wake Sylvie. She may be gazed on with impunity; a good mirror, the changes in her are all benign. For instance, she is no longer a spinner like her friends, and this allows a patronising admiration: 'she is almost a young lady since she has begun creating fine lace, while her family have remained simple village-folk' (p. 603). Thus the social mobility contingent on her having to work is aesthetic and vaguely flattering to him – and 'almost' keeps her safely unmarriageable without seeming to make her available to others. Sylvie invites him to go with her to a great-aunt in Othys; on the way he quotes passages from *La nouvelle Héloïse* while she picks strawberries.

At the aunt's house, they dress up in her perfectly-preserved wedding clothes. '"Oh dear, I'll look like a funny old fairy!"' (p. 606), cries Sylvie. The hero corrects her: '"the fairy of legend, who is eternally young!"'. Again their differences are stressed but tamed: her keen sense of the changefulness of fashion is subsumed by his delighted nostalgia; her realistic sense of time masked by his myth of eternal youth. The marriage that class makes unthinkable is mimed as 'we were husband and wife for a whole fine summer's morning' (p. 607). These costumes out of the aunt's past are, like the faded souvenirs of the uncle's cynicism, tokens rich with meaning which the protagonist can take but not quite leave. What he is free to don is too close to desire to put off: Sylvie as eternal sprite, Aurélie as demi-rep, these preserve him as a 'bridegroom of the last century'.

A later recollection supervenes. One evening the hero went with Sylvie's brother to the old abbey at Châalis. Chancing there upon a modern-day mystery play, they see a figure, probably Adrienne, dressed as an spirit risen from the underworld. Her cardboard halo glows as with real light, her voice is more powerful and as Italian as ever. Once again hints of the actress inform the portrayal of the nun: for each the situation of voice and costume fades into a divine remoteness onto which the protagonist can but intrude. But the uncanny accompanies this memory too: perhaps his desire invented it all. 'This memory may be just an obsession' (p. 609), the narrator admits; 'luckily' (another studiedly casual adverb) we are back in the coach which is halting to let us out. He arrives at the party just as it is ending; Sylvie is dancing with a young man, but she greets her old friend and they leave together.

As they walk home, the protagonist accuses Sylvie of ceasing to love him. She makes no apologies: 'my friend, I had to be sensible . . . things don't always work out as we wish in life' (p. 610). But her resignation is still flattering; she assures the hero that if he had returned earlier things might have been different:

> 'You told me once about *La Nouvelle Héloïse*, I have read it now; I got a shock when I saw the first line: "Any young girl who reads this book is lost/damned [perdue]". But still I read on, trusting to my good sense [raison]. Do you remember the day we put on my aunt's wedding-clothes? . . . The illustrations in the book were also of lovers dressed in old-fashioned costumes, so in my mind you were Saint-Preux and I saw myself in Julie. Oh, why didn't you come back then! But they say you were in Italy. The girls there are much prettier than me, I'm sure!' 'There are none with your look and your pure features, Sylvie. You are a nymph of ancient times who[7] does not know herself' (pp. 610-11, ellipses Nerval's)

Sylvie has misquoted the opening of Rousseau's novel; it is more damning: 'no chaste girl ever read a novel . . . Any girl who ignores this title and dares to read a single page is lost [une fille perdue]' (p. 610, n. 1). Worded thus, the opening is less a warning than a condemnation: those who allow a page to penetrate their minds are by definition already not virgins, for a reading woman is an unchaste woman. In Sylvie's version, the woman has a choice: by opting to read she may, in their terms, become 'perdue' but she can also by-pass their intimidation by a confidence in her 'raison'. It is this that the hero most urgently rebuts: you are not a reasoning being to whom I come too late, but a timeless creature forbidden to know herself. Her 'look', the reading gaze, is subsumed into the visible of her face, 'the pure

130

features' of his memory.

At this point, the hero throws himself at Sylvie's feet and weeps, confessing his irresolution and hinting at the baleful spectre of Adrienne; he begs Sylvie to take him back and save him. She begins to respond, turning 'her tender gaze towards me . . .' (p. 611, ellipses Nerval's), when his performance is interrupted by a violent burst of laughter. Sylvie's brother has arrived, his native 'rustic jollity' supplemented by the night's drinking; beside him stands the rival, whose 'honest face and deference mingled with embarrassment' (pp. 611-2) make him no threat.

On parting from Sylvie, the hero pays a nostalgic visit to his uncle's house, where everything has decayed or grown old. The landscape is still full of monuments to culture, however, for this is the site of Rousseau's grave. In homage to the latter, the narrator laments: 'you gave us the milk of the strong and we were too feeble to make use of it' (p. 614). Thus Rousseau as mother/wetnurse has been abandoned by the young men, who dream instead of thinking. What he does not add is that it is the disobedient daughter Sylvie, who trusted to her reason and read, who is really the rightful suckler at the breast of the patriarch. Again a 'denatured' mother-daughter configuration is implicitly set up on the failure of the father-son bond.

With the deflationary laughter of the brother and rival, a new phase is announced. The hero begins to notice less pleasing changes in Sylvie. She is no longer his girl: nowadays she dances with a peasant, not just annually at festivals with him. No longer in aspic, it seems she may be doing more than just reading. As the visit progresses, everything he discovers spells out her emancipation however modest from the figure he liked to think her. Representative of the real, she has become too real to represent. Specifically it is those changes which suggest she has come to resemble him that disturb him most.

He goes to her house; she is wearing 'a young lady's outfit, almost in the fashion of the city' We can see how the 'almost' has changed value now: her being a 'young lady' is no longer flattering because it threatens an intrusion into his urban space – does not everybody call him 'Parisien'? Sylvie is still ingenuous and her smile is still charming, 'but the pronounced arch of her eyebrows sometimes gave her a serious look'.[8] Her bedroom furniture is modern, a new mirror replaces the old looking-glass. Worse, Sylvie has stopped making lace. She shows him an 'iron tool that looked like a long pincer'; this fearsome machine is for making gloves. "'Oh, you are a glove-maker, Sylvie?'" (p. 615), the hero gasps.

The scene that follows marks the point of no return. They go out for a walk and exchange nostalgic banter: "'do you remember when we were children and you were taller than me?" "And you were better-behaved than me!" "Oh Sylvie!'" Here for the first time, we see a role reversal between them, in which Sylvie is both taller and bolder; the identity of height between the boy-hero and Adrienne suddenly no longer makes her small. At this point Sylvie reminds him of his 'milk-brother' (the child of his wetnurse) who once rescued him from drowning in the river, after first assuring him it was safe to cross.

The rival (for we soon discover he is Sylvie's dancing-partner) both led the hero to and saved him from death by water. This stands for the original sharing of milk which the natural child creates and the foster-child borrows. Some wetnurses, believing they could not produce enough milk for two, would let their own babies die in order to feed the child they were paid to nourish. In this relationship, then, we find a knot of envies over the mother's body – the woman again a kind of whore, for she may give more to the child she is paid to feed, but always a real mother only for her natural infant, to whom her first feelings flow. Behind the foster-mother stands the absent figure of the foster-child's natural mother who, by refusing her breast, prefers class to maternity, putting a political displacement into the child's earliest encounter with the female body. The conviction that a woman who is poor is available has come, then, not only from the patriarchal admonitions of the uncle but also from the *dea abscondita* of the refusing mother. All this is implicit in the figure of the rival-double 'milk-brother'.

They stroll on. Sylvie shocks the hero by remarking that the land-scape reminds her of Walter Scott: "'you've been reading a lot in the last three years!" he retorts, "I prefer to forget books; what I like best is to go with you to visit this old abbey where as children we played hide-and-seek among the ruins'" (p. 616). Her reading is a threat to the preserved image of infancy that he has invested in her; as we see a page later, it makes her too much like him for the flattering reflection to magnify. When he asks her to sing a folksong, she refuses because "'nobody sings those things any more'". Instead 'Sylvie modulated a few notes from a new operatic aria . . . She was *phrasing!'*

(p. 617, ellipses Nerval's).

The woman's voice is essential to her mythic qualities in Nerval. Young girls singing folksongs their mothers taught them recur elsewhere in his autobiographical writing (pp. 458-60); both Aurélie and Adrienne are characterised by public singing, and their voices have a 'penetrating' splendour that Sylvie's is supposed to lack. In accusing her of the over-sophistication of 'phrasing', the narrator is indignant not just that she sings the wrong kind of thing but that she presumes to take artistic control of her voice. Phrasing is something [male] writers do; and the hint that her artistry is derivative embodies an even deeper threat, as we shall see in a moment. Rattled, the hero shows off his erudition as he has so often before, but Sylvie is no longer impressed: '"you *have* read a lot more than me . . . How clever you must be!"' she accuses; and he is stung by her reproachful tone. It is not so much that she resents his pretension as that she exposes it. Her voice is unseemly.

When he makes her sing Adrienne's song, only Sylvie's reluctance breaks down the complementary double the protagonist wants her to make with Adrienne. But even passively her attitude undermines him and his project; his culture-games have suddenly become unseductive. 'I tried to talk of what was in my heart but, I don't know why, all I could find were common expressions, or even suddenly some pompous phrase from a novel – which Sylvie might have read'. This is surely the key moment of his education. The utterance of his [sincere, whatever that means] desire is newly impossible because it is clothed in aesthetic derivation; and Sylvie, literate and even articulate now, might be able to recognise the costume and so doubt the motive. The 'vagueness of the passions' stands exposed like a naked Emperor before the speaking, thinking woman.

The hero changes the subject again and asks what became of the nun. '"Oh, you really are dreadful with your nun . . . Well, . . . well, it all ended badly"' (p. 618, ellipses Nerval's). Sylvie, master of her words, refuses to say more. All at once she ceases to be desirable: his thoughts turn back to Aurélie, the actress. Here named for the first time, the latter has become easier to face. She is accompanied in his imagination by a man, 'the young lead with the wrinkled face', the strange double of the old-young self who will prove another worthy rival. By eight he is back in his seat at the theatre.

After spending several months in Germany, the hero returns to

Paris with a play for Aurélie to act in. With a flourish of rhetoric, he announces his initiation into the mad, terrible world of theatre: 'my sanity was the determination to conquer and fix my ideal' (p. 622). She agrees to star in his play, and admits '"I have never yet found a man who could truly love me". O woman!' the narrator cries, 'you are looking for love . . . And what about me?' (ellipses Nerval's). But the analogy is one of resemblance rather than reflection: Aurélie turns out to be not promiscuous but monogomous – '"if you really love me *for myself,* you will realise that I can only belong to one man"' – and this is not, after all, what the hero wants. Her singleness may undo the uncanny of his double passion but it also makes her valueless to him. He does not of course love her for herself.

A few weeks later, the melancholic young man of the opening scene has gone to join the army, and the protagonist and Aurélie (between the lines) become lovers. The relationship founders the following summer, when the hero takes the troupe to the Valois. The director is the wrinkled lead actor, who has now become a friend, and from close to, looks less old, even attractive: 'he was still slim, and could make quite an impression on a provincial audience, for he had a certain passion'. The protagonist takes Aurélie to Senlis and they visit the lawn where he first saw Adrienne, but 'she showed no trace of emotion' (p. 623). So he tells her the whole story about the nun: 'she listened gravely and then said, "You do not love me! You expect me to tell you that the actress is the same as the nun; you are trying to create a drama, and the ending won't work. Go away, I don't believe you any more!"' Thus Aurélie refuses the doubling and, using the imagery of her art, rejects a passion that makes her derivative. In splitting open the pair-identity on which he relied, insisting on her uniqueness, she proves that he does not love her and is himself a shadow, an unreality. The actress falls in love with the director: 'Aurélie said to me one day: "Here is the man who loves me!"' (p. 624).

Both these women resemble the hero too much: Sylvie has become a reader both derivative and creative like him; Aurélie has turned out to be a similar kind of 'idealist' in love. For this reason, they cease to be of any use as mirrors: the reflection is not laterally inverted, does not magnify his figure but, like a certain painting by Magritte, shows the viewer's mute back instead of his speaking likeness. Sébillotte's comment represents the protagonist's delusion here: 'this sensible young woman who "takes the realistic view" scarcely resembles the old Sylvie ... How could she be expected to understand the illusions that plague the heart of a poet?' (p. 162). On the contrary, both girls, by having the same kind of impulses (who hasn't?) can understand the 'poet's heart' all too well – and this is not what he wants. Arthur Symons, confusing character with original, typifies the critics' view of what is supposed to be a clash of 'ideal' and 'real':

> the Jenny Colons of the world are very simple, very real, if one will but refrain from assuming them to be a mystery ... The picture of Gérard, after many hesitations, revealing to the astonished Jenny that she is the incarnation of another, the shadow of a dream, that she has been Adrienne and is about to be the Queen of Sheba; her very human little cry of incomprehension, *Mais vous ne m'aimez pas!* and her prompt refuge in the arms of the *jeune premier ridé*, if it were not of the acutest pathos, would certainly be of the most quintessential comedy.[9]

Incomprehension again. But what if Jenny/Aurélie is not 'very simple'? That is unthinkable for both the author-protagonist and his critic doubles, for then 'very human' could not be contrasted to 'the heart of a poet'. What keeps them apart is a vital (false) gap of understanding, a sanctioned difference of knowledge.

The uncanny is almost easier than this, and it is certainly more picturesque. Poulet however highlights what 'enigma' and secret (symptoms of the uncanny of which we have seen much in other *récits*) really signify: 'the real person, as opposed to the imagined person, is a soul dissembled; individuality always harbours a secret' (p. 74). Enigma or secrecy, that old black continent of womankind, is simply a function of the gaze upon the other, when it disavows the other's fundamental analogy to the self. The knowledge that the other is a like self is strenuously evaded: the uncanny is preferable, just as the boy in Freud disavows the completeness of the female body in an elaborate displacement of castration-fear onto her body. The woman is not a different man but another 'I'.

In the last chapter of *Sylvie*, as throughout *Dominique*, we find a stress on the position of the narrator as mature adult and writing as the garnering of experience: 'these are the illusions [chimères] that charm and lead one astray at the dawn of life. I have tried to set them down [les fixer] in no particular order, but many hearts will understand me. Delusions fall one after the other like the rind of a fruit, and the fruit is experience' (p. 624). But this rings false. First because we know that the hero too gazed behind rather than ahead, regretted rather than desired and saw a past always already lost and derived. Second because in appealing to the group of [male] implied readers who will understand him, the narrator is reneging on the explicit knowledge of Aurélie and Sylvie. He has left irony behind, come up front – thus the last chapter draws attention to its status as writing in the title 'Final page' – and restored the discredited ivory-tower complementarity of the pink and blue: 'Ermenonville! . . . you have lost your unique star, that shimmered for me with a double brightness [éclat]. In turn blue and pink like the deceitful star of Aldebaran, it was Adrienne or Sylvie, the two halves of a single love. One was the sublime ideal, the other sweet reality'. Here he latter, tucked again under the myth of an absract concrete, is as safely locked away as the former.

We glimpse a present-day friendship between the protagonist and Sylvie, now married and a mother: they call each other Lolotte and Werther and smile to think that 'pistols . . . are no longer in fashion' (p. 625). Shared references to books are now the stuff of reassurance. But something still rankles. The narrator intervenes on his flow to add, with the usual pretence at casualness, the *coup de grâce*:

> I forgot to mention that the day Aurélie's troupe put on a performance at Dammartin, I took Sylvie to the play and asked her if she did not think the actress looked like somebody she knew. 'Who on earth do you mean?' 'Do you remember Adrienne?'
>
>   She gave a great burst [éclat] of laughter, adding 'What a ridiculous idea!' Then, as if to reproach herself, she went on with a sigh: 'Poor Adrienne! She died at the Convent of Saint-S..., in 1832.' (pp. 625-6)

Once again, the woman has the last word; once again too a woman dies, though not the same one. In this reappearance, the old mocking Sylvie both kills and revives. Her 'éclat' of laughter definitively disrupts the 'éclat' of complementarity just as it blows away the uncanny double. The resemblance between actress and nun is only in the protagonist's eyes, they are not in any sense 'the same'. But also, by her sigh of sympathy for the dead Adrienne, she aligns herself with her in friendship, no longer split off by the protagonist's fantasy of their mutual jealousy; the complementary pairing is refused, the women group together not by his agency but by their own. Adrienne's death may not be the only reason she is pitied; Sylvie's earlier 'it all ended badly' is still unexplained. Did Adrienne leave the convent and return? fall in love? die in childbirth? commit suicide? pine away?

Something of her fate remains a secret amongst women. And finally, in Sylvie's voice, we have the triumph of the order of clock-time and the routing of the 'comprehending' reader. A date closes the text; but what does it mean? Long ago, before any of the other events happened? at a date that has some other, unrevealed significance? recently enough to hold a special irony? Since there are no other dates in the narrative, there is no way of reading what is clearly meant by the narrator as a definitive gesture of closure. The last laugh is with the ironic stance of the text. Narrator and reader are no longer friends, and doubles only in the fact that each fails to understand; like the ending of *Mademoiselle de Maupin*, this last word leaves the male partners in ignorance, the women after all together and in knowledge.

My last nineteenth-century *récit* is Fromentin's only fiction, *Dominique* (1863). But before turning to it, I want to take a brief look at a text in which the themes and pattern of the genre appear in another medium, poetry. Victor Hugo's monumental *Les Contemplations* (1856) is shaped like a confessional narrative. The first half ('all pink')[10] is dated to precede and the second half ('all black') to include and follow the death of the author's elder daughter Léopoldine in a boating-accident a few days after her wedding. The theme of father-daughter desire is less common in fiction than that of son-mother; retroactive on the Freudian turning-point of the abandonment of the seduction theory, it belongs to real life (so the argument goes) rather than to phantasy, to the structures of social power rather than the infantile imagination. But the male Romantic poet is not just an 'child of the century', he is also a patriarch made or in the making. In this text, power and desire struggle over the figure of the woman and the unacceptable fact of her death. The whole object of writing is to resurrect her and keep her for ever inside the text.

The key moment that opens the second part of *Les Contemplations* is not Léopoldine's death but her wedding. The effort to 'give her away' is enacted in a pair of poems in which blessings vie with expressions of resentment and reproach: the 'naked foot . . . of love' (p. 222) is bleeding, the departing child is told: 'go, . . . / Take with you happiness and leave us tedium!' (p. 223). Thus the daughter is both lost and abandoning; she leaves first, and the death that follows her leaving horribly fulfils the repressed curse of her father's jealousy.

So the text is an expiation, a wail of self-pity and a continued howl of anger at the girl who doubly got away. Drowned with her husband in a sort of amniotic *Liebestod*, she must be brought forth from the grave and repossessed by the poet. His persona thunders through the text, as in everything else he wrote, but he is not sure where to place her; at the end, never quite captured in the book, she becomes the implied reader, in a border-line compromise between the autobiographical impulse to confession and the urge to recapture her in fiction.

The early poems, some shifted out of chronology to fill out the happy section, represent love, youth, delight; two daughters appear as a dove and a swan; butterflies are winged love-letters, and the world is God's book, the poet his privileged reader. Here as later, the key doubling is with the deity: author too, he lets the poet read and pass on his occult expressions, and without the literacy of the latter, the natural world would remain uninterpreted. Thus the position of 'contemplator' is really that of speaker: Hugo's persona is at once reader and teller, God and witness, all the doubles centre in him. At the same time the poet is presented as male mother to a daughter-text: he lives both in the 'them' of his fictional creatures, and in the 'her' of his 'creation' (p. 30).

The interpretation of God's world as his word lets the poet use natural creatures – bushes, birds – to voice his own arguments; he poses as their mouthpiece, 'the interlocutor of the trees and the wind' (p. 68). The girl, like the thoughts of love, is just one more flying thing. Infant bereavement is mitigated in the image of the bird escaped through a cage-door left open (p. 159), for 'is the child not a bird?' (p. 166; and see pp. 183 and 430). But there is also a premonitory hint of darkness embodied in the negative closure of 'Lettre' and its glimpse of 'sinister birds' (p. 84). This epithet will recur.

After the elliptical epitaph marking the daughter's death, a quarrel with God begins, in endless poignant verses of complaint. Léopoldine is the 'angel that fled away' (p. 225), stolen by a 'jealous God' (p. 226), or abandoning in her own right a father that was her private God and author: 'I composed that young soul' (p. 233). In perhaps the most interesting poem of the volume, the 'strophe of the poet' becomes the Proserpine to his Pluto.

A bright natural creature, she (apostrophised in the second person) is caught in the flowery meadow by 'the poet, . . . searcher of the dark abyss' (p. 319) who seizes her 'in flight' and carries her off, ignoring her cries and sobs, and now keeps her

> . . . captive et reine en même temps,
> Prisonnière au plus noir de son âme profonde,
> Parmi les visions qui flottent comme l'onde,
> Sous son crâne à la fois céleste et souterrain

> [. . . at once captive and queen,
> Imprisoned in the blackest place of his profound soul,
> Among the visions that flow like waves
> Beneath his skull both celestial and underground]

where she sits in calm despair and whilst, close by, the black crowd of his dramas

> Des sombres passions feuillettent le registre,
> Tu rêves dans sa nuit, Proserpine sinistre. (p. 320)

> [Leaf through the register of sombre passions,
> You dream within his night, sinister Proserpine.]

In this poem, the pretext-metaphor is soon left behind and the other pole of the comparison seems to develop alone; it is only with effort that we remember this is supposed to be about a strophe, not a kidnapped girl. With his familiar displacement technique anxiously accented, Hugo's poet appears here in the third person – not for the usual effect of false modesty, but to permit those 'sombre passions' of violence, desire and sequestration to be acted out as another's. Using the 'tu' to address the girl, the 'I'-position is implicitly yet another person's: that deity who sees everywhere or even perhaps the distraught Ceres. By the latter possibility, the author lends an extra ambiguity to the description of the girl's violent abduction: we are invited at once to pity and to enjoy the spectacle of her cries and tears. His soul, his skull is the underworld. She is a flying thing pinned down – by whom? God has been blamed for the death of the daughter but here she is the father-poet's prey, and his creativity has come to depend on her as captive, dreaming for him, grouped in his unconscious with the thoughts he needs her to express. Implicitly also Eurydice, or Pallas Athene birthed from Jupiter's brain, it is no wonder she is 'sinister', like the birds negatively shadowing the idylls of 'Autrefois'.

In the later poems, it is the 'I' who flies: 'Ibo' is all about a phallic thrust into the heights of knowledge, the challenge to God cheekily punned in the phrase 'to rob [voler] God' (p. 338).[11] The persona is 'he who goes' (p. 339), the 'winged dreamer', the 'distant eagle' (p. 401), 'carried towards the azure' (p. 403), even 'a pilot' (p. 427). In the final piece, 'A Celle qui est restée en France', the daughter becomes the intended reader and the text is a flight of black and white birds. Sent from exile to the daughter buried in France, it is a winged envoy from the underworld to freedom, as if she now had a more real life than he. Though he dedicates his book 'to the tomb' (p. 459), it is a tomb that his imagination prises open, as he pictures her nudging her husband in their common grave, anticipating his arrival. He will then take over from the deity, Jesus to her Lazarus: 'love will twice violate the secret of the mortal shadows' (p. 461).

Though God is still cited as the writer who turns 'the pages of my soul' (p. 462) he is effectively superseded by the resurrecting poet and his risen daughter. In what was the final image, the book as flying phallus enters the grave and dies: 'take this book . . . Between your vague hands let it become a ghost' (p. 466). Thus the death of the woman, dimly desired, results in the lifelessness of the man, as in many of my other texts. Hugo was not satisfied with this and added a 'sublime finale' (p. 800), in which, nominally 'in the presence of the Being' (p. 468), he thunders down peace on all creation. Male doubling, the writer as God, ends with the last word, but only to cover up the image of the woman, desired, murdered and both recipient and essence of the poetry; dimly alive, she still 'dreams in his night'.

This text falls in the interim between *Sylvie* and *Dominique*, the former a quarrel with filial desire as hallucination, the latter dedicated to the establishment of the fatherly pose of maturity. In *Les Contemplations*, we see the pits and dangers of paternal desire; in *Dominique* maturity is undesire.

Written consciously as a latecomer to the genre, this text gathers together all its features except the death of the woman – though in this case, the promise to set down 'our story' was made two months posthumously to the original.[12] Comparisons between the text and the life are particularly instructive here. Fromentin himself was no orphan; his mother outlived him. Jenny Chessé, the Creole model for Madeleine, was nearly four years older than he, had three children and died aged twenty-seven. Their meetings, held when her husband was away, were almost certainly sexual trysts, and the nominal chaperone, Lilia, appears to have been passionately in love with Fromentin herself. Most important, Fromentin apparently tired of the affair two years before Jenny's death, so that the stimulus for the text (completed only fifteen years later) was her dying, oddly repressed from *Dominique* because, perhaps, it carried too much remembrance of neglect. Guilt, in this text, is spoken of but never properly shown; we know the young Dominique was a bad lot because the middle-aged narrator has become wise by outgrowing him. But it seems his only vice was a conceited measure of himself combined with an inability to escape selfconsciousness. As far as Madeleine is concerned, we are apparently to believe that he heroically renounced her to save her from losing her virtue.

Dominique is all about unfinished business. But the business is apparently between the narrator and his past self, not the living woman he repulsed. In this text more than any, the male doubles crowd protectively around him, hiding his real guilt from view.

The narrative is skirted by the most sympathetic of frame- narratives which opens with Dominique's direct assertion of his maturity: 'certainly I have nothing to complain of . . . for, thank God, I am now nothing special – supposing I ever was anything out of the ordinary' (p. 5). The gentleman already protests too much; supported by the loving endorsement of the frame-narrator, this declaration insists that having an ordinary life is in his case not the luck of the draw but 'an act of modesty' (p. 6). The dullness of Dominique's actually very seigneurial existence and his similarity to everybody else are repeatedly stressed so that we shall see, under a grey cloak, the glow of his exceptional nature peeping through. Obscurity, modesty, renunciation of desire, these are rewarded by the good life because they are always just this side of his deserts. Two dichotomies intersect here in a suspect way: the superficially retrenched versus the truly impressive Dominique; and the wise grown-up versus the foolish youth. That the former of the second pair cannot quite let go of the latter is under-written by the first pairing: after all foolishness had something of genius, renunciation is both wisdom and loss.[13]

The frame-narrator meets Dominique out hunting. He later learns that Dominique is mayor of the commune, an honour inherited with 'the ancient respect attached to his name' (p. 14); an affable, discreet man, he can count 'as many people grateful to him as there are inhabitants in the commune' (p. 15). His popularity, then, is coextensive with his power; everyone is in his debt. As we shall see in the central narrative, he is so much the centre of the fiction's world that there is nothing, landscape or people, which does not radiate from him. His name reifies his position: he *dominates*. Even the season suits him. The peasants doff their caps, inarticulately reproaching and thus proving his famous modesty, and 'nothing would have distinguished him from these men of toil, had they not addressed him as "our master"' (p. 18). His shadowy wife dispenses charity, but what she writes he signs.

The frame-narrator departs for a year and when he returns the friendship is even more passionate. They confide in one another; he stays in Dominique's house, sleeping in his childhood bedroom. One day he is taken up to the hero's study, whose walls are covered with scrawled maxims, dates and initials, ceasing suddenly on the date of his marriage; and here he reads forth Dominique's soul:

> A great concentration of mind, an active, intense self-observation, the instinct to reach ever greater heights, to dominate himself without ever losing sight of himself . . . feelings that arise and touch this young heart egoistically feeding off its own substance, this name entwined [qui se double] with another, verses bursting forth as a spring flower blooms, frenzied leaps towards the lofty heights of the ideal, and finally peace entering this stormy, perhaps ambitious heart, tortured with illusions . . . The soul of thirty years still throbbed with passion in this narrow room, and when Dominique was there before me . . . somewhat distracted and perhaps haunted by a murmuring echo of the past, I wondered whether he came here to conjure up what he called his own shadow, or to forget it (pp. 36-7)

This is the picture we are to keep in view when reading Dominique's own narrative. The manly thrusts of his self-loving, self-abusing mind – 'to dominate himself' contrives nicely to imitate both gestures – are vowed to silence but rigorously audible. And there is another presence here, desperately repressed: Madeleine is only the 'other name' that doubles his, and 'a certain echo' released by the tinnitus of his past. We are constantly told that Dominique's phallic figure is both single and double – the woman is the as-yet-unknown third party, a mere pretext for his quarrel with himself – and this Faustian dividedness is both his sorrow and his heroism, hardly his fault.

A childhood friend, Olivier, comes to dinner; very wealthy and living in solitude, he is the same age as Dominique but looks younger, an inveterate dandy and Parisian by election who has chosen to bury himself without family in the country. He never reads books, but affects contempt for those who write: 'he held . . . the banal opinions of the disillusioned, though he had never done anything to justify counting himself among them' (pp. 42-3). Olivier is like Lorenzaccio: his character appears 'slightly obscured by the dusts of solitude; its original features beginning to show wear'. He has not, as Dominique has, preserved a perfect self underneath the surface but is ruined all through, seemingly because he has not written any bad poetry to merit his resignation.

The configuration of four in *Dominique* is the 'family circle': Dominique, Madeleine, Olivier and Julie. The latter two are the ones who [nearly] die. Olivier is a particularly interesting figure: male, he is under the narrator's doubling control, thus we have frequent stress on the symmetry of his balance with Augustin – Alpha and Omega, they dance carefully around the hero, orphans like him, Augustin wise beyond his years, Olivier a wise child, Olivier full of 'sophisms and impotences' (p. 45), Augustin all virile striving. But at the same time he carries many of the aspects usually assigned to the woman in the *récit*. His is the articulate intelligence that twice in the narrative voices a clear critique of Dominique which is left echoingly uncensored. He is introduced in the opening frame, very much like Manon and Carmen, to allay any trust we might place in him and also to draw forth from Dominique as double the zomboid fate that attends so many other heroes. His attempted suicide in the 'present time' of the text is, like the usual death of the woman, the stimulus that allows Dominique to return to the fathers, confessing to the frame-narrator and afterwards flinging himself purified into the arms of Augustin. So Olivier, both double and mirror, plays the dangerous role of the 'other who knows', something the women cannot be allowed to be. The fourth of the quartet is Julie who even more than Olivier carries the burden of the uncanny. For she loves Olivier as Dominique loves Madeleine, with some important differences that will be discussed presently. Uncanny chiefly because in this couple she is the one to desire, she feels and evinces female sexuality and is thus an object of horror to all the men of the text. The couple Julie-Olivier functions as a complex mirror to the couple Dominique-Madeleine by reversing its gender structure and exposing the politics of Dominique's obsession. Finally, at the heart of the four is the pair of sisters Madeleine and Julie, whose implied parallel (both, eventually, mad with desire) is what gives Julie her dramatic uncanniness, but between whom there is also a bond of affection and loyalty that the narrative is careful to marginalise.

Olivier comes to Les Trembles, a welcome but patronised guest; Dominique's wife wants to marry him off. He however is alive to the risk of 'wedding the freedom and happiness of another' (pp. 44-5); the others shake their heads pityingly. It is after this discussion that he attempts to kill himself, and ends up cruelly disfigured. Punished for Dominique's complacency, he limps out of view leaving a note that endorses the latter's virtue: 'you have been not my best friend but my only friend. You are my life's excuse. You will bear witness to it. Farewell, be happy, and if you speak of me to your son, tell him not to be like me' (p. 47). Like the woman, he leaves a last word, but his refusal to be a double will go unheard under the more audible flattery of the echo of Dominique's discourse.

Dominique begins his tale with the 'family romance':

> I can truly say I had no family . . . my mother had scarcely the strength to feed me before she died.[14] My father survived a few years more but in such a poor state of health that I ceased to feel his presence long before I lost him, and so for me his death goes back much further than its real date. Thus I really hardly knew either of my parents, and the day when, in mourning for my father who had just passed away, I found myself alone, I noticed no real change or suffering. I attached only the vaguest meaning to the word 'orphan' that was repeated all around me as if it signified misfortune, and it was only the tears of my servants that I showed me I was to be pitied (p. 50)

This emotional anaesthesia is presented with studied casualness; Dominique is to be a child of nature, hatched out of an egg and no victim of maternal deprivation. But we note that the people who weep for him are his staff, and their paid devotion is implicit in the description of the 'wild child' (p. 51) that follows. The boy is parentless but carries a name (orphan, heir) that places him. Even though he spends his time running through the fields setting traps for birds, he is never quite alone: the unschooled 'sons of the neighbourhood peasants' accompany him, and seem exactly like him, except that he loves nature and their role is purely functional. After all, the land they hunt on is his property. Dominique's famous isolation is entirely political: the spoilt darling of Mother Nature, he remains 'alone of my rank' (p. 53). And the hunting is also in dead earnest, for while it is 'no education' it is a training for adulthood – the 'mature' Dominique also spends his days killing wild creatures. As Barthes points out, 'mature wisdom is exploitation without expansion':[15] Dominique has no need of expansion for the world is an exact fit. I shall argue that, in this *récit*, nostalgia stands for the reassertion of the infantile myth of omnipotence, this author more falsely than most wrenching history into a flattering fiction, and that in the place of desire we find a bitter effort to force the woman into the orbit of the hero's centring self. Like Echo, she draws near of her own accord, for she (eventually) desires; but once he has got her there, he has all he wants and discards her.

The dead mother, then, is here neither blamed nor missed; father too has no influence worth telling, except implicitly to leave Dominique master of all he surveys. 'The name of the father', both status and orphanhood, settles the hero into a snug place in the symbolic from which he can enjoy the maternal landscape as both sensitive and exploiter. The estate, parental idyll in which mother and father are diffused into place and name, is the Eden of infancy: all else will be a fall. But even it, after all, is a displacement, and even as a child Dominique is looking back, valuing sites that 'recalled my past, an impression that I enjoyed even at that early time' (p. 56); for to control so completely is to have lost the mother's body.

Into this idyll comes the momentary interruption of a very different character, the tutor Augustin, over-read but poor. Here and elsewhere typified as the virile father-figure, his character is nevertheless curiously castrated: 'this incomplete personality, who however had not too many gaps, had the advantage of possessing many dominant qualities that took the place of the gifts he lacked; thus his nature appeared whole and one would not have suspected any emptiness in him' (p. 54). Augustin's secret 'hole' is the lack of a name: he has neither money nor legitimacy, and all he ever achieves by dint of ambitious hard work is in vain: forever unglamorous, as unsexual as Homais, he guarantees that the bourgeois ideology he incarnates will never appeal.

The seasons pass and the boy romps while Augustin writes dramas, like some Balzacian genius waiting for recognition. The boy fails to understand how anyone can be interested in these unknown characters, for he has so completely what he wants that he has no interest in other existences. Then the time comes for him to go away to school, and suddenly the anaesthesia wears off. 'With the most inconceivable horror, I saw the day approach when I must leave les Trembles . . . I suffered a state of morbid sensitivity that went quite beyond reason; no real misfortune could have made me feel worse' (p. 63). Here is the screen bereavement that in other texts comes with the death of father or friend. Dominique begins to have an imagination of sorts: obsessed with his own trauma, he writes an essay on the departure of Hannibal from Italy that moves him to tears: thus far and no further will he feel for other people.

Augustin 'shook my hand with a gesture of virile authority' (p. 67). Aged retainer André is more sympathetic. In the return to les Trembles which closes his narrative, Dominique's reinsertion into the symbolic will take place in a reversal of these two encounters: the motherly old manservant as first embrace, the virile educator as second and last.

The hero arrives in town to live with his aunt; the house is large, the garden small. Without the maternal Eden, he is as 'absent' (p. 71) and passive as the other heroes after their matricide. School begins and he makes friends with another new boy, the elegant Olivier. At his aunt's house, old-timers reminisce about the awful days of the revolution, while the four young people play cards and whisper. A sort of dynastic union between Dominique and Olivier makes the latter's cousins family. Of these two girls, only the elder is described at any length, and entirely in terms of absences: the convent school she has recently left 'showed in her repressed manner, awkward gestures, look of embarrassed selfconsciousness . . . Her white complexion had the chill of a life lived indoors and without any emotions, her eyes were half-shut as if she had scarcely woken up. She was neither tall nor short, neither thin nor fat, with an undefined figure that had still to develop its form; people said she was extremely pretty, and I repeated this view without taking notice or believing it' (p. 79).

Madeleine starts as Amélie, Adrienne and Alissa end up: in the effigy of a nun. Everything in this description makes her invisible because unobserved: she is perceived as unsexual, unshapely, faceless, above all unopened. Whereas Sylvie or Alissa, with their arched eyebrows, are full of hope and expectancy, this girl is as anaesthetic as the child Dominique – and not without reason. For her repression comes from the same adult narrator who recalls his infantile bereavement with careful indifference, and he is here preparing her for a final stage of mature sexuality that he wants us to find aberrant.

The young people seem to make up a charmed circle of four, and the narrator recalls them at this time as being 'without a real care in the world' (p. 80). Possible? All motherless adolescents, they are presented in two quite distinct ways: the boys with their gaze wandering outward or inward, are sensitive, *disponible*. Of the girls we learn nothing. Yet this quartet, for all its inequality of presentation, is set up essentially to give the protagonist a second 'family romance', another Eden in which the set of four dwell in childish innocence, undivided by desire; the narrator will explicitly or implicitly refer to it in all the vicissitudes that follow, for it establishes the prelapsarian myth of incest that Olivier will refute and Dominique cling to. We are back in the world of *Atala*. For all her unawakenedness, Madeleine is Eve.

The spring he is seventeen, Dominique gets the pathetic fallacy with a vengeance. He walks in the suburbs and all around him the birds and the bees are active. In an ecstatic mixed metaphor, he longs to 'lose myself in the very body of this great countryside all bursting with sap' (p. 87). Arriving home, his excitement beams forth from his features, and his aunt takes a closer look: 'with the gesture of an anxious mother, she drew me into the fire of her clear, deep eyes. They disturbed [troubla] me horribly: I could not bear either their gentle appraisal or the penetration of their love; I was seized suddenly by a strange confusion, which made the vague questioning of that gaze unbearable to me' (p. 88). The motherly gaze excruciatingly exposes his as-yet-objectless desire: with the repeated negative of 'bear' the narrator stresses the pressure and penetration he feels from the woman's eyes. This theme recurs in the figure of Julie, whose gaze haunts and pursues Olivier, implicitly making him the zombie he becomes. Women's gaze is phallic, threatening; Madeleine, who has no look, is the only safe object. We shall see how, in pursuing her to make her speak desire, Dominique ends arousing her dangerous gaze, and runs away just in time to save himself.

On his next walk, he meets the sisters with their father; Madeleine's blank eyes and light voice make him shiver. He flees home and that night, pours out words onto paper without censure or hesitation. Here as later, writing substitutes for sexual ejaculation, keeping desire objectless; he finally falls asleep 'in a state of delicious exhaustion' (p. 91).

Soon after this, Madeleine goes away for a long trip; Dominique is relieved. During her absence he visits her room, making fetishes of her private objects, all 'pale and sweet things' (p. 98) like herself. Then she returns, radically changed. She turns on both young men 'her direct, frank gaze' (p. 106); she is tanned, lively, her voice fuller – as in Adrienne, female maturity is judged in masculine vocal terms – and 'her whole appearance had somehow diminished in volume while acquiring a more firm, more precise character ... This was Madeleine beautified, transformed by independence and enjoyment ... by the excercise of all her powers' (pp. 107-8). But strength and precision in the woman make her phallic, an inadequate mirror: 'I detected in her an ever more visible superiority to myself: I had never before measured so exactly and with such feeling the enormous distance between a girl of about eighteen years and a schoolboy of seventeen' (p. 108).

One day his three friends do not come to their usual rendezvous; Dominique rushes to their house and looks in from the garden, the outsider on a new group of four. An unfamiliar figure, 'still young, tall, perfectly correct in his demeanour, Olivier aged thirty-five but with less delicacy and more stiffness' (p. 119), turns slowly at times towards Madeleine, who is bent, out of the light, over her embroidery. Julie sits motionless and silent, staring at the stranger; her gaze stands in for both Dominique's violent curiosity and the unimaginable of Madeleine's desire. The hero falls in a tremble and through his sobs, repeats: '"Madeleine is lost [perdue], and I love her!"' (p. 120).

This phrase will reappear, significantly altered, more than a hundred pages later. The lostness of Madeleine and her desirability belong together at this stage as an index of the innocence of the hero. 'Lost' and 'lost to me' (p. 121) are the same. Dominique, like the motherless pre-oedipal infant that he is, has assumed 'that Madeleine had no feelings and loved nobody' (p. 122); how could she, especially, love a stranger who had appeared from nowhere in her life? The very concept of exogamy is impossible. At the same time, he is conscious of no jealousy, 'certain of my powerlessness [impuissance], condemned more than ever to keep silence, feeling no resentment of the man who was not taking anything from me, since I had been given nothing'; there is no animosity towards the rival, for the hero is a child, castrated, voiceless.

The wedding takes place on a freezing day at the end of winter; Julie is pale as death and trembling 'with cold and emotion' (p. 127). All the hero's response is subordinated to hers:

> What a strange child she was in those days! dark, slight, nervy, with the impenetrable air of a young sphinx, and her gaze, sometimes questioning, never answering, her absorbant eye! This eye, perhaps the finest and least seductive that I have ever seen, was the most striking feature in the physiognomy of this over-sensitive [ombrageux], suffering, proud little creature. Large, wide, with long lashes that never let a single bright point show through, veiled in a dark shade of blue that gave it the indefinable colour of summer nights, this enigmatic eye dilated without light, and all the rays of life were concentrated there, never again to spring forth (pp. 127-8)

This remarkable description carries the full sexual anxiety for which Madeleine's marriage stands. In Julie, the image of the eye as infinitely absorbing and ungiving focuses the phallus's fear of the female genital. In making it beautiful but unseductive, the narrator pretends to withstand its fascination, as two-dimensional, an object of interest not penetration; but the rays of life all come towards it, drawn in by its colourless hole. Dark, shadowy like the 'little creature' for which it is metonym, it is also large, wide, striking, it dilates like a penis, it mirrors the object it kills. The image is both castrating and a fearful portrayal of fatherhood: for the rays that do not emerge are an ejaculation accepted by the female body and therefore no longer the man's. Where the seed remains, there is a rival child. It is no wonder that Madeleine will be condemned to childlessness. This is another instance of the pool in which Narcissus drowns; what lies within it is a mirroring he cannot bear to desire.

Julie's sorrow is understood as a farewell to their common youth; while the narrator notes her 'insights that terrified me' (p. 128) he interprets her reaction as something far simpler than his own. Even (or especially) on this occasion, women cannot have their own desire, nor can one sister be bereaved by another's departure. As for the bride, she is disembodied, ghostly. In her white she is both her own ghost and that of his youth, 'virgin, veiled and gone for ever'. It is the hero who is 'more dead than alive' (p. 129) as he greets her by her married name and she gazes back with 'her terrifyingly sweet eyes'. Like René on a similar occasion, Dominique makes an unseemly display and quits the scene. All night he battles with his thoughts and around midnight he hears, across unimaginable distances, 'a brief high-pitched cry, which even at the height of my heart's convulsions, made it beat like the cry of a friend' (p. 131). Thus displaced onto the landscape in the repeated call of the curlews, the primal scene is fantasised as murder, orgasm and a cry for help.

When Dominique graduates from school, Madeleine comes to the prize-giving. The incongruity of his youth with his feelings is a humiliation he does not want her to witness; she is in summer clothes, laughing and talking with her married women friends; the gap between them now is less her age than his virginity. Each is embarrassed. Then she leaves for Nièvres and he, completely *disponible*, goes with Olivier to Paris.

The city is alien, nocturnal; it horrifies Dominique and suits Olivier perfectly. The latter berates his friend: 'you are forever looking back . . . It is your fate always to regret and never to desire. You must make up your mind, my dear chap' (p. 142). He visits Nièvres and finds Madeleine further expanded, 'in more spacious circumstances, with the freedom of manner and the breadth of habits' (p. 146) that go with riches and responsibility. Dominique resolves to suppress his passion, but finds himself gradually resenting her ignorance of it. In his imagination he sets up a choice: if he is to live, to survive the drastic sacrifice he has made for the woman – what sacrifice? his future, apparently – then she must pay the price of being told how he has protected her, and thus become unprotected. Telling Madeleine is the first step to forcing her to face him and take account of him. Madeleine must be made to *know*, and all there is to know is him.

Olivier realises it is time for a pep-talk. Dominique protests that whatever his friend is about to say he has said over and over to himself. Olivier disagrees: he points out that Madeleine is legitimately happy and has everything to look forward to; Dominique is a special friend to her, nothing more. Born eight years too late to lay a claim to her hand, he watched another man come along and '"take what did not belong to anybody"' (p. 155) without protest, since for all his sensitivity, he is sensible too. To go on bothering her now is pointless. Why not find someone else to love: '"Madeleine is not the only good, pretty, warm-hearted woman in the world, made to understand and value you . . . I can't think of a woman, as long as I consider her worthy of you, who would not have the right to say to you: 'The true, unique object of your devotion is me!'

Olivier is here vouchsafed one of the few fair and lucid speeches in the whole genre of the *récit*. He does that rare thing of stepping into the woman's point of view and imagining how things look from her angle. And though he borrows the conventional view of her as the property of her husband, he also suggests a self-identity for her (and for other women), a right to choice and happiness that Dominique's viewpoint ruthlessly discounts. He is wrong about the latter, though. The very idea of replacing Madeleine offends him because – as we have seen many times before – the unique beloved represents the mother and to double her would be promiscuity in the woman or madness in the man.[16]

Augustin intervenes, offering the 'willpower . . . straightness '. . . rigorous intellect . . . iron constitution . . . rigidity of his counsel' (pp. 162-4) that make him father in all but name. But for a time Dominique joins Olivier in an orgy of urban decadence. Then he hears that Madeleine is staying in Ormesson, and takes his leave of his latest mistress who, eyeing him in her mirror, smiles a farewell: '"you are not your own master"' (p. 1.3).

For two months, Madeleine and her family stay as Dominique's guests at les Trembles. She pays him the ultimate compliment: '"your region resembles you"' (p. 171). He integrates her into the landscape, trying to create a retroactive Eden, a kinship 'almost of birth and family'. Showing her his favourite places, he looks for 'the precise echo, the exact unison for the cord vibrating in myself' (p. 172). Thus she is to blend, as mirror, into the maternal landscape in which he is pervasively present and above all Dominique wants her to present him with a reflecting gaze, to see and recognise 'my deeper, hidden nature'.

One day all five of them climb to the top of the lighthouse; they are paralysed by the height, the massive view, and 'the enormous tower' (p. 176) swaying at their feet. Madeleine gives a cry, but it is Julie who faints: 'she was standing motionless beside Olivier, her trembling little hand placed next to the young man's, tightly clutching the rail, her head bent towards the sea, her eyes half-shut, with the bewildered expression of a person suffering from vertigo and the paleness almost of a dying child'. Julie's passion for Olivier, here graphically expressed in a 'little death', cuts significantly across the configuration of four. She loves as irrepressibly and unrequitedly as Dominique but with none of his aggression. Yet the text chastises her (and her beloved) for a desire that is repulsive because female. She for ever and Madeleine acutely suffer the joint punishment and guilt that come, in the *récit*, to women's desire. They approach too near and burn too bright, like Echo. We shall learn later why Olivier 'cannot' return her feelings; we shall see her behave with irreproachable control, doing nothing to follow or challenge him, instead internalising her desire into an anorexia of silence and self-consumption. Her total passivity is the exact reverse of Dominique's aggressive pursuit of Madeleine – yet her desire is shown as so dangerous that the terms used to describe it are always powerful, active, menacing. Olivier's failure in life is somehow her fault, as if her self-sacrifice had robbed him too of something or her phallic eye had emptied him of strength.[17]

By contrast to the scene of the lighthouse, Dominique's most intense moment is spent observing the relaxed body of Madeleine asleep in a boat. Like Albertine, she is thus available unopened to his sexual gaze; like Marcel, this is all he really wants: 'I would find it [difficult] to say whether I wished for anything beyond this modest, exquisite view which contained at once every restraint and every attraction' (p. 179). For she is here immobilised by his gaze, contained as within a womb in water. As we come to see more and more clearly, Dominique's wish is not a sexual desire but a fantasy of containment: Madeleine must be his to look upon, held in the orbit of his space. Eyes closed, she is his thing; gazing back, she will threaten.

Madeleine comes to live in Paris and here suddenly she is visible to other people as the hostess of a fashionable salon. When she gives her first party, the hero is shocked by her 'splendid, indiscreet' (p. 186) *décolleté* and touched when she returns his blush and slips on a lacy scarf. But he becomes moodier the more she seems to be enjoying herself: the angel is turning into an 'accomplished woman'. At the end of the ball, the quartet groups itself together, emblem of the lost past and the twisted tensions of the present. Dominique blames his beloved for the social whirl into which he now plunges; he follows her everywhere, feeling unjustly robbed of his property, and harangues her on the immorality of smart society. Madeleine smiles wistfully. Unwilling perhaps to play the mirror, it is possible that she does not agree. For she, unlike Brigitte or Ellénore, is perfectly comfortable in society: conventional enough, she has done nothing to offend it, and she is unlikely to see the force of a diatribe so visibly motivated by personal frustration.

From this point on, Dominique's passion is all aggression. His energies are concentrated into the single aim of making the woman speak. Like Amélie, she is held to have a secret (in this case explicitly her knowledge of his desire) that she must be made to tell; like Brigitte there is no cruel intrusion that she does not somehow, in the name of this motive, deserve: 'some perverse impulse made me want to embarrass her, beseige her, invade her last reserves' (p. 196). The narrator stresses his swordplay, her parrying, his arrows caught and blunted by her discretion. He becomes obsessed with her as the enemy, determined to 'make myself master at last of this mind that was so sure of itself' (p. 198) and discover 'whether the heart of my old friend was still living' (p. 199). Penetrating to the core of the woman means destroying her, reducing her mind to the outer clothing within which the heart (his image) is wrapped. He abandons her for several weeks, then finds her red-eyed, subdued, almost conquered. She hazards some sisterly advice: happiness consists perhaps in the will to be happy. Dominique leaps up, crying, '"May God grant it, dearest Madeleine!"' (p. 203), and the sound of her name spoken with such fervour shocks her like a blow: 'from the depths of her breast, I heard a sort of agonised exclamation of distress that never reached her lips'.

So he hears, as he wished, a sound from within (pain? pleasure? same sound) and she brings forth the troublesome object, without however quite expelling it. He wonders if he should tell her all; then he looks up. Madeleine is cowering in her seat, her hands crossed, deathly pale, her eyes fixed on him 'like two stars' (p. 206) expressing not so much her suffering as her terror at 'the useless/unnecessary [inutile] anxiety she perceived in me'. In this ambiguous but mirroring gaze, he recognises his ideal: 'sublime in her anguish, suffering and rigour . . . with a heartrending look of pity, indulgence and authority' (pp. 206-7), she is the phallic mother at bay. Destroyed but erect, she signals him to silence, and leaves the room.

There are two further steps to the final victory over Madeleine. The pair begin a dangerous game whose pretended object is to cure his unfortunate passion. Madeleine plays nurse, hinting (with a reversal of the fundamental structure of *René*) that she feels half responsible for his problem: 'nothing', the narrator exults, 'was more delicious, more touching and more awe-inspiring than this bizarre complicity by which for my sake Madeleine wore out her strength but failed to give me back my health' (p. 210). Throwing aside all caution, they meet only when her husband is in town. One day he realises she is exhausted and, for reasons best known to himself, tells her the cure has worked and he no longer loves her. To his surprise, Madeleine changes in a flash from the tireless carer into 'a new, strange, incoherent creature, inexplicable and elusive in mood, embittered, gloomy, irritable and over-sensitive [ombrageux]' (p. 220). When he visits her, she seems only to be kept standing by the firm support of her husband. Indeed the game really depends on the latter, for it is the titillatory romp of mice playing while the cat is *not* away, a childish substitute for adult sexuality. Madeleine is being destroyed by this evasion of desire not just unspoken but not really felt.

In the meantime we learn that Augustin, manly as ever, has married a mousy little woman who waits for him in a humble suburban house. Olivier's refusal to find the couple edifying annoys Dominique. But Olivier is preoccupied by the fear that he has been glimpsed by his cousins and uncle in the company of his mistress: '"Julie has eyes that would find me even where I am not"' (p. 232). Aware that Madeleine once planned his own marriage with Julie (so that the sisters might never be parted), Dominique observes a change in the younger woman:

> her excessively touchy [ombrageux] character was daily getting more angular, her face wearing more impenetrable expressions, her whole appearance taking on a more defined character of obstinacy and obsession with an *idée fixe*. She spoke less and less; her eyes, rarely questioning now so as never to have to answer, seemed to have drawn back inward the one spark of life that had been a means of contact with other minds (pp. 234-5)

Dominique perceives Madeleine's concern for her sister, but only to contrast the two women, one warm, the other icy. Both the hero and the narrator fail to remark the lesson available in the different behaviour of the two couples.

Olivier refuses his cousin's love because '"I've always known her. We more or less slept in the same cradle. Some people might find this sort of brother-and-sister relationship alluring. As far as I'm concerned, the very thought of marrying someone I knew as a little

doll seems as ridiculous as the idea of joining together two toys'"
(pp. 237-8). The incest-bond that repels Olivier is precisely what
attracts Dominique. In the terms of the text's argument, Dominique
is right, for only endogamy and return (in his own case, going back
to les Trembles as true mother) can bring contentment; Olivier will
be condemned to an unfulfilled future. But he is too clearsighted to
indulge in the game of doubles. Extricating himself from the narrative's very assumption, he explains why he no more would than could
change places with Dominique. The latter loves Romantic intrigue,
indulging simultaneously in the extremes of self-castigation and risk:

> Your life is traced out in advance, I can see it all: you'll go on right to
> the end, you'll carry on your adventure as far as you can take it without
> doing anything dastardly, you'll luxuriate in the delicious sensation of
> being within a hair's breadth of sin and avoiding it. Would you like me
> to go on? One day Madeleine will fall into your arms, begging you for
> mercy; you'll have the incomparable joy of seeing a sublime creature
> swooning with lassitude at your feet; you'll spare her, of course, and then
> you'll go off, with death in your soul, to spend the rest of your life weeping
> over her loss (pp. 240-1)

Olivier starts by correctly diagnosing Dominique's immature sexuality with its fascination for itself and the titillation of 'not going too
far'. He moves on to an implicit critique of the whole thematics of
fatality in the *récit*. Exactly predicting the hero's future, this speech
appears uncensored and uncommented by the grown-up Dominique
who seems not even to observe how little notice he took of the
prediction.

The second crisis is not long in coming. Seated behind Madeleine
at the opera, the protagonist thrills to share her eroticised response
to the music. Then a former mistress of his enters the box opposite;
Madeleine must have intercepted the woman's bold stare, for she
turns on him 'the fire of her gaze, the most immediate and clearsighted that I had ever confronted' (p. 247). As they part, she murmurs
'"you are torturing me, you're tearing me to pieces"' (p. 249), and
matches action to words by chewing on her bouquet of violets, ripping
it in half and flinging one half in his face. The violence of this gesture
sends Dominique wild with joy; he runs through the streets in exul-
tation. The narrator comments: 'Madeleine was lost [perdue] and all
I had to do now was dare' (p. 250).

The epithet 'perdue' has come full circle: the unavailability of 'lost to me' has been replaced by the alternative meaning: damned, condemned, a fallen woman. The woman has rejoined her namesake, she *is* available. So far is the maternal figure now sexualised, he is sure he can have her. But not for a while. When Dominique goes to see his beloved the next day, he is refused entry. A 'banal, perfectly dry' (p. 251) message asks him to leave her alone, and in fury he quits Paris.

The interim is filled with actions and achievements in the world of men: the narrator treats his younger self to a stream of phallic epithets: 'energy poured out of me . . . my willpower . . . sought a new obstacle to overcome . . . my mind exploded with plans' (p. 252); yet at the same time, in Balzacian mode, 'I did not spend, I amassed' (p. 253). Dominique dabbles in politics, publishes, becomes famous, but none of it means anything. One day he finds a portrait of his beloved in an exhibition: her gaze bespeaks both expectancy and reproach. A pool of 'extraordinary vagueness' (p. 260) in 'the vigorous incision' of the painter's technique, she stands captive, powerfully gazing but aestheticised as visible. Not long after this, Olivier informs him Julie is very ill and he departs for Nièvres.

It is November; he finds Madeleine as icy and pale as the portrait. Julie fell ill nursing a village child who is now dead. Cadaverous but agitated, all that is left of her are her 'cavernous eyes, wider and blacker than ever, in the obscurity of whose orbs there flamed a dark inextinguishable fire' (p. 267). Julie is recovering; her very suffering gives her the power to live. Thus chastity in a woman, enforced rather than elected, has its own mysterious strength, a self-destructive power that nevertheless resurrects; female desire, refused and hoarded, becomes, like the childbed separation, a focus of both death and life.

Released from the fear of her sister's death, Madeleine seems suddenly to lose her mind. She has begun uncannily to express what Julie keeps silent, throwing 'her heart at my head as she had done that evening with her bouquet' (p. 269). She is taking the active part; Dominique is consternated. On mad horse-rides, she streams along ahead while he gives irritable chase; then reins in her horse, stares at him, her whip between her teeth, her cheeks livid, her eyes bloodshot, emits a few chilling laughs and takes off again. The gaze, the grin, the laughter of the madwoman coming out of her attic, are versions of the autonomy we have seen in the malign wit of Mérimée's heroines or Musset's prostitutes, or more gently, in the corrective humour of Sylvie. Madeleine is becoming real, no longer a saint and thus, in the narrator's eyes, a fantasy whore, whip and all. The horse plays phallus for her, horrifying her admirer who finds in her too much strength for the mirror he requires. That night, he prowls down the 'interminable corridor' (p. 272) to Madeleine's room: she is awake, the key is on his side, but he is 'literally benumbed', and does not go in. Undesire is taking shape in his mind: 'the one thing I had no doubt of, but which left me undecided, was that if Madeleine sinned it would kill her, and I would certainly not survive her by an hour' (p. 273).

Their mutual murder, it seems, is in his hands. He claims the sexual act would kill her, but it is his own life he preserves when – 'I cannot say what it was that saved me' – he fails to enter. The next morning, he announces his departure; Madeleine is 'in a horrible state of disarray, with a physical and mental agitation that pained me to see' (p. 274). In a crucial parenthesis, they visit the dead child Julie had nursed; Madeleine asks to see the cradle and tries to kiss the body. 'Going home she wept a great deal, repeating the word "child" in a tone of acute distress that told me much about a secret sorrow which was eating away at her life, and of which I was pitilessly jealous.' Jealous – of her for experiencing a real bereavement? of the husband disappointed or failing a desire for parenthood? or, more bitterly, of the child she wants? His pitiless jealousy is directed at a sorrow in which he has no part; her love for a child he is not, even if it does not exist, arouses Dominique's own childish instinct for cruelty; she shall be punished for a replacement that she has not even been vouch-safed against him.[18]

As he whiles away the moments before leaving, she appears before him and asks him to help fold her shawl.[19] They approach each other, and she falls into his arms.

> I seized her and clasped her against my chest, her head thrown back, her eyes closed, her lips cold, the beloved creature half-dead and swooning under my kisses. Then a terrible spasm made her shudder; she opened her eyes, stood on the tips of her toes to reach my height and, throwing herself with all her strength upon my neck, she in her turn began to kiss me.
>
> I seized her again; I forced her to defend herself, like a struggling prey, against my desperate embrace. She sensed that we were lost; she gave a cry. I am ashamed to say it, but this cry of true agony awakened in me the only human instinct I had left: pity. I realised confusedly that I was

killing her, without being quite clear if it was her life or her honour that was at risk. I cannot boast of an act of generosity that was almost involuntary, so little part did human conscience/consciousness [conscience] play in it. I loosed my grip as a beast might stop biting. The beloved victim made a last effort; it was useless/unnecessary [inutile]: I no longer held her (p. 276)

Then she walks very slowly backwards to the door, without taking her eyes off him as if (the narrator surmises) to control his evil impulse, 'with a terrifying pantomime that still today fills these ancient memories with all manner of anxieties [terreurs] and shame' (p. 277), and leaves the room.

In this extremely powerful and disturbing scene, it is impossible to distinguish the motives of hero and narrator; the wilful misreading surely belongs to both and there is no hint of authorial irony. Dominique has to be the oppressor so that he can be the saviour; found in a situation where the woman's desire so completely outsizes his own, he desperately cleaves to the idea of his domination, even to the extent of reversing the significance of her parting gaze. The wordless confusion in Madeleine's mind (she is, in Freud's muddling terms, the active pursuer of a passive aim) is surely illustrated by her zombie-like figure after she has flung herself into his arms. He kisses the effigy; it awakes, opens those eyes and kisses him back. At this point he forces her, as much as he can, into the role of victim. His mind-reading is perhaps not inaccurate: she may indeed be realising there is no hope for them, even in an embrace. Her cry, echo of the primal scene, and of the 'spasm' with which she just became active, arouses in him enough sadism for the 'manly' response of pity. He is relieved to recognise that he, not she, is the killer. As he throws her off, modestly abjuring self-congratulation, she makes a last effort – and the double meaning of 'inutile' here underlines the alternative viewpoints, for what is she trying to do: get away or stay in his arms? The 'beloved creature' has become the 'beloved victim'; but the eyes, as they back away, still dominating him to this day, avenge their misreading; the power of her desire remains figured in his involuntary memory as 'all manner of anxieties and shame'.

Familiarly, the woman leaves the scene erect and with gleaming eye, and the man, in a comical mix of epithets of weakness and potency, faints away 'while remaining standing', then drags himself to his room and collapses 'stiff on the floor'. At dinner he glimpses his ghostlike face in a mirror; when Madeleine comes down, she is as sick-looking as he. They exchange their last words, she trembling but authoritative: "'I have put between us the one obstacle that must separate us for ever'" (p. 278). Free to tantrum now that she is maternal, he throws himself sobbing at her feet, and in 'a last impulse of weakness or pity' (which?), she at last utters the word he wants to hear, an avowal of love which is "'the forbidden word that will separate us'" (p. 279). For if the gaze carries the taboo of female desire, the word is controlled by patriarchy's laws, and endorses separation.

Dominique runs to Augustin, then Olivier and he part, each haunted by the desire of a woman, the ties of the quartet finally broken. He sees his kindly aunt at Ormesson. Finally four days and nights after the crisis, he arrives on foot at les Trembles and, flinging himself in the asexual arms of gnarled old André, 'my heart . . . gave way of its own accord and burst into a flood of tears' (p. 283): a final ejaculation that will meet no equal love. The pale narrator finishes his tale to the frame-narrator; gradually he recovers his age and calm. The little tasks of everyday resume. The text ends with the arrival of Augustin, representative of dull maturity. Just as the bastard has atoned for the sin of his mother by the obscurity of his wife, so Dominique now subsumes Madeleine's desire under the charitable Mme de Bray. He of all the quartet is vouchsafed parenthood, and he alone speaks, the witness (by his lights) of all their failures. The frame-narrator pronounces him 'a mind whose truest originality lay in its having followed exactly the ancient maxim *Know thyself*' (p. 290). The circle is closed, the doubles draw near, and the woman is buried alive.

Chapter 6: *L'Immoraliste* and *La Porte étroite*

'At times I am afraid that what I have suppressed will take revenge'
(Gide)

Alongside these introspective narratives, of course, the large-scale realist novel was developing in France, and with it what is known as the 'scientific analogy': an image of the creative writer as truthful in the modern manner of the scientist, an aspiration towards something called 'objectivity'. Two key texts in this tendency are the 'Avant-propos' (1846) to Balzac's *Comédie Humaine* and Zola's essay 'Le Roman expérimental' (1880). Balzac proposes an ethological comparison based on the work of Geoffroy de Saint-Hilaire, stressing the dependency of human types upon the environment. The writer's job is to be the accurate recorder of social history. Zola too has a scientific model, the philosopher of medicine Claude Bernard; following his theory, literature is to use the 'experimental method', testing hypotheses and seeking proofs.

Objectivity, in this view, is not just desirable but also possible. Like the dramatist of Stephen Dedalus's analysis, the writer resembles 'the God of the creation, . . . within or behind or beyond or above his handiwork, invisible, refined out of existence, indifferent, paring his fingernails'.[1] There is, I think, little to choose between the God-writer of Joyce or Flaubert ('everywhere present, but nowhere visible')[2] and the scientist-writer of Balzac or Zola: both are deemed to be at a healthy emotional distance from what they write and both have a power that is quintessentially masculine.

Gide wrote a great deal about subjectivity – or, in his terms, sincerity – but he still nursed the myth of objective writing, for example in an image taken from his favourite science of botany, in which he compares the character of Michel to a dormant 'shoot' taken out of the soil of his own personality. 'Here is my simple recipe for creating a hero: take one of these shoots, put it on its own in a pot – you will soon find you get an excellent individual. NB: try to choose (if it is true that one can choose at all) the shoot that bothers you the most. You will get rid of it at the same time'.[3] In this argument, which is not without its disarming illogicalities, Gide is taking the phantasy of authorial 'indifference' and 'invisibility' and transplanting it to the genre that seems least to invite it, the confessional *récit*.

160

His prized method is irony. Irony of this kind must both be signal-
led and also have a certain snobbish discretion: you and I can see it's
there but the stupid reader will miss it. So the signal cannot be blatant
but passes in whispers between the alerted, and is above all felt to
emanate securely from the author. We perceive something out of
line in Michel's narrative, assume the author is a good guy like us,
and side with Gide against the character. The author's wisdom
depends on an impression of distance: 'to me this *I* is the height of
objectivity'.[4] Or more exactly, the author becomes divine as we perceive the protagonist to be humanly erring.

In what, then, does the signal of Michel's error consist? It will
help to answer this question if we begin by looking at an earlier work.
The story of *L'Immoraliste* was, Gide claimed 'born between the lines'
of *Les Nourritures Terrestres* (1896).[5] The usual understanding of this
is that Michel acts out the theory of the earlier text and reveals its
moral weaknesses. I want to suggest instead a structural relation that
brings us closer to the central problem they share, that of the failure
of desire. *Les Nourritures Terrestres* is a self-negating text: both prefatory and closing words advise the implied reader Nathanaël: 'throw
this book away – and go out'.[6] At the end the narrator adds: 'you are
in my way now; you are holding me back; I exaggerated my love for
you, it preoccupies me too much' (p. 248). What is to be cast away
with the book is an over-urgent relationship with a reader modelled
on the desired boy of the paederast dream. The massively repetitious
length of the text is surely a result of an internal censor on the
utterance of Gide's real theme, the release of homosexual desire: the
text never comes, is never satisfied, is always 'expectancy [attente]'
(p. 161*ff*). And in it the chain formed of couples who never coincide
(Ménalque – the narrator – Nathanaël – the intended 'real' boy
reader) defers to the point of failure both direct encounter and completion of embrace. At one end of the chain stands God as all-inclusive
and inconclusive object of desire; at the other, the only thing able
to bring these notes to a stop is the sudden intervention of an
unnamed 'she' who, in the 'HYMN by way of Conclusion' (p. 247),
dedicated to Gide's wife Madeleine, gets to speak two paragraphs
within quotation marks. With the assumption of the female voice,
Les Nourritures Terrestres can arrive at silence.

This is the structure that *L'Immoraliste* turns around and rewrites.
A page or so before the end, complaining that 'something in my will

is broken' (p. 471), the narrator declares: 'at times I am afraid that what I have suppressed [supprimé] will take revenge'. We can understand this remark in two ways: first, that Michel is haunted not just by a failure in himself but by the wife he has done away with – though how she, in her weakness, can be an object of terror we have yet to see. Secondly, that the author, who has again betrayed the aesthetic of sincerity by failing to write what he meant, leaves the motif of homosexual desire merely implicit, signalling his cowardice.[7] In examining *L'Immoraliste*, I want to see how these two suppressions work together.

Gide's 'objectivity' depends on our certainty that Michel is subjective – deluded, foolish, speaking falsehood, though not actually lying of course, for then we could not read him. But wherein do we infer this wrongness? A typical critic takes it that Michel's avowed Nietzschean quest is a cover for 'egotism and the selfish pursuit of pleasure' (Davies, p. 9). This indeed does seem to be what the text is after, and Gide's own comments on Michel's 'excess' endorse this view. But if we read with care we find that Michel does nothing to justify it: his problem is not self-indulgence but the failure of desire, lack of consummation.[8] Moktir, Ménalque, Charles, Alcide et al. provide him with beckoning models, but he does not follow, much less embrace them. Nothing he says is precisely indictable; no student can point you to the line where he betrays self-delusion. Rather, Michel's errors are etched upon the body of Marceline. This is her role as mirror: we know he is bad because she suffers. Her suffering is physical, most often presented as a shedding of blood. Gide from on high is a cruelly moral God who punishes Marceline for Michel's failures to act, in order that these should appear as sins of his flesh.

Michel claims to be powerful and virile; he is not, partly because he must be weak in order for the author to be strong, partly because the text is so structured that each failed encounter is with a stronger (usually younger) man who can only reflect negatively on him. Clearly he desires not so much to pursue this series of male doubles as rather to destroy Marceline – for it is she who really has what he wants. At the start of their marriage, she is the one with strength: she has health and poverty, two key attributes in the world of *Les Nourritures Terrestres*. She ends up agreeing that she is one of the weak, and dies vomiting blood. After her death, Michel survives in a familiarly powerless and zomboid state, as if even beyond the grave something of her remained to diminish him. His night spent with Ménalque, Moktir's theft of her scissors, the poaching, eel-catching or voyeuristic obsession with peasant incest – all these result not in consummation but in the shedding of Marceline's blood. There is perhaps a kind of shadowed vampirism that seeks in women's menstruation or parturition a strength of desire that the male lacks. The liquid imagery is not fortuitous: Michel drains Marceline so as not to spend himself. Or perhaps draining her is the nearest he can get to spending himself, the only kind of desire he knows.

In the opening frame, we discover the protagonist surrounded by nurturing male friends eager to insert him into the symbolic: 'how can Michel be useful to the State?' (p. 369). He has summoned them simply, he says, in order to speak. He begins his story by reminding them of his wedding. Whereas Gide became engaged to his cousin more or less at the deathbed of his mother, in an act of endogamy whose doubling significance is clear, Michel loses his austere huguenot mother at the age of fifteen and is brought up by an academic father. Though it is the father's death that yokes together this girl and the young man who has 'never loved any other woman' (p. 373), the confusions of an incest bond are obvious in the contradictory declarations, 'I knew my wife very little' (p. 372) and, three pages later, 'I knew her too well to see her with fresh eyes . . . I had seen her grow up' (p. 375).

The hero is another infant prodigy, reading six ancient languages as a child and publishing his first article under his father's signature: the world of the patriarchate is at his feet. At twenty-five, he has, familiarly, gazed only upon ruins and knows nothing of life. Self-regarding – 'I cherished all my finer feelings' (p. 374) – he is also, like the others, distanced from himself: 'I knew nothing of myself'. He is unselfconsciously rich; Marceline is poor. He has delicate health, she is robust.

On the boat, with the phrase 'for the first time' four times repeated in a page, Michel begins to notice his wife. She returns his gaze 'fixedly' (p. 375) and smiles; Michel recognises 'that this where the monologue ended' (p. 376). As she speaks, he finds he can no longer maintain an unconsidered prejudice about the foolishness of women: 'in her presence, it was I who seemed to myself awkward and stupid'. The discovery that 'the person to whom I was attaching my life had her own distinct life' comes as such a surprise that he wakes several times in the night to gaze down at his new wife asleep in the lower bunk. Marceline already presents to Michel a mirror he cannot control; for the moment he feels excited by the newness of it, and he will never openly admit to himself how fatally it disturbs him; but it is a sign of his anxiety that he can only comfortably enjoy her otherness, like Dominique, when she is asleep. The separate beds indicate a distance that is not simply circumstantial but also defensive.

In North Africa they are tossed about in a coach in cold and windy weather; Marceline asleep, Michel coughs into a scarf borrowed from her waist, and on waking finds it dark with blood. He makes sure Marceline sees nothing but then, resenting her ignorance, announces that he has spat blood. She faints; he leaps to help her, even more irritable: 'wasn't it enough that *I* was ill?' (p. 379). The doctor rights the balance: Marceline is fine, Michel is dying.

Determined that he shall recover, Marceline takes charge. Michel reaches Biskra 'as if dead' (p. 380) but there the love and care of 'Marceline, my wife, my life' save him. His rebirth is of her making, he gazes at her like the newborn at its mother. Then one morning she introduces another infant into the home, an Arab boy who clings to her in reaction to Michel's cold reception. But the latter notes the child's 'winsome animal grace' (p. 381) and that he is naked under his shabby robe. 'Really, am I supposed to take an interest in *that?*', (p. 382) he ponders and, as if in answer, the boy's 'gandourah, which had slipped a little, revealed his charming little shoulder. I feel the need to touch it. I lean forward. He turns round and smiles at me.'

Here as elsewhere, everything happens to Michel, he is never the instigator. The marriage was not his choice; the illness appears from nowhere; Marceline tries to preempt him, then saves him, then brings him the children who will become his allies against her. The very 'need' to touch is provoked by the (involuntary?) lowering of a garment. For the second time, Michel spits blood, this time 'a horrible clot' (p. 383) which makes him not weak but angry. Examining the clot like the product of a miscarriage, he compares it with the 'beautiful bright blood of Bachir ... And suddenly I felt a desire, a wish, more violent and imperious than anything I had felt before: I want to live! I *will* live' (ellipses Gide's). Desire belongs to the boy; the false birth of the vomited blood is feminine and shocking; life is something to be gained by an aggression of the will. Not Marceline's nurturance now, but Michel's own determination shall oust the disease, 'an active, numerous enemy, dwelling inside me' (p. 384). To be born is to cast out the gestation of a negative self. Mother and infant are both him. A sort of childbed murder begins, as early as this, to hint at a horror of the female function and a violent urge to appropriate it.

'It's a matter of willpower', the narrator avows, 'I put myself in a state of hostility . . . I went over my willpower, like one learning a lesson; I studied my hostility' (pp. 384-5). This manly violence, supposedly directed against the illness, falls largely on the head of Marceline. If he is to recover by his own efforts, she must not be allowed to pray for him, for this would give both God and her the credit for the cure. As he comes more and more to rely on the boys, Marceline is eased out of the way; one day she is even robbed. Moktir is 'the only one of my wife's protégés who did not irritate me (perhaps because he was beautiful)' (p. 394); Michel watches his reflection in the mirror stealing Marceline's scissors. His heart beats with joy; though he pretends he has seen nothing, from this day on 'Moktir became my favourite' (p. 395).

This theft is a famous turning-point. In his assent to a petty crime against his wife, Michel is of course 'changing sides', but not in a straightforward way. Letting the boy appropriate the woman's tiny weapon is not recognising a fellow rebel but accepting a new master; when the narrator swears he felt no 'revolt' he means against Moktir. At the same time, in the incongruous last word here: 'when I had given Moktir enough time to rob *me*' (my italics), he hints that the mirrored boy makes not his wife but himself weaker.

The rest of the honeymoon is spent in narcissistic reverie: insomniac with objectless desire, Michel cradles one hand in the other and finds it wonderful just to be alive. But these moments must be protected from the wifely gaze: she seems an obstacle to the free passage of self-admiration. In Michel's mind, Marceline's mirroring nurturance threatens his sense of masculinity, just as the sickly boys she favoured, menacing doubles of himself, 'frightened me' (p. 394). Already and henceforth, he plays the wild child, she the indoor mother.

On the journey home, the drunken driver of Marceline's carriage whips the horses into a fury; he is overpowered by a furious Michel who that night consummates his marriage. 'It appears, when I recall it now, as if that first night were the only one . . . so sufficient does one night seem for a great love to express itself, and so obstinately does my memory recall it alone' (p. 405).[9] A cynical reader might observe that this one night is necessary for Marceline, like so many fictitious wives, to conceive and incur an obstetrical trauma; what is certain is that Marceline gets the leavings of her husband's failure to realise his desire for the bestial coachman. Comparison with a similar passage in *Si le Grain ne meurt* highlights a constraint here which suggests that the heterosexual marriage is limited to one night only 'to express itself' so that all that follows can be a parting from Marceline.[10] For an instant, as in the childbed death, 'our souls were mingled' (p. 405): everything afterwards is separation.

Michel's country estate, La Morinière, belongs to the lost summers before his mother's death; her property, it has come down through the father's inheritance. Here Marceline gestates but it is the steward Bocage who produces a son, whom Michel follows into the wild while his wife is resting. Charles catches eels in his bare hands – a vulgar Freudian image that needs no interpretation – and shows Michel around an estate coextensive with his body: 'every day we continued our walks; the estate was vast, and when we had thoroughly searched all its corners, we would start again more methodically' (p. 414). Charles is as critical of his master's ignorance as Oliver Mellors is of Connie's. Marceline and Michel together watch him taming an unbroken colt (with a minor change of gender, another anticipation of Lawrence). In this scene, as earlier in that of the coachman, both man and animal are sexually charged: 'the colt . . . set off again with an even trot, so beautiful, so supple, that I envied Charles and told him so' (p. 417). The possibly heterosexual Charles promises to make the animal 'as gentle as a [female] lamb' for Marceline, whose condition of course does not permit her to ride.

Vulgar Freudian imagery here and elsewhere plays a special role in the strategy of Gide the 'indifferent' author. It is important that the motif of homosexual desire be implicit and never overt, not just for public censorship or the author's private failure of nerve or sincerity, but also because only thus can the latter seem subtle, discreet, distanced. As a million undergraduate essays affirm, Gide 'lets us judge for ourselves', by which they mean that he pulls us rather than pushing us or that we do not see the strings. The *deus absconditus* is naturally a bigger tyrant than the inert idol. But this irony cannot afford to be too subtle because we must see the point clearly enough to join the conspiracy of polite silence, noticing desire and divining in it the failure of the Nietzschean quest. Then we are less likely to perceive that what the text is really about is undesire, not only Michel's but also Gide's.

So Michel and Charles ride about together, and Michel indulges in the displaced pleasure of domination over his workers: 'I enjoyed organising and commanding' (p. 418), 'ordering people about . . . and using my authority [dominer]' (p. 419), though his given status needs the supplement of Charles's native dignity to boss the peasants about. The supine Marceline 'took as much delight, it seemed, in feeling me live as in living herself' (p. 418); thus he replaces the kicking foetus without even having to stay indoors; yet she also manages to get in his way: 'Marceline's love, stronger than words could express . . . was almost anguishing to me' (p. 420). Like our other misloved heroines, her soul seems simple because his is not: she must love. But above all, she like Charles has strength.

In the autumn they settle in Paris; Michel heroically spends money and socialises though, like Dominique, he finds urban life uncongenial. He too complains to the woman: '"These people are all exactly the same . . . When I talk to one of them, it feels like talking to several". "But, my dear," Marceline replied, "you can't expect each of them to be different from all the others." "The more they resemble each other, the more they are different from me"' (p. 423), Michel growls. If Michel depends on these indeterminate doubles to prove his own individuality, it is via Marceline that he voices it. Her assent to the social charade, like Madeleine de Nièvres's, is necessary for him to articulate his disinctiveness. This is shown up sharply when among the mannequins there appears the charismatic Ménalque.

Michel knows him already (we are not told how) but, before his own marriage and Ménalque's 'shameful, scandalous lawsuit' (p. 425), always disliked him. Now he is interesting: those who rebuff him are treated to the superiority of his disdain. Apart from the whiff of Wildean scandal, the glamour of this double – his piratic handsomeness, his cool, his Malrauxian travels on behalf of the government – explains the 'secret influence' that attracts Michel to him; and he is older, an educator, a substitute father holding open the library door. Ostracised by the bores, he represents a seductive outsiderhood, and flatteringly invites the hero to a coupledom deferred from *Les Nourritures Terrestres*. After a moment's hesitation, Michel visits Ménalque at his hotel, where the latter, considering 'sobriety . . . the most powerful intoxication' (p. 426), does not drink but plies Michel; then he produces, tarnished and rusty now, the scissors Moktir stole from Marceline. So Moktir knew all along, and the doubles have spoken of Michel, perhaps laughed at him, amongst themselves. Together or individually, they know and are more than he: "'you thought you had him, but really it was he that had you'" (p. 428).

The next time they meet, Ménalque argues against 'moral agoraphobia' (p. 432) and Michel finds himself replying with Marceline's remark: "'my dear Ménalque, you surely can't expect each of them to be different from all the others'". His interlocutor gives him a penetrating look and walks away; the echo of the woman's speech, become 'my phrase', is stupid. Here again (like Ellénore) Marceline seems to intervene, but only via Michel's appropriative obsession with her: already she haunts him where he thinks he is *tête-à-tête*, and specifically because what she is to Michel, Michel is to Ménalque. In a last attempt, the patient Ménalque challenges Michel to share the night before a journey; separation from Marceline and her kind ('all these people of principle') is to be consummated.

The wife begins to suffer even from this unuttered threat – 'a few days after that party, Marceline became unwell' (p. 433) – thus Michel can, by keeping the rendezvous, sin against her without committing any more irrevocable infidelity. Pinned down by her 'condition', which was after all Michel's first wound, she submits to his leaving her for a night. As he walks to Ménalque's hotel, he rehearses the supposed conflict:

> as soon as I was in the street, my anxiety [inquiétude] took on new strength; I pushed it away, struggled [luttai] with it, angry at myself for not being able to get rid of it properly. Thus I gradually reached a state of extreme tension, strange over-excitement, very different from and at the same time very close to the painful anxiety that had given rise to it, but closer still to a feeling of happiness [bonheur]. It was late; I was walking in great strides; thick snow began to fall; I was happy at last to be breathing a keener air, battling [lutter] against the cold, happy to be against the wind, the night, the snow; I exulted in my energy (p. 434)

I have marked the originals of many key terms above, because this passage is an excellent example of the narrative sleight-of-hand by which the motifs of male desire ('strength . . . struggle [lutter] . . . great strides . . . energy') are built up out of a primary aggression against the female. What the hero is irritably fighting is Marceline, and the feminine pronouns pertaining to 'inquiétude' stress this but show also that he is fighting a feminised part of himself. He has to vanquish this inward soul before he can thrust forward with the phallic happiness that he pits against the masculine nouns of 'air', 'froid' and 'vent'. Then at the very end, the nouns change back into the feminine again and the fight is between 'la nuit, la neige' and the self conceived as 'énergie'. We have already seen in Lorenzaccio how the 'feminine' soul-self becomes confused with the mobile separable self of the phallus. In this image of male desire as conditional upon vanquishing the woman, we find the essence of Michel's real goal: engagement with a feminised self.

Ménalque plays devil's advocate; in particular he voices the temptation of murder: "'my dear Michel, every joy awaits us, but it always wants to find the bed empty, to be the only one, it expects us to arrive like a widower'" (p. 436). Here the feminine gender of 'joie' (not, say, 'plaisir') disguises homosexual invitation under a generalised fantasy of adultery; but the key element is an actually rather conventional monogamy that requires the wife to die. When he arrives home, Michel finds his wife laid out, pale as death, surrounded by medical instruments in a room darkly reminiscent of the torture-chamber, and 'I saw, I thought I saw, a cloth stained with blood' (p. 438). She has lost the baby, and 'before me there was nothing but an empty hole into which I stumbled headlong'.

The black hole emptied of a rival child is the wound he has made and will be entrapped by.[11] The soiled cloth rapidly becomes a metonym for the whole woman; a few months later phlebitis and embolism produce a 'horrible blood-clot' (p. 439) which she vomits up like some grim afterbirth, and 'sickness had entered Marceline, it inhabited her thenceforth, marked and soiled her. She was a ruined thing'. Penetrated by his reified phantasy, she becomes a less-than-whole object, the castrated female who endorses his phallic manhood. The use of woman as mirror is very plain here, even to the identical terms of this second clot of blood. Following this deadly symmetry Michel can kill her by the trajectory that cured him. Good Marceline will serve bad Michel in her dying as she did in her nursing.

They return to La Morinière. Here, Michel is attracted to the peasants as doubles – 'it was as if I could feel through them' (p. 441) – but this is less empathy than voyeurism: still a virgin in such matters, the hero 'lovingly contemplates their pleasures'. It is also, like Dominique's, a political relation. They act, feel and suffer for him as well as working for him: their labours and exhaustion feed him with a painless vicariousness. This relationship is described as education (he 'learns', they 'teach') but its furtiveness – 'I prowled, followed, spied' (p. 442) – specifies that what he wants to learn is vice. He contemplates a drunken itinerant and is furious when Bocage dismisses him; he is riveted to hear the gossip about the incestuous but silent Heurtevent family in which brothers and father once joined forces to rape a servant-girl. Charles is now too respectable, so paternal Bocage helpfully conjures a second son more to the master's new taste who introduces Michel to the 'dreadful pleasure [volupté]' (p. 447) of poaching on his own land – another vulgar Freudian hint at the delights of masturbation, which above all stresses the safety of the act: for Michel, unlike Alcide, runs no real risk. Serious Charles reproaches the master for neglecting the estate; learning at last, Michel decides to sell it. At this point the narrator notices Marceline again: she is pining, for, like the rest of the property, she has been ignored. Promising more loving attention, her husband takes her away to Italy.

In this third section of L'Immoraliste, everything is on the slide. The very obvious symmetry guides us to diagnose Michel as deeper and deeper entrenched in the mire of vice; yet as ever he judiciously avoids pleasure. Only on the last page does the homosexual significance of his desire appear in a stage whisper. As they travel, his resentment of Marceline's illness is expressed in such formulas as '[she] was like a rest for someone who did not feel tired' (p. 454). Trying to reflect her devoted nursing, he shows that he is aware of having caused the disease: 'before she nursed me Marceline had never been ill'; but he is both repelled and fascinated by her mirroring of his past self. No wonder he comments, with splendid illogic: 'one should only sympathise with the strong' (p. 455). Her coughing irritates him – 'will she never stop? . . . I'm sure I coughed better than that'; and her weakness is measured against his new strength. In Italy, he is tumescent with deprivation: 'my abstinence went to my head I was intoxicated with thirst as other people get drunk on wine . . . An enormous reserve of love filled me to bursting; sometimes it flowed from the depths of my flesh to my head, and corrupted my thoughts' (p. 458). Here we see the ideology of undesire, central both in *Les Nourritures Terrestres* and here in the voice of Ménalque: as for Dominique, it is non-consummation that excites, or even more, the act of refusing desire. 'Full of anxiety and expectancy' (p. 459), Michel watches Marceline's life drain away as they move compulsively southwards, and he spends money like water because he knows that tomorrow without her he will be able to indulge that delicious indigence.

Marceline is now suffering above all from 'fear of my ideas', and this 'fear' is especially necessary to him since by allowing his bundle of conscious and repressed urges the dignity of a title, she suggests the very consistency and purpose he lacks:

> 'I understand,' she said one day, 'I understand your doctrine – for that's what it is now. It's a fine one, perhaps' – then she added, in a sad, low voice, 'but it does away with [supprime] the weak.'
> 'Quite right too,' I answered in spite of myself.
> Then, shocked by my brutal remark, I seemed to feel this delicate creature turn in upon herself and shiver . . . Oh, perhaps you are thinking that I did not love Marceline. I swear that I loved her with passion. She had never been or seemed to me so lovely (pp. 459-60, ellipses Gide's)

We are familiar enough with the protestation in the last line: feminine humiliation and saintliness have provoked it in several of our narrators. And indeed, Marceline must be precious to the protagonist, for his need to reduce her is much more urgent than his desire for the wild boys who maybe form couples behind his back. Marceline is (like the labouring ladies of many male writers' Acknowledgments) the gaze in which, negatively, his ideas seem formed.

Their two lives, by now too symmetrical, cannot coexist: 'the less I respected myself the more I venerated her' (p. 460). One day he brings her the tribute of an armful of almond blossom. He expects her to be overjoyed; she bursts into tears and complains of the scent; he seizes 'those innocent fragile branches, I break them, take them out of the room, fling them away, exasperated, my eyes bloodshot' (p. 461). Her extreme sensitivity to sensation is read as another aspect of weakness: 'the smallest pleasure could sate [soûlait] her; a little more brightness and she could not bear it. What she called happiness, I called repose'. Now we get very little sight of Marceline's unmediated character, but such a scene as this suggests, in addition to the intelligence and conventional sociability we have been told of, something different from her main monotonous nurturance. Pleasure comes so easily to her that she can enjoy what leaves Michel hungry: this would imply a more sensual nature, not less. So that where he finds himself shunning the very *jouissance* he pretends to pursue, her mirror suggests a possible pleasure that he neither knows nor allows. In this inverted image of the bouquet-scene in *Dominique*, it is again the woman's desire that is both expressed and crushed.

As they continue south, there is another coachman, 'delicious as a fruit' (p. 462): Michel, fired by the boy's admiration for Marceline, kisses him. Here we can see the reversal of the earlier scene with the nasty coachman who stimulated a desire displaced to the wife – for it is this boy's interest in the woman which makes him desirable, so that Marceline, at the very stage in which Michel is supposedly rehearsing separation, has become more and more essential as mediator of his desire. Where she began as his pimp – innocently introducing the Arab boys, of whom he chose precisely those she cared for less, or sending him out of doors to play with, successively, Charles and Alcide – she now comes to embody something he both evades and seeks in the male objects of his interest. They must repel her (like Ménalque) but also contain some dim reflection of the desire of her; this is why, when he finally sleeps with another, it will be a woman, and Moktir will have stepped into Marceline's mediating role.

As for the men, it is no longer beauty and youth he seeks but corruption for its own sake. Michel, daring not speak the name of his desire, becomes the phallic eye, following the down-and-outs with both prurience and envy: 'I imagined their existence just beyond my reach. I wanted to follow them further, to penetrate their drunkenness' (p. 463). At the hotel, he force-feeds Marceline rich dishes while fantasising the crusts of bread and bits of cheese they enjoy 'while here on my table there is enough to satisfy [soûler] them for three days!' This is not, as he believes, a charitable impulse, it is rather the image in them of her desire ('the smallest pleasure could sate her') that fascinates him.

They move on to Biskra where each tree and building is viewed through an observation of Marceline's silent reaction. So tied are they that all his excursions are measured by their distance, their separation, from her. The boys, when he finds them, have grown ugly; one is married but only as a front for other debauches. Moktir, however, just out of prison, is lovelier than ever; Michel invites him to accompany them to Touggourt.

As they enter the desert, both admire the 'inhuman' look (p. 468) of the landscape whose sand and light destroy her. Marceline lies down and cannot eat; Michel stays till nightfall, gazing at her. He feels exhausted himself, as if no more effort is possible. 'I scarcely dare to look at her; I know that my eyes, instead of seeking her gaze, will focus horribly [affreusement] on the black holes of her nostrils; the expression of her agonised face is atrocious. She does not look at me either. I feel her anguish as if I could touch it. She coughs a lot; then falls asleep. Now and then a sudden shiver shakes her.' Black holes again; here they replace her eyes, the maternal gaze that might speak concern or desire. Her face is objectified, expressing without intention. This scene of looking precedes the final betrayal. The narrator dwells on it while the hero, typically, hesitates; but this time Marceline will not mediate the homosocial pursuit for him. What he demands of her she does not give; instead, even in sleep she continues to stir as if alive.

Michel slips out, joins Moktir and is led to a brothel where Moktir's mistress takes him by the hand into a room with a low bed. 'A white rabbit, shut up in the room, is scared at first but then, tamed, comes and eats out of Moktir's hand. Coffee is brought. Then, while Moktir plays with the rabbit, that woman draws me down, and I let myself go to her as one lets oneself sink into sleep . . . ' (p. 469, ellipses Gide's.) The foreplay is all Moktir's, the act the responsibility of 'that woman', the passive Michel slips into coitus as into Marceline's sleep.

Once again, Marceline has uncannily bled for him; he tiptoes home to find her half out of bed, 'her sheets, her hands, her nightgown . . . awash with a stream of blood; her face is soiled with it; her eyes are hideously enlarged; and no cry of agony could be more terrible than her silence' (pp. 469-70). The use of her eyes restored, but without the faculty of speech, she stares out of a ghoulishly bloodied face while 'I search her sweat-soaked face for a tiny space where I could place a horrible [affreux] kiss' (p. 470).[12] This time she refuses her rosary: the divine rival is gone. Like Carmen or the ghost she will become, she falls asleep 'but her eyes remain wide open'. Then, stifling, in a parody of seduction, she seizes and tears at her nightdress; 'towards early morning, another vomiting of blood . . . ' (ellipses Gide's).

Narcissus and Echo

With this, the untold death of Marceline, Michel comes to the end of his confession. He is now far removed from this past – 'these three months make all that seem ten years ago' – and the separation seems consummated. But alone now, like so many of the others, he finds his freedom meaningless. Begging his friends to act for him, he admits: 'something in my will is broken ... At times I am afraid that what I have suppressed will take revenge' (p. 471), and ends, with careful casualness, by describing a new sexual conflict:

> The child who ran away when you arrived brings me [my food] evening and morning, in exchange for a few pennies and caresses. He is shy with strangers, but with me he's as loving and faithful as a dog. His sister is an Ouled-Naïl; every winter she goes back to Constantinople where she sells her body to passers-by. She is very beautiful; in the first few weeks I sometimes suffered her to spend the night with me. But one morning, her brother found us in bed together. He appeared very annoyed and didn't come back for five days. And yet he's well aware what his sister does for a living; he had talked of it before without any sign of embarrassment ... Could he have been jealous? – Anyhow, the rascal got his way, because since that incident, partly out of boredom, partly for fear of losing Ali, I've given that girl up. She doesn't object; but whenever I happen to meet her, she laughs and teases me, saying I prefer the child to her. She says it's he that is really keeping me here. Maybe she's got something there ... (pp. 471-2, ellipses Gide's)

Ali becomes less of an animal, gaining a name, when he shows a jealousy Michel obtusely refuses to understand; it is left to the woman to speak the latter's desire for him. The obvious reading of this ending is that Michel is empty and purposeless because he has still not had/ said what he really wants. So far gone, the wife murdered by his horror of her heterosexual body, he still cannot manage without her to realise what we have perceived in every line. The boy's sister parodies Marceline's tender pimping but even then Michel only half-hears. But this, I suggest, is not the whole answer. Michel is frozen not simply by dishonesty but also by too many equally urgent impulses.

He wants, as ever, to be carried. A first choice is between the child's fierce desire and the male group's willingness to return him to the patriarchate. A second is between the boy's mute wanting and the girl's articulate knowing, both with equal claims on him, and each essential: the truth which his text has suppressed cannot exist outside the female voice and knowledge which mediates it. Or finally, he may remain (as in the text he precisely does) hovering before choice, the undead host of the strengths of his buried wife, the widower to whom joy still does not beckon.

The female voice continues to haunt Gide's later writing. In *La Porte étroite*, the usual line goes, we find the companion volume to *L'Immoraliste*, that other extreme which provides the 'objective' author with his median position. But the symmetry of the two texts is based on a fallacy, for the reflection of the first in the second has undergone an important distortion. Most critics get uncomfortable with this text because it presents them with an awkward dilemma: which one 'is' Gide this time ('is' with irony of course)? He must be Alissa, because she is the central character; but on the other hand she is a woman and that won't really do, and besides, biography instructs us to identify Gide with Jérôme. But on the other hand, Jérôme is such a wimp . . .

These are the pitfalls of 'sincerity'. We can avoid them by continuing the reading of woman as mirror from *L'Immoraliste* to *La Porte étroite*. From this point of view the second text has gone on to a further stage: the woman whose fault it all somehow is, who dies because she mediates but also freezes desire and because he wants to possess the strengths of her body, here takes the central role. Her fault becomes the crucial issue, her death begins to be the literal suicide it will become in *La Symphonie pastorale*. In all these three *récits*, though the woman is now wife, now protagonist, now adulteress, it is she who dies and he who speaks. Each time but the most explicitly in *La Porte étroite*, error is invested in the woman, yet there is some virtue in her that the man desires. Jérôme tries in vain to reach Alissa, but the author succeeds in another way. Both in 1909 and again four years later, Gide expressed the pleasure and ease that he had found in appropriating the woman's voice.[13] Readers of Schlumberger's *Madeleine et André Gide* will recognise how extremely close to Madeleine's own writings these letters and journal are. Thus the appropriation and destruction of Marceline which were Michel's real secret vice reappear here more directly in the tactic of the author.

And what happens to the male chain that signifies the failure to act or speak desire? It is hidden on the surface in the ostensible theme, the problem of Protestantism. In Catholicism, a continuous line of 'fathers' forms a hierarchical ladder between the worshipper and the deity. In the Protestant universe of *La Porte étroite*, this is replaced by Alissa's painful search for a dyadic relationship which is perpetually undercut by an obsession with adultery.

When we open the text, which has no frame-narrator but begins and ends in a present time, we find Jérôme's motive for writing: not to 'make a book of' (p. 495) his memories, but for the sake of 'the last pleasure I hope to find in telling them [les dire]'. They can be spoken now but only in writing; and the bizarre epithet 'pleasure' is perhaps explained by the fact that, with Alissa voiceless, they are now his alone to utter.

Jérôme, a much more directly autobigraphical protagonist, lost his father at the age of eleven and has been raised in a Huguenot matriarchy by his mother and her English companion, both of whom always wear mourning. What we learn of the protagonist before he meets the woman is, as usual, revealing. His mother, one day long after the father's death, dares to come down with a mauve ribbon on her bonnet. Her son cries out, '"Oh mama . . . that colour doesn't suit you at all!"', and the next day the black ribbon is back in place. Here already we see the power of the 'ineffectual' Jérôme over a woman who is supposed to have made him so:[14] at once arousing and undermining her sexual vanity, he keeps her monogomous to the absent father. This acute awareness of female sexuality as a transgression of the oedipal triangle is the crux of what will thereafter be defined as Alissa's problem.

The boy is delicate and they spend their summers at the home of his uncle near Le Havre. There are three cousins, the youngest Robert (quickly subsumed in another cousin, Abel), Juliette a year younger than Jérôme and Alissa, the eldest by two years. The summer his father dies, he notes that both he and Alissa 'ceased to be children' (p. 497).

But at this stage, Alissa is less important than her mother, the double she will carry like an albatross for the rest of her life. Her mother is the obverse of his: where the one wears black, the other is more at home in scarlet, and her light, low-necked dresses scandalise both mother and son. A beautiful Creole – the staple of the forbidden exotic of female sexuality in French – she lounges about with 'her childish air' (p. 498) and her unopened books of poetry; orphaned and abandoned, she entered the family like Heathcliff, disrupting it with her bizarre ways and, engaged at sixteen to the banker Bucolin, was thankfully passed across by his cousins Vautier who could ill afford to keep her. Gide's actual aunt had no such exotic history; the fiction provides a careful family romance for the endogamy of Jérôme-Alissa [Gide-Madeleine]: this cuckoo in the pastoral nest is an eroticised cousin who comes out of darkness and goes back to darkness but is the source and model of the soulful Alissa. The mother-daughter relation that is initially the man's phantasy is as crucial here as in earlier texts, not least because the doubled body carries a multiplied threat of the power of 'the desire of the mother'. She provides another, sexualised maternal figure for Jérôme; and if the mother and son kill each other by mutual desire, then it is fitting that the daughter should die for her womanhood.

Lucile Bucolin carries a tiny mirror at her waist, and never looks at other people. But the year Jérôme starts to grow up, she catches him one day, strokes his cheek and starts undoing his collar. Then, asking him if he is ticklish, her hand descends further . . . 'Suddenly I gave such a jump that my shirt tore; my face aflame . . . I ran away to the end of the garden, where, dipping my handkerchief into a little tank, I applied it to my forehead, washed, scrubbed my cheeks, my neck, everything that woman had touched' (p. 500, ellipses Gide's).

The phrase 'that woman', used of the two Arab prostitutes in *L'Immoraliste*, again indicates the excessive but necessary activeness of female desire. What Jérôme tries to hard to scrub off, however, is not only repulsion, nor just the stain of implication. This is the only scene I know in Gide where an adult's attempted seduction of a child is presented as shocking; elsewhere, in *Corydon* and *Les Faux-monnayeurs* in particular, the sexuality of the paedophile is given as educational, pedagogical not predatory. But here we see exemplified the misogyny that underwrites this apologia: a woman's touch defiles. Alissa's mother takes over the guilt not just of the half-aroused Jérôme but also of the author who, once again and all the more completely in this text, is suppressing sincerity, desire and the woman.

When Lucile leaves home it is not, as it is for so many Gidean heroes, a righteous bid for selfhood, but rather, as for Laura or Sarah after her, a betrayal caused and soon punished by sexuality. Not her but her daughter's body will answer for her *disponibilité*. This deadly mother-daughter bond, though, is much more obviously than in *Atala* mediated by the envy of a son. Before she leaves we get a first description of Alissa. Like Dominique's Madeleine, she is pretty but the hero does not notice it. She resembles her mother, except that 'the expression of her gaze was so different that I did not become aware of this likeness until later' (p. 501) – when? why? we are never told. The most striking features in her ambiguous face are two:

> her smile, already almost sad in expression . . . and the form of her eye-brows, so extraordinarily high above her eyes, raised in a great circle . . . I like to imagine that Beatrice as a child had wide-arched eyebrows like these. They gave her gaze, her whole being, a questioning look that was both anxious and trustful – yes, a look of passionate questioning. Every-thing about her was inquiry and expectancy . . . (last ellipses Gide's)

Alissa here has all the qualities of *disponibilité*: the 'expectancy' typical of *Les Nourritures Terrestres*, the inquiry of a Bernard or a prodigal son. Her air of questioning suggests a readiness for dialogue; but adultery intervenes. At the moment of his discovery, Jérôme fore-closes the dialogue: declaring that here 'this questioning took posses-sion of me, became my life', he coopts and silences it. For whatever Alissa knows may make her solemn and anxious but it has not stopped her being confiding and passionate; it is only when *Jérôme* knows that the question is closed. Glimpsing his younger cousins playing at the foot of the chaise-longue while an unknown lieutenant amuses his aunt by mocking their father's name, he recognises the horror of adultery in a parricidal sacrilege visited on the implicated, innocent children. Again a flavour of heterosexual paedophilia is the most telling aspect of sin. Jérôme finds Alissa praying and weeping for her ignorant father; he is thus righting the obligation to another absent father when he calls God to witness that he will devote his life to 'protecting this child against fear, against evil, against life' (p. 504). His older cousin is now an infant to be sheltered from the violence of maternal incest, and God now the marriage-broker brought in to seal their coupledom.

This complicated logic informs the text. The triangle set up here – Alissa, Jérôme, God – is specifically a displacement of the primary one of adultery, for 'life' here clearly stands for female sexuality. The expression on Alissa's face, which for the narrator barely hid her resemblance to the wicked mother, is to be coopted by the couple Jérôme-God who will henceforth prevent its desire from finding speech or a hearing. For God as third party is no Pindar and does not aid dialogue but prevent it. He has been brought in not to seal an understanding between the couple but as a double of the father whom women must wear black for, to enclose Alissa in an apparent monogamy little less restrictive than the one from which her mother has escaped. There is no escape for Alissa from the outlawed impulse to heterosexuality. The narrating Jérôme retells her story in such a way as to invert her outsiderhood into his: the text narrates Alissa's cruel and deluded adultery with God, and his exclusion. Yet, familiarly, she dies in punishing isolation, not he.

The Sunday after Alissa's mother runs off, the pastor, another uncle, gives a sermon on the text, *'Enter ye in at the narrow gate'* (p. 505). The hero is seated a little behind Alissa and, staring fixedly at her, feels as if 'I were hearing through her the words I listened to with such desperate attention'. Frantically fantasising his cousin's thoughts, he sees 'the broad path' as her mother's room/body and the narrow gate as the door to hers. His desire penetrates with sado-masochistic intensity into her space: 'I saw that narrow door through which we must strive to enter. As I plunged into my dream, I imagined it as a sort of mill through which I passed with great effort, in an extraordinary agony that also contained a foretaste of heavenly bliss': rarely (except in *André Walter*) can a Biblical text have been read with more precise sexual interpretation, even to the extent that unde-sire for Alissa is subsumed into a phantasy of anal intercourse. He has a second fantasy, not recognised as contradictory, in which he and Alissa advance, all clad in white (the reverse of mourning and colour of her mother's dress), 'hand-in-hand and our eyes fixed on the same goal' (p. 506). It is in the misunderstanding between these two visions, one conscious the other unconscious, that the tragic future is prepared. What Alissa is feeling, we do not know. The hero does not speak to her, 'thinking I should merit her better if I parted from her at once'.

'This austere teaching found [in me] a soul ready to receive it' – you bet it did. The mixture of lust and repression, combined with a 'sympathetic' compulsion to appropriate the autonomy of the woman, form the hero's ready conspiracy with God. At the same time, he is still somehow free – 'like all fourteen-year-olds, I was still unformed and open [disponible]' – in a way Alissa no longer is. She is doubled by adultery, he is its observer. Watching himself as obsessively as our other heroes, a good scholar, rather dull, he has the usual mixture of self-absorption and self-criticism. In the boys' world of school, he mixes with Robert and his other cousin Abel, a sort of

Olivier, 'a graceful, indolent boy for whom I felt more affection than respect' (p. 507);[15] but his real thoughts are devoted to Alissa, that pearl of great price whom he wishes to 'merit' rather than 'possess'. Like Dominique's Madeleine, she is not expected to have any feelings of her own. For his homage, she gets simplicity: 'everything in her artless soul was of the most natural beauty. Her virtue was so easy and so graceful that it seemed a mere letting-go [abandon]'. In this description we find both a lightness improbable in the daughter of a broken family and also a hint ('abandon') at the mother's taint, perceptible through displacement from body to soul.

Jérôme's dying mother, unlike both Gide's and André Walter's, neither joins their hands nor separates them, but commends their common future to God. When she dies, Jérôme unexpectedly feels almost the anaesthesia of Dominique: the narrator perceives that he is already anticipating the replacement of mother by cousin. But this does not happen; instead, Alissa sends a letter, vaguely worded but full of a sense of her own bereavement. Jérôme cannot understand, invests the mystery in Alissa and fails to see that her grief is, unlike his, unmediated and that she has reservations about their marriage which do not preclude tenderness. Alissa repeatedly offers her cousin a familial closeness that suggests Olivier's mistrust of endogamy. Where he sees in her a double of her own mother, she suggests the alternative of a double with his which her own father underlines when he points out a likeness between Jérôme and himself, Juliette and Tante Plantier and Alissa and Jérôme's mother. Much later, the uncle will voice a circumstantial similarity between Alissa and his adulterous wife; but here he agrees with her, hinting at an incestuous impulse that Jérôme will not admit, and showing clearly that the *hantise* of adultery originates in the boy.

The younger sister Juliette plays messenger between the pair: Jérôme confides in her the feelings he dare not utter to Alissa. It is clear that the constraint of direct speech is equalled only by the ease of a mediate relationship: far from disrupting an idyll, the third parties are essential to the structure. But Juliette intercepts the 'sweet dissemblance of love' (p. 516) with her own desire. Like Fromentin's Julie, this sister carries the full burden of female sexuality once the mother has departed, and is punished for it by a despised, portly happiness.

Alissa, for her part, is haunted by separation: in a nightmare she recounts just before he leaves, he is dead and she cannot reach him, and each must make 'all our lives . . . a great effort to get back to each other'. There is both dread and wish-fulfilment here, but it also reproduces (without the bliss) his phantasy of the narrow gate. Like the other women, she is made to anticipate her own death as necessary: '"do you believe death can separate?" she said . . . "I think it could do the opposite: bring together what has been separated in life"' (p. 517). Jérôme, though he reproduces these remarks as an awful premonition of her dominance, is the one who declines to get engaged: '"I'm interested in too many things . . . I want to put off as long as possible the moment when I have to choose one thing and not the others"' (pp. 517-8); he wants both to cling to Alissa and to be *disponible*, a son and not a husband.

A key problem with the supposed complementarity of *L'Immoraliste* and *La Porte étroite* is that the homosexual motive, simmering in the former and realised in the life to which the latter text is much closer, is entirely excluded here. But the failure of desire narrated in both *récits* is inextricably linked to a homosexual motive, however incomplete: the man betrays the woman because his desire negates her, goes past without seeing her, is repelled by hers. Distinct from my nineteenth-century examples, where the incest-desire for the mother was more directly apparent, it is mediated in the texts of this chapter by a homosexual motive which seems primary. The woman is mother because the man's desire is a boyish rebellion that makes her old. But the male bond also always fails, and it is as if the impossibility of any desire is still, finally, the woman's fault. Michel never reaches his male doubles, Jérôme finds no consolation with God, Meaulnes cannot make it up to Frantz, and Sartre's heroes seek a posthumous embrace with their fathers in an atheist's afterlife. In every case it is the woman who is punished for this, carrying a secret in her body that is the real object of pursuit. Even where Narcissus loves his like, then, he seeks that double in the mirror of the mother's body and the reckoning is always with her.

Alissa is a surrogate mother to Jérôme and he wants to get away from her while staying umbilically tied. It is this, rather than her inhibition, that makes them forever separated, linked only by a set of mediators who are all blighted. Jérôme walks with Juliette down the garden avenue; confident in being heard he utters the Narcissistic wish: 'if only we could bend over the soul we love and see as in a mirror the image we place there!' (p. 518). Juliette weeps, realising that he will ruin her sister's life; he registers neither this nor her own desire for freedom. All the narrator will expose is her flattering passion for him and Alissa's sensitivity to it; this is understood as the latter's motive for refusing him. His semi-frivolous words are reified when, entering Alissa's room without knocking (less 'effort' than in the original fantasy!) he is reflected in her mirror; she gazes at him there. His stumbling proposal is declined and from his departing coach he watches her watch him depart. Both these instances of mirroring perfectly demonstrate Jérôme's motive: invested in Alissa, his image of himself must stay and he must go.

Abel, the *raisonneur* who has ambitions as a writer, perceives Juliette's cultivation (she has picked up Italian from Jérôme as her sister picked up Latin) and among his irritating babble he makes a couple of sharp criticisms: 'you, the master of the slow approach' (p. 528) and 'the egoism of you and Alissa is amazing'. But the author does not allow him and Juliette the satisfaction of a match, for the tragic misdirection of love requires that each be frustrated – punished, one might almost say, on behalf of their counterparts in *Dominique*. Here, besides, the structure of four is only apparent: in the two sisters grouped around the protagonist, we have another instance of the triangle, on the edge of which Abel briefly hovers.

Jérôme and Alissa correspond; viewing from his end, we see how fraught the mediate communication is: he suspects that she is covering something up yet is himself convinced that 'I let nothing of my anxiety show through in my letters' (p. 530) – a biased symmetry of male reader and female writer that will persist until the reproduction of Alissa's diary. At Christmas, the crisis breaks: Juliette tells Jérôme that Alissa wishes her to marry him, he retorts '"that's madness!"' (p. 536), and Juliette outbids Alissa in self-sacrifice by becoming engaged to her stodgy admirer Teissières. The latter stands for the horror of exogamy – 'taller, stronger, higher in colour than any of us, almost bald, from a different class, a different background, a different race from us, he seemed to feel alien among us' (p. 538) – a parody of the oedipal father so aristocratically portrayed in *Dominique*, and also, implicitly, a caricatural incarnation of Jérôme's own supposed rival, God. In a last view of the failure of Alissa's attempted doubling, the collapsed Juliette is carried to bed by tante Plantier, Teissières, Abel and her sister, all tenderly concerned. This anticipatory contrast with the isolated death of the latter underlines her damnation.

After this crisis it is a long time before they can see each other again. The narrative proceeds by reproduction of passages from Alissa's letters, for 'my memories often become confused from this point, and I can check by them' (p. 541). There is a certain false naivety here. What the narrator does in using Alissa's written voice will gradually become apparent. A letter from Alissa to tante Plantier passed on by the latter to Jérôme irritates him by its easy, relaxed manner of talking about personal matters between the couple. Jérôme wishes Alissa to use language only as she uses it to him: she must not link with or care for any other interlocutor than him. Abel consoles him: "'the whole letter is really addressed to you . . . it's your fault if Alissa writes to that good woman as a substitute . . . it's you she's saying those things to'" (p. 544). But he is wrong. The stylistic tics which annoy Jérôme are signs that Alissa is aware of the titular reader of her letters and wants both to love Jérôme and to be able to address other people.

From here on, long passages of her writing are selectively reproduced – only those, presumably, that demonstrate her concern for the hero. He has irritated her by leaving her initial in the margins of literary passages he thinks she will like ('*I was a bit annoyed at first to see you offering me what I thought I had discovered for myself*', (p. 545) and see Schlumberger, p. 59), for by doing this he is preempting her as reader, and we shall see later how deeply this marks her. She asks him not to visit this summer, but reveals how often, involuntarily, she waits for his step. Alissa believes intensely in a sort of empathy that is rather like prayer: possible only in the absence of the interlocutor, it strives to create a secondary, imaginary presence more powerful (because it is fantasy) than the real. As for her cousin, he reads her conflict as flattering and it helps him find 'the strength to resist' (p. 548). Many critics berate him for his passivity: shouldn't he just go and lunge? But this is to mistake Jérôme's own ambivalence: he wants to be wanted but also to be free, obsessed, reading texts that mirror him. The narrator does not reproduce his own letters. Instead he stresses how boring everything in his life is apart from this epistolary love. But he is travelling, and it is left to the letters of Alissa to tell us so. His experiences appear reflected, more exciting by displacement, in her image of them. When she avows that she does not wish to see him just now, it is just as difficult for us as for the narrator to diagnose Alissa's motive. What is certain is that remaining immobile while he travels and reflecting his adventures in her textual gaze is something that Jérôme wants from Alissa: the proof of this is that the narrator reproduces that relationship in *his* text, in which her words, containing him, become his book.

'To tell the truth,' he admits, 'I bore [this] rather severe discipline most cheerfully' (p. 550). A year has passed since they last saw each other, and Alissa's letters build the absence into a far greater presence: '*I was not away from you one single day* ... *Unless I can trust in you, Jérôme, what will become of me? I need to feel you are strong, to lean on you. Do not weaken*' (pp. 550-1). As in *L'Immoraliste*, the man's strength depends upon the woman's weakness; and her avowal of humility, while playing the part of the severe matriarch who nevertheless encourages him to fly the nest, is exactly what the hero requires. Their apparent reciprocation depends increasingly on her willingness to reduce herself to his mirror: '*my brother! I am not really myself, more than myself, except when I am with you* ...' (p. 552, ellipses Gide's). By 'with him' Alissa means enacting this imaginative reflection: she is retrenching into an exclusively epistolary existence, just as the narrator has described his own, but while he as reader finds his image in her text, she as writer subsumes her self in his.

Thus although the woman's voice dominates this text, it is only in the form of a highly circumscribed, coopted writing. No less than Jérôme preempts her reading by annotating the margins of her books, he makes it impossible for her to write except of him. Alissa's famous self-destructiveness sets in at about this point. But we can interpret it otherwise than as the inexplicable anorexia the narrator diagnoses. Her imagination, dedicated to reflecting his adventures, has impoverished her own senses: '*when you wrote to me from Italy, I saw everything through you; now I feel as if whatever I look at is something I am stealing from you*' (p. 553); so far has he taken her over that she feels herself no longer entitled to any but vicarious experiences. This impoverishment is further reflected in an inability to pray: where Jérôme has appropriated her self, there is no God. The effort to project herself elsewhere is futile: Juliette is now happy without her; with nothing to do but long for him, Alissa is isolated, obsessed with an 'attente' that, far from the excitement of *Les Nourritures Terrestres*, is simply a nervous consciousness of her captivity:

The closer we get to the day of our reunion, the more anxious my anticipation [attente] becomes. It's almost apprehension; it seems now as if I were dreading your arrival, which I longed for so much. I try not to think about it; I imagine your ring on the bell, your step on the stair, and my heart stops beating, or starts to ache . . . Above all, don't expect me to be able to speak to you . . . My past life seems to end at that moment; I can see nothing beyond it; my life stops . . . (p. 555, ellipses Gide's)

A death-wish invested in the lover haunts this document of ostensible desire: the threatening tread makes her mute, then blind, then kills. Where the narrator of *L'Immoraliste* perceived marriage as the end of the monologue, Alissa sees her lover's presence as silencing her. His reply is omitted; we simply see her agree that it will be better not to prolong this meeting: *'what would we have to say that we have not already written to each other?'*. So it is Jérôme who chooses to limit their encounter and keep them in the mediate relationship of writing.

The meeting is strained, less by the presence of other people than in the rare moments they find themselves alone. The fantasy of silence and death has been reified. It is clear that sexual constraint and their mutual dependence on the exercise of her imagination have made speech impossible; this loss seems to threaten their very existence as a couple. In an anguished letter, begging him not to see her again, Alissa confesses: *'I felt . . . as if our whole correspondence was nothing but a great mirage, as if each of us, alas! had only been writing to themselves'* (p. 559). Here, Alissa anticipates the isolation that will attend her last days, when prayer suddenly becomes a monologue spoken as if to a mirror. For authorial irony is here, as in *La Symphonie pastorale*, directed above all against the diarist as a Protestant. Protestantism is supposed to be a dialogue with God. Alissa's problem is her intense wish for direct speech and the fact that she comes increasingly to find every pair a three; there is always interference on the line. The failure of the religious dialogue is Gide's most damning stroke as author-God: Alissa will finally find that even this speech is impossible, preempted by Jérôme, and die voiceless and alone.

Apart, she writes now, she loved him more.[16] When Jérôme replies, he blames everything on her for, by articulating the failure that he had only tacitly recognised, she has made it 'real' and given it substance. Now whatever stops him from communicating will be her fault: *'Alissa! as soon as I try to argue, my words turn to ice . . . the more I love you the less I can speak to you'* (p. 560). He asks that they should stop writing to each other and meet in person at Easter. Without waiting for a reply, 'I was able to plunge back into work'.

At the next meeting, the real difference between them is demonstrated before they even speak: he approaches slowly, savouring the instant before she sees him as 'the most delicious perhaps, sweeter than the happiness that follows' (p. 561-2), while she jumps up, puts her hands on his shoulders and gazes smiling at him. They then agree at his instigation that on a signal from her, he will leave without a word of protest: her signal, his instigation. One day he hazards the beginning of a proposal; but Alissa refuses happiness for '"sanctity"' (p. 564) – a word she pronounces 'so low that . . . I guessed rather than heard it'. He guesses, because he already knows: Alissa is the saint he has made her. That evening she gives the signal and he departs.

To abandon Alissa is to is obey her: in this way she appears the free partner, he the weak captive. But in an exchange of letters that follows this mutual disappointment, we see how fixedly he looks to her for a self-image and how her very 'abandonment' is giving him one:

> 'It often seems to me', I wrote, 'that my love is the best part of me; all my virtues hang upon it; it raises me above myself and without it I would slip back to the mediocre level of a very ordinary character. I will always think the hardest path is the best because that is the path by which I hope to join you.'
> What did I add that made her reply with these words:
> *But, my dear, sanctity is not a choice, it is an OBLIGATION* (the word was underlined three times in her letter). *If you are the man I believe you to be, you too will not be able to evade it* (p. 565)

Whatever it is he added, he does not tell us; thus Alissa is blamed for the stringency of the image she returns him. Her words are reminiscent of those of Amélie from the coffin: in both cases the man's sinlessness is presented as forced on him by the assumption of the woman. For the rest of the text, Alissa casts back, from an increasingly opaque surface, a picture of holy virtue which follows logically enough from the first turning-point when he swore to protect her from desire. He is left to submit to the mirror he has made.

Alissa's terrible power rests, of course, in her repression: both abandoning and liberating mother, she preempts the son's rebellion by forbidding the incest of a return to her body. But this was forced on her by her cousin's original obsession with the transgression of female desire. It was he who foreclosed her questioning. Just as his mother had to wear black, so she must never know what her mother knew. Her refusal now is the deadly consequence of that first imposition.

She does what she is required to do: withdraw so that he can form a couple with God. The hero sees her silence as a test; the narrator (who now knows, by his lights, how much she loved him) terms it a 'ruse', the false clothing of a true passion. For at their penultimate meeting, Alissa seems all repugnant surface. Warm, smiling, but badly dressed and with a new unflattering hairstyle, she no longer plays the piano and has replaced her classical library by a collection of ill-written tracts which approximate to direct conversation: "'they are humble souls speaking to me in a simple way, expressing themselves as best they can; I like their company'" (p. 569). Here, after all, he will not fill the margins with her initial. Jérôme is appalled by her looks from which all poetry seems gone, her voice which has become clear and monotonous – "'Alissa!'" he complains, "'why are you tearing off your wings?'" (p. 570). But the truth is, Alissa has long since had no wings: earthbound and circumscribed, she has stayed still while he soared. Now she is reifying the metaphor: he must be God's high-flier, while she remains humbly below. Jérôme sees her as escaping his grasp – 'Alissa eluded me all the time . . . I was dispossessed' (p. 571) – and himself as in 'mourning' (p. 572) for his lost happiness. She replies in kind: "'you are in love with a phantom . . . an imaginary figure'", and he is the murderer of the ghost: seeing his reaction to her changed appearance, she taunts him that he loves her less, though nothing has changed in her, just because she has grown old. His protests ring false. He leaves, condemning Alissa as a fallen idol, a failed mirror: 'left to herself, Alissa went straight back down to her level, a mediocre level, where I stood myself, but where I no longer desired her' (pp. 573-4).

Jérôme departs for his silent travels again, seeing Greece and the Middle East in a couple of lines of narrative. More than two years pass; then, almost casually, he wanders to Fongueusemare and enters her garden. He finds her thin, 'dreadfully [affreusement]' (p. 576) pale, in mourning for her father. She seems psychically to have anticipated his coming, and throws herself into his arms. Swearing he could marry no-one but her, her face shining 'with a superhuman, angelic beauty' (p. 577) – echoes of the 'never had she seemed so lovely to me' – he takes her in his arms 'almost brutally' and 'crushed her lips with kisses'. Their embrace resembles that of Dominique and Madeleine:

> I held her a moment as she lay unresisting, half flung back against me; I saw her gaze veil over; then her eyes closed, and in a voice whose truth and melodiousness could never be equalled, she cried:
>
> 'Have pity on us, my friend! Oh, don't ruin our love.'
>
> Perhaps she also said, 'Don't be a coward!' or perhaps I said it to myself, I do not know any more, but suddenly, throwing myself on my knees before her and clasping her devoutly in my arms, I cried:
>
> 'If you loved me this much, why did you always push me away?'

It was Alissa who clung to him when he arrived; this second embrace is described even more one-sidedly than Dominique's. She does not kiss back; every reaction is his. His desire is an attack on the angel; the voice that emerges when the eyes close sounds to him clear and beautiful, and the accusation of cowardice may have been his own; it is he who lets go. Only later do we get an idea of the desire Alissa is so bad at expressing but which Jérôme, on his knees now, does not really want to perceive.

Alissa swears it is too late, only divine love would be perfect enough now. In her final gesture, 'she gazed at me for one more moment, at once holding me and keeping me at arms' length with her hands on my shoulders, her eyes filled with unutterable love' (p. 578). She, familiarly, walks away still looking, while her lover collapses sobbing outside the locked gate. The narrator adds: 'but to hold her back, to force the gate, to penetrate somehow or other into the house, even though it was not closed to me – no, still today when I look back and relive all that past, I know I could not have done that, and whoever does not understand this has not understood anything about me' (p. 579). Like our other protagonists, he leaves her empty-handed. The implied reader is required to understand. The love she cannot speak is the narrator's last word.

A few weeks later, Juliette writes to say that Alissa has died, far away from all of them in Paris. Jérôme receives Alissa's diary, begun soon after Juliette's marriage. Aside from a frame-ending, in which Jérôme takes his leave of the grown-up Juliette and sees her baby daughter, named after Alissa, the rest of the text consists of uncommented excerpts from the latter's posthumous writing. She wants her diary above all to be no *'flattering mirror'* (p. 583) but a place where she can form a conversational couple with God. Yet everywhere Jérôme's image intervenes like an adulterer. For, as we have anticipated, she finds him internalised in her view of herself: *'sometimes when I listen to him speaking it is as if I can see myself thinking. He explains and reveals me to myself. Would I exist without him? . . . All my virtue is just to please him'* (p. 584). What Alissa dreads as an abhorrent narcissism is really the penetration of Jérôme into her own self-reflection.

Jérôme's view of her (as we know from his account) is inseparable from the taint of desire embodied in her mother. One day, she finds the nearness of her cousin's body *'strangely disturbing'* (p. 585); later she reclines in her mother's couch, thinking of the latter, and when her father comes in, he stares and begins speaking of his wife. That night, Alissa is obsessed with the past *'rising up in me like remorse'* (p. 586): to be seen is to be the bad woman.

The shade of adultery always present, Alissa at first sees herself as the obstacle between Jérôme and God; she resolves to make him love her less, for (in a mixture of contempt for herself and for him): *'would I love him as much if he were satisfied to stop at me?'* (p. 587). Here too, her modesty reflects his pride, her withdrawal his repulsion. She vows her love to silence, convinced that two cannot walk abreast up the narrow path to God; but there is another reason for her inability to speak. Everywhere the immediacy of language has been invaded by Jérôme. Her impulse to style – *'the culpable wish to write well'* (p. 588) – seems derived from him; she tries to write badly (as we have seen her try to read badly) *'to escape from the rhythm of his phrases; but to struggle against him is still to think about him'*. When she attempts to pray, God himself seems to be setting Jérôme's image in the way of communication.

The narrator clearly reads this, and expects us to, as a love so intense that Alissa's heroism is absurd, both ruthless and masochistic. The 'truth' revealed by her writing is supposed to be that out of a crazy saintliness and a horror of sex, she withdrew from him, yet pined away unto death. But we can read something rather different in this cry for help. The original adulterous triangle is everywhere ruining her attempts at dialogue; the male couple formed by Jérôme with God conspires in her very text to disempower her.

As the diary continues, Alissa comes to admit this: *'My God, you know that I need him in order to love you'* (p. 591).[17] We read her side of their last encounter: beforehand, a passionate expectation of his arrival and afterwards, intolerable bereavement. In that crisis, she recognises how both male partners have abandoned her: Jérôme incapable of reading the feeling behind her inarticulacy, and God as disrupter of their couple: *'in secret I was false to the words God placed in my mouth ... jealous God, you dispossessed me'* (p. 593). The last resort is to accept God's stern conditions: she flees the place that is full of her failure, to search for *'somewhere where I shall see nothing but You'*.

In the grim nursing-home where she takes refuge, Alissa begins her final 'attente', this time a desperate hope for the reign of God *'to enter me!'* (p. 594). The attempt to cry out in direct speech to God goes unanswered; she returns to the written form of the diary *'to reassure myself, calm myself'* (p. 595). Then finally she recognises that there is no implied reader. Her last words are: *'I'd like to die now, quickly, before I realise again that I am alone'*. Alissa's punishment is to learn that she is in neither a triangle nor a couple, but entirely isolated. For the first time, she writes not in the second person but the first. She is shut out from what, without her, reverts to the familiar failure of the male couple. Jérôme will form no union with God. When he takes over as narrator – not to confess to anyone but simply for his own 'pleasure' – he appropriates not only Alissa's voice but also the authority of God-the-writer. His lonely atheism is the last refusal of 'the desire of the mother', the final, self-directed mode of desire.

There is no room to go into detail here, but the final appropriation of the woman's voice in Gide takes place in the directly confessional text he published after his wife's death, *Et nunc manet in te* (1947). Here he chose not to publish Madeleine's letters or diary, but to print the sections from his own diary that he had censored out of respect for her in her lifetime. The insistent tone of *mea culpa* ends, as Schlumberger argues, by making her seem older, more abused, more grim than she probably was. At the same time he attributes to her saintly authenticity the impossibility of communication while she was still alive: thus like Alissa (and our other devoted ladies) she is pure and simple. In retelling the painful events when she revealed that she knew about his affair with Marc Allégret and, while he was away with his lover, burned all his letters to her, he biases the account towards his appalled sense of desecration. If for Madeleine the letters were '"the most precious thing I had in the world"' (*Journal 1939-1949. Souvenirs*, p. 1146), for her husband she had wantonly destroyed his finest writing. By her action she had, he laments, 'wiped out [supprimé] the unique ark where my memory might hope, later, to take refuge' (p. 1145). This book, then, is surely his riposte to the 'I am afraid that what I have suppressed will take revenge', turning it round so that finally it serves him. In this text, the haunting voice of his guilt becomes – as in all confessions – the somewhat flattering image of his truthfulness.

And what of 'sincerity'? His favoured image of the 'creature of dialogue' (p. 547) comes of a Goethean dialectic in which *Polarität* (polarity) presupposes *Steigerung* (rising/synthesis); internalised, this means a war of selves that can justify the claim to be authentic – as he draws all opposition into the self, Gide evades the quarrel with others that would be insufficiently poetic. In his own interpretation of *L'Immoraliste* and *La Porte étroite* as the two poles of excess between which the author sits, we find the same phantasy of splitting the self with a nice symmetry to produce the presiding authorial third party. We have seen that these *récits* are not two halves of a whole but rather versions of a project that takes shape in all his writing. Unuttered desire as failure appears in the male chain which never closes in consummation, and always at fault is the woman whose strength must be coopted and destroyed. The battle that is enacted in *Et nunc manet in te* as autobiography goes furthest towards the false goal of sincerity. Madeleine, who in Gide's rewriting becomes the figure of saintly authenticity, is contained in his confession; the implied reader/confessor absolves him: he is her pure mirror. The Eden of pre-Saussurean utterance, in which I can mean what I say, seems restored; writing is monologue. But only through the death of the woman. The first person, after all, is speaking in her voice.

The *récit* is properly a Romantic genre but, perhaps unsurprisingly, it is not entirely dead; in the last section of this chapter, I want to look at a number of other texts, more or less consonant with my original definition, in which the modern variant of undesire for the woman combined with a failed impulse towards male bonding is centrally developed.

Alain-Fournier's *Le grand Meaulnes* (1913) is very much a *récit*: it has a pattern of male doubles, a beloved woman who dies, a frame-narrator and a central narrative. But it would be difficult to decide for certain who is its protagonist: many hints make this rather the

story of François Seurel's doomed ideal than Meaulnes's. Even the
central narrative of Meaulnes's adventure is told by the narrator
François in the third person and with certain privileges of omniscience. In this respect, the structure rather resembles that of *Frankenstein* than that of most of the nineteenth-century *récits* and the prob-
lems of male doubling take a central position.

Meaulnes suffers from 'this inability [impuissance] to be happy'
(p. 237)[18] because he is more attached to Frantz than to the latter's
sister Yvonne. The lovely girl glimpsed in the 'lost domain' appears
to be the object of his quest, and is certainly the object of François's
passionate identification with that quest, but when François finds
her and brings her to Meaulnes, he is disappointed, even repelled,
for she arrives metonymic not of the magical past but of its loss.
Yvonne fails to answer Meaulnes's desire, not simply because she
now stands for daylight reality and the courage of poverty, but because
it is Frantz he wants to have and be. Just as Frantz himself is 'a strange
. . . charming creature' (p. 236), so the reflection that Meaulnes gazed
at in an iced-over pond, the 'charming, romantic creature' (p. 93)
clothed in dreamlike travesty, is a self he pursues through the medium
of the quest for the woman.

Meaulnes wants to preserve Frantz, find him, restore him to his
domain; he parts from Yvonne the morning after their wedding so
that he can bring back to Frantz the fiancée that both have 'perdue'
– Frantz in the primary sense of 'loss', Meaulnes in the secondary
meaning for he has cast her into the hell of prostitution. So intense
is the doubling in this text, Meaulnes has almost married Frantz's
betrothed, Valentine, but when he realises who she is, he throws her
out with the accusation: '"what harm you have done us, you who
wouldn't believe in anything. Everything is your fault. You're the
one that has ruined [perdu] everything, everything!"' (pp. 302-3).
The woman is at fault because, by refusing to represent Frantz's
dream, she undermined the fantasy, the common secret that keeps
boys boys.

The 'us' in the above quotation rings strange, linking two supposedly rival males together in the very reproach to the absconded
bride; this pronoun and its ambivalences haunt the whole text. François's narrative opens with a reference to a 'we' that points to his
family; on the next page 'we' means first himself and his mother,
then, a few lines later, everyone but his mother. For most of the text,

even when referring to experiences that strictly belong to Meaulnes alone (pp. 267, 282, 285), the narrator uses 'we' to unite Meaulnes and himself; but elsewhere the companion is an interloper: 'someone came and extinguished the lamp around which we gathered as a happy family' (p. 21). Meaulnes both gives life and takes it away. Adolescence seems to be coextensive with his presence but, because he does not know how to grow up, he robs both Yvonne and François of the adult happiness they might have enjoyed.

If we continue to consider this François's story rather than Meaulnes's, we can see in what a complex way the narrator manipulates his double. The schoolboy comrade represents for the hero the mobility he, as a crippled and protected child, has lacked; Meaulnes both travels and desires for him, bringing home a mystery for them to digest and develop together. But at a certain point, Meaulnes leaves François behind and the latter begins to grow up, allows Meaulnes's rival Jasmin to point the way to the domain, finds Yvonne framed significantly among his own extended family, befriends her, brings Meaulnes to her, sees them marry and is left 'to prowl' (p. 244) obsessively outside the honeymooners' window. That the boys' world is reasserted precisely now – Frantz returning to disrupt the marriage he envies and to call his boy to find his girl – reflects the interests of François's jealousy. Yvonne runs out, a humiliated bride, to fetch her husband back to the one night that will ensure her childbed death, her disarray suggesting an otherwise repressed female desire. Thenceforth, she is the object of friendship, a mediate passion that fails to protect her from a destruction by her brother's profligacy and now completed by the paired abandonment of Meaulnes and Frantz.

Passion is so fraught with the imagination of male camaraderie that even the gesture given as 'that caress to which he should have been able to reply' (p. 255), the sign of Meaulnes's desire for his wife as mediated by the vicarious narrator, is the same touch of hand on shoulder that marks the comradeship of boys (pp. 45 and 104). But the 'young woman so ardently sought and loved' (p. 284) is sought and loved by François, who carries her down to her coffin and tells her story – not as his own but, in the dangerous name of friendship, as Meaulnes's.

The woman appears as mother in a nostalgic recollection of infancy (bizarrely shared between François and Meaulnes, pp. 75 and 269) in which she is glimpsed tranquilly playing the piano. This image of the matriarchal musician reappears in Meaulnes's dream (p. 69), in his first sight of Yvonne (p. 91) and on their wedding-night (p. 245), when it is expanded to mark the turning-point of girl to woman, the loss of virginity and threat to female narcissism that marriage represents in the narrator's imagination (pp. 245-6). As Yvonne takes over the doubling of mother as pianist, Valentine is left the role of 'young housewife' (p. 314), despite her original *disponibilité*; she also plays, dressed up like Ganache as a pierrot, the mediate figure of the innocent thief, both 'suffering and mischievous' (p. 294). But if these two women poised between girlhood and adulthood (pp. 90 and 184) take over the ambiguities of the mother and suffer for them, the surviving echo in this text is Yvonne's and Meaulnes's daughter.

Daughters are rare in fiction: when they appear it is usually as the just deserts of adulteresses fit only to reproduce themselves.[19] The baby Alissa in *La Porte étroite* marks the indirect survival of the sterile heroine in the offspring of her sister. The daughter in *Le grand Meaulnes* causes the death of her mother but, as double, is also her residue. Into the couple formed by her and François, Meaulnes comes for a second time as interloper. The narrative ends with him robbing the narrator of 'the only joy he had left me' (p. 315) and leaving with his daughter 'for new adventures'. The boys' world is at an end, broken up by the female child they all want to father. The double ends (as his name suggests) in the ambiguous image of a *roi des aulnes* (carrying this child as he once carried François), the double who robs his master of everything. Thus the mythology of male friendship and possibility of heterosexual desire coexist here as they do in Gide as failures for which the woman dies and the man remains with nothing but his text.

Four other fictions offer more insights into aspects of the *récit*. Breton's *Nadja* (1928) is less the story of the eponym than a quest to discover the narrator's self. The text begins: 'who am I? If, exceptionally, I were to resort to an adage, might not the answer after all be to discover whom I "haunt"?' (p. 9).[20] The woman, then, is not the phantom but the host, the place wherein he will be reflected. And sure enough, when Nadja belatedly enters the narrative, it is to discover the protagonist to himself. In her gaze he finds visions of himself, heading for the stars, terrifyingly powerful. Like Carmen and Ellénore, Nadja obligingly predicts her own doom at the hands of the hero's ambition which, at the same time, she flatters and nurtures. Asked who she is, she disembodies herself as a part of him, 'the wandering soul' (p. 82), but in his eyes she has that supreme quality of the heroines of *récits*, *'simplicity'*. When they keep running into each other on the Paris streets, he reflects: 'it is clear she is at my mercy' (p. 106). She is 'a free genius' (p. 130), but only because 'it happened that she took me for a god, believed I *was* the sun'.

The relationship finally comes apart when he reacts with violent resentment to her over-detailed and 'somewhat ironic' (p. 135) account of being beaten up by a man to whom she had taken 'a mischievous pleasure in refusing herself' (p. 134). She weeps flatteringly when the protagonist says they can no longer see each other, but 'finds in her very tears the strength to exhort me to follow my resolution' (p. 135). It is hard to see exactly what Nadja is being punished for here. Perhaps not so much for submitting to a beating, having first had the cheek to say no to an admirer, as because of the way she speaks about herself. Like Mérimée's bad women, she has dared to be ironic. For this she is condemned to play the self-sacrificing heroine, awash with resignation. She ends up languishing in a psychiatric hospital; while the narrator pauses to inveigh against such institutions, he is careful not to visit or rescue her. His future lies, instead, in the prefatory coincidence of the meeting with Eluard, or in the aptly named 'Hotel of the Great Men' (p. 24). For in the male grouping of the Surrealists, a woman's place is in the dream.

Bernanos's *Journal d'un curé de campagne* (1936) is the narrative of a saint not unlike the protagonists of Stifter's and Grillparzer's Novellen. But he of course is a celibate whose only legitimate union must be with God. He begins his diary with a certain sense of guilt: like Alissa he does not want a trace of narcissism, for the journal could be 'a clouded mirror in which I fear I might see a face suddenly appear – whose? my own perhaps . . . a rediscovered, forgotten face' (p. 1036, ellipses Bernanos's).[21] This face emerges in the text, not through the hazardous communication with God but in the frame of the gaze of women.

In the course of the narrative, the motif of young women's gaze as vicious and predatory becomes gradually subsumed under an image of maternal charity, the two combining by the end to create a figure of the Virgin as both mother and girl. This female gaze that belongs to mother and daughter together is adumbrated early in the text, first in the image of the Church as tenderly gazing mother, then in a series of metaphors in which the parish, the village, truth, injustice and poverty are likened to female figures with dangerous or significant looks (pp. 1045, 1052, 1061, 1063, 1067, 1071, 1077 and 1080).

The priest remains in love with his parish, though it is like a wife who has long since got the measure of him. His parishioners' children especially seem to have the knowing gaze of the sexually experienced; and it is only much later that he contemplates the mixed-up Séraphita with the same sympathetic view as the lonely homosexual Sulpice. For women are dangerous to look upon, their faces both excessively mobile and strangely hard (pp. 1053 and 1088).

The wildness of Séraphita confounds the priest but a certain class-pride makes him rise to the challenge of Chantal and her mother the countess. These two women are powerful and voice desire as demand – "'everything, and all at once'" (pp. 1148-9), "'I want to give all or nothing, that is how we daughters are in this family'" (p. 1163) – but in them he divines and exploits a depth of suffering that awakens the unexpected authority of 'paternity' (p. 1170). They both resemble and hate each other in a vicious spiral of incest: the daughter violently jealous over her foolish father, the mother bitterly mourning the death of an infant son. In bringing the countess to the state of cathartic serenity where she dies at peace, the curé becomes both her father and the replacement of that beloved son, just as she, the first time we see her, is dressed in a mantilla like his own mother. But Chantal is more directly punished, for the wilfulness of the young rich is hard to forgive; the incarnation of the Virgin is finally found instead in the Samaritan Séraphita and in the tenderly self-sacrificing figure of the mistress of the curé's disreputable double, the ex-priest Dupréty/Dufréty. This young woman submits in sublime humility to her lover's snobbery and pretension, nursing his vanity as devotedly as his body, though she herself is as ill as he. She resembles her mother, who died on her feet after years of torment at the hands of a drunken husband. This mother-daughter bond, an exact reverse of the other, stands guard like the infant Madonna over the death of the curé: he recognises in himself the same female-proletarian tenacity and will to survive through suffering, and finds the maternal gaze of his infancy restored, completing the circle of the mirror: 'for the first time in years, the first time ever perhaps, I feel as if I were facing my youth, looking at it without mistrust. I seem to recognise its face, a forgotten face. It [elle] looks back at me, and forgives me' (p. 1254). Thus the 'forgotten face' that he dreaded to find in the mirror of the diary is, after all, the mother's gaze. His actual death is presided over by the patriarchy, however: a brief closing frame presents the letter of Dufréty to the curé de Torcy, and the latter will, the priest knows, cast out Dufréty's mistress in order to save her unworthy lover for the Church. The secret we understand to die with him is a mute knowledge that the true image of sanctity is embodied in the mother and daughter, not in their 'fathers' or sons. Sanctity – but not, after all, endurance: the women do not survive, any more than the priest who now mirrors them. Martyred and obscure, they survive only in his imagination, that is, in his text.

In Sartre's *La Nausée* (1938) and Camus's *L'Etranger* (1942), heterosexual undesire is elevated into the text's fundamental argument, there as metaphysics, here as ethics. The isolation of Roquentin and Meursault is axiomatic, the residue of a Romanticism no longer so overtly proud of itself. Their universe is grim, banal: both make lovelessness a way of life.

Roquentin's nausea is the product of a sense that the defining lines, the phallic precision of the material world have suddenly become precarious: images of pregnancy, abortion, rape and birth inform the text, bespeaking a horror at the 'viscous' contagion of the feminine in the very possession of a body.[22] It is, of course, also about writing, but if we recall the description of books in *Les Mots* as 'these boxes that open like oysters . . . [with] the nakedness of their inner organs, their pallid, musty pages, slightly swollen, covered in tiny black veins, that drank up ink and smelt of mushrooms' (*Mots*, p. 37), and reflect that 'the library was the world in a mirror' (p. 44), we can see that the problem of writing is inseparably linked to the image of the mother's body.

In his autobiography, Sartre claims that, having never known his father, he has no superego, and makes his infancy seem entirely matriarchal, but his mother was domesticated not as wife but as daughter; hence the *hantise* of brother-sister incest to which Sartre disarmingly refers in a note (p. 48). For the library is the grandfather's and so is the mother.

Elsewhere in Sartre's writing, there is a repeated attempt to chart a homosocial reconciliation of rebel son with ambiguous father on the far side of the grave. In *Les Mains sales* (1948) the hero Hugo opts for a martyr's suicide in order to restore to the paternal Hoederer the wrongness he had in life and the political murder that history will otherwise deny him. In *Les Séquestrés d'Altona* (1960) Frantz descends from his upstairs cell and goes off to join his father in an incongruous suicide pact. But in the earliest of the plays, *Les Mouches* (1942), the crime is an entirely unsuicidal matricide.

Back in *La Nausée*, the whole of nature is (as in the balmy days of Romanticism) a maternal body from which we cannot break free. Where the Romantic longs either for consummation or at least attention, Sartre's protagonist wants to be born out of the material world altogether, to kill the Triffids that colonise towns. In the public gardens, the hero finds nature burgeoning relentlessly until, by a sudden act of will, he emerges in a moment of birth. The garden smiles at him, relieved perhaps at escaping by the barest of luck from a childbed death that would have blown up the world.

Roquentin manages to solve his problem by fantasising, through the aesthetic 'being' of a jazz record, a kind of male motherhood without taint of the flesh. He leaves for Paris gestating a novel; though Sartre later argued that nothing could come of such an ambition,[23] and though debate continues over the ironic status of this ending, there is no doubt that it momentarily restores the phallic myth – the story is to be 'as hard and beautiful as steel' (p. 210) – that Roquentin had feared was slipping from his grasp.

As for Meursault, he dies, in his author's observation, because "'in our society any man who does not weep at his mother's funeral risks being condemned to death'" (p. 1920).[24] Fond of disguising ambivalences under paradoxes, Camus elevates filial indifference into a capital crime for a number of reasons. It displaces the guilt for both Meursault's crime and his punishment onto the hypocrisy of society, so that he dies a martyr and the Arab's murder disappears into thin air, thus washing away any stain of politics from the sunny landscape of thirties' Algeria. It makes Meursault seem innocent and frank, when in fact his speech is fraught with nervous apologies (pp. 1125, 1126, 1137) or evasive lies told 'in order not to have to speak' (p. 1126). His very silences are supposed to alert us to a truth too deep for words, to suggest that perhaps after all he did love his mother but is too modest to display it.

Meursault is the Romantic hero turned carefully inside out, so that we will appreciate him freshly. He does love his mother, of course, if thinking of her at certain disturbed moments is a sign of love. She pops into his mind when he tells us about Salamano's sado-masochistic relation with his dog; he remembers her in the final climax where he is affirming the truth of the absurd by opening his arms to the 'tender indifference of the world' (p. 1209); and she is tied up with his every temptation to apologise and then cover it up with a dismissive 'it means nothing really'. Twice, in particular, the thought of the mother is linked to a conviction of fundamental guilt. To Marie, he reflects that it is meaningless to apologise for his mother's death, for 'in any case, one is always a bit at fault' (p. 1137); and to his lawyer, he observes, '"no doubt, I loved mother, but that means nothing. All sane people more or less desire the death of those they love"' (p. 1170). One both loves and hates one's mother, and she no doubt both loves and hates her child. The exasperating inarticulacy of a silent mother is converted, in Camus's autobiographical narrative 'Entre oui et non', into an affection too deep for demonstration, or in *La Peste* into a gently beaming presence appreciated by the son's friend Tarrou if not by him; but in the play *Le Malentendu*, the mother is her son's murderer, and she shows the jealous Martha that this is an index of how much he meant to her: 'a mother's love for her son . . . that survives twenty years of silence' (pp. 165-6) is reborn because 'he is the one I killed' (p. 167).

Camus's later writing moves towards a homosocial grouping that pretends to be political, but a good look at *La Peste* confirms that just as no Arabs seem to get the plague, no women do either: they nurse, cling and wail, but are admirably resistant to the bacillus – no doubt because, as its feminine gender indicates, the plague partakes of their threatening femininity, just as it mimics in its terrorism the repressed presence of the natives.

Meursault guns down the Arab because, like the inmates of the old people's home, the latter has a mute gaze that speaks judgment. The hero himself loves to stare, especially at the clear sky (pp. 1136, 1142, 1160) and in prison, he gradually learns to stop gripping the bars and admit that even entrapped in the trunk of a hollow tree he would enjoy what he can see. Contracted to the sheer motion of the eye, desire could be content with an immobile upward gaze. This image of a phallic thrust in perpetual readiness but never leaving ground has echoes of Camus's mystifying ethic of lucidity: a state of tireless awareness, never used up, never lost.

The sky is a special case: it does not stare back and refute desire by judgment – except, that is, when the sun gets in your eyes. One Sunday on the beach, the stare of an Arab and the glare of the sun coincide fatally on the bright blade of a knife, and this is when Meursault kills. Immediately before he fires for the first time, the narrator uses two key metaphors: 'that burning sword gnawed at my lashes and dug into [fouillait] my painful eyes . . . it seemed as if the whole sky opened up and rained down fire' (p. 1166). Blades in the eyes and the sky raining fire: these two images point to the myths of Oedipus and Sodom, both instances of pre-ordained guilt and specifically, the stories of men punished for the two desires of son-mother incest and homosexual buggery. At the point where these two myths come together in the concerted attack of black man and sun-god (the one holding the phallic weapon, the other pouring forth), the sea is heard in a noisy *jouissance* and Meursault at last lets go and shoots. Whom he is shooting is indeed an open question. For if the undesired mother is killed in effigy, it is to her 'tenderly indifferent' embrace that he turns in the end, seeking in it the image of himself as purged, pure and free. Here if anywhere Meursault becomes 'l'homme absurde', a real man.

As a last instance of the motifs of the twentieth-century *récit*, let us look at the longest one of all, Proust's *A la Recherche du temps perdu* (1913-27). There is no room here to go into detail but it is striking that, while this author preempted his fellow homosexual Gide by speaking directly (though not in the first person) about the social psychology of male homosexuals, especially about the secrecy, glamour and sordidness that issue from its outlawed status, yet he develops the central theme of jealousy primarily and most fully in reference to man-woman couples. The viewpoint is exclusively that of the male lover; the woman is pursued by frantic researches, chased not just spatially but also temporally, so that there shall be no place in her present or past that he has not explored and known. Desire is above all epistemophilia, with the typical motive of aggression upon the mother's body. What Marcel discovers when his mother spends a whole night in his bedroom is that 'it seemed as if with an impious, secret hand I had traced upon her head a first white hair' (I, p. 38).[25] To love her is to destroy her, for if she gives in he is no longer the model of willpower that she wishes him to be, and by a chain of mirror-logic his failure in her eyes becomes her disablement in his.

The woman is whole, then, only so long as she reflects the man as strong. If she ceases to do this, she becomes tainted. As Marcel grows up, his desire is always for that image of himself as good, stable and whole which the original transgression of puberty has mutilated. Girls glimpsed at railway stations, Gilberte in front of a hedge of hawthorns, are required to hold and present his image in their eyes or his name between their lips, for this alone (momentarily at least) can make him real.

When Swann falls in love it is with a woman who is not even his type – an arbitrariness that is only skin-deep for it is clear that the beloved will represent the mother just as the narrative of Swann's affair is anticiped by the drama of the goodnight kiss. One's mother is never what a character in Rebecca West calls one's 'sort'.[26] Swann falls in love because one evening when he looks for Odette she is not there, and from that moment the relief that only she can give must be pursued through the cityscape and back into her sleeping past. What he finds when he gazes thus into secret corners is not his reflection – for her assent to him is always out of the question – but the image of what she desires: other men, caricatures of himself, and finally the hint of a lesbian relationship.

What is ultimately sought in the woman is that doubling of desire that refuses the man as object: her secret centre, perceived as lesbian *jouissance*. In Marcel's passion for Albertine, his necrophiliac jealousy pursues even beyond her death the trace of her love affair with Andrée, who resembles him. What he seeks in the female mirror is the image of himself as a woman.

This homosexual desire, then, passes through a violent engagement with the mother's body in which the looker's image is sought not in his doubles but, after all, in hers. For the woman's desire and the woman's knowledge belong to her mode of doubling, the mother and daughter pair which is where Narcissus's quest comes to an end. It remains, in the last chapter, to see what this means, and to bring Narcissus and Echo back together again.

Chapter 7: Men's mirror and women's voice

> 'For if she begins to tell the truth,
> the figure in the looking-glass shrinks'
> (Woolf)

What can we say, then, having looked in detail at ten texts and briefly at thirteen others, about the place of women in the French *récit*? I want to begin by recapitulating some common motifs, and then I shall broaden the argument to the theoretical issues in psychoanalysis and feminism which these themes and structures point to.

The women in the *récit* all, overtly or covertly, stand for the depriving mother of the childbed death. It is implicit in the quarrel with the heroine that she and the hero cannot coexist. Either she abandons the man by her 'betrayal' real or suspected, or she is killed by him in order to enact an abandonment understood as axiomatic – often both these themes occur in the same text. Thus even where the woman is at her most solid and present (desired or undesired) she is always also a ghost. Her voice, like Echo's, is posthumous and only audible because disembodied.

A sister often appears, either as a directly desired figure, as in *René* or *Atala*, or as a problematic and indirect object of desire, in *Dominique* or *La Porte étroite*. She stands for the mother and is also in an implied relation to her for, as I shall examine later, the mutual murder of the mother-son relation is underwritten by the phantasised alternative of a doubling desire between the mother and the daughter he is not. An envy of women is perceptible in this *hantise*, for it hints that somewhere – perhaps between Sylvie and Adrienne or between Rosette and Madeleine, or between the actual sisters Madeleine and Julie, Alissa and Juliette – there is a pairing of the same sex which differs from the relationship of the protagonist and his doubles. Where it is fraught, as in the jealousy of Juliette or Sylvie, or the unreasonable demands of Atala's mother, a unity of feeling seems to override the conflict and even the death.

Many of my protagonists look back to a matriarchal Eden: nature serves as a lost place of nurturance in *René*, *La Confession d'un enfant du siècle*, *Sylvie* and *Dominique*; but even in these texts there is a sense that the hero's childhood is already mediate, symbolic and patriarchal. In *Adolphe* and *L'Immoraliste*, the hero has been brought up by his

202

father, a figure both over-educating and neglectful. Fathers give cynical advice, offer homes empty of mothering, or appear in surrogate form as the critical frame-narrator *(Manon Lescaut, René, Adolphe)* or the figure of God who presided over a theological upbringing *(Manon Lescaut, Carmen, La Porte étroite)*. The 'vagueness of the passions' analysed by Chateaubriand traces a mediate culture back to infancy: the hero has read too much to be able to live, is always already in the symbolic. The result of this is his ubiquitous inability to engage in conversation, and the frequency of letters, of third parties interrupting or mediating communication with the beloved, and of the sense that the two can never uncomplicatedly enjoy each other's looking and speaking presence. This patriarchal infancy is not incompatible with the motif of the childbed death: as I argued in my reading of *Adolphe*, the 'descent to the mothers' which produces nausea is a repressed presence within the paternal landscape, for every child has, somehow or other, been born. What happens is that the separation of birth is felt as so urgent and unforgiveable a trauma that writing poses as its own origin, authorship becomes the only acceptable parturition.

So we see no point of inauguration, even in those texts informed by a nostalgic longing for Eden; the triadic structure everywhere undermines the possibility of the couple.[1] This phantasy comes from outside the pages of the text: René or Dominique speak, but Chateaubriand and Fromentin are writers. The fatherhood which produces texts is necessarily a mediate relation. We can see how this works if we examine the role of autobiography in these fictions, so often proposed in a communication to the original beloved as 'our story', but a story that becomes a highly-crafted betrayal of the historical relationship. Madame de Staël appears disguised as the hysterical Ellénore, George Sand as the virtuous Brigitte, Madeleine Gide as misloved and prematurely old: all these are ploys to disempower the presence of the original, to kill her like Laopoldine into fiction. The author's attitude to his past self is similarly rewritten in a variety of ways. In every text, sympathy and critique coexist, integrated or appended, in- or outside the frame. God or the double plays father just as the author does, and the naughtier the son is the more gratifyingly confession brings absolution.

Irony, as I outlined in the last chapter, is a way of being God. The position of Gide or Mérimée invites the kind of deconstruction I gave it because it is brightly signposted, an aspect of the biographical ambivalence I have just described. But occasionally something rather different happens. In *Mademoiselle de Maupin* and *Sylvie*, the critique of the protagonist is voiced not by a male figure but by the women themselves. It is interesting that they form couples to do this, not necessarily on the level of plot, but by speaking the same belittling viewpoint from two female positions. This suggests the possibility that, where pairs of women are implied or presented in other *récits*, what they might have done is speak such truthful bitterness. Here is one reason why the pairing of women is psychologically abhorrent to the protagonist and why these texts are so stringently directed at a (sometimes internalised) male reader. For a woman to read the *récit* is to trespass on its fantasy. The 'family romance', like the Oedipus complex, cannot permit her as knowing subject. There is a hint that the mother's desire is terrible not so much because it is directed towards other men, fathers or sons, but because it has something to do with other women.

In an earlier book I suggested that the Oedipus complex might be twisted around a little to reveal the political assumptions behind its bonding of males. Following the *fort-da* and the curiosity of children of both sexes about where babies come from, it is reasonable to assume that both boys and girls begin their psychic life intensely anxious about separation from the mother and with an envious sense of her power. The girl comes to realise that in adulthood she will be able to restore the mother-infant dyad in her own body while also having an independent will; this can console her for separation.[2] The bonding of males which inaugurates the symbolic order in the life of a boy would then be compensatory not of an original hatred towards the father but of an original envy and resentment of the mother. Castration is accepted as a preferable alternative to feminisation, for feminisation is disappointingly impossible and castration is sanctioned by the fathers and brings (eventual) power. Father invites the son to pass through an initiation period which will end in full membership of the club. They agree – this is the crucial password – to despise women, to identify their bodies as lacking and to mark women as exchangeable others in a male system. The confessional *récit* stands at the doorway to the men's social club: the hero narrates to the father who, sympathetic or severe, accepts his word and absolves him. One explanation for the grouping of men around a usually isolated woman in these texts is that they are proclaiming the exclusion order on mothers and sisters. Language then becomes something men sanction and ordain. But what goes on in the gynaeceum? Could it be that there is talking in there too?

In her recent book, *Between Men: English Literature and Male Homosocial Desire*, Eve Kosofsky Sedgwick presents a scenario seemingly not unlike that of the *récit*: 'the scene wherein male rivals unite, refreshed in mutual support and definition, over the ruined carcase of a woman'.[3] In a sense, this is what happens in my texts, for the uniting of male author and implied reader, of frame-narrator and central narrator and of the group of doubles who flank the protagonist, is enacted over the dead body of the woman. But I want to begin my concluding argument by distinguishing the structure of the *récit*, as it has emerged in this study, from Sedgwick's schema.

Sedgwick starts from René Girard's model in *Mensonge romantique et vérité romanesque*, where all desire is defined as triangular and 'in any erotic rivalry, the bond that links the two rivals is as intense and potent as the bond that links either of the rivals to the beloved' (*Between Men*, p. 21). She goes on to argue that in this structure, the beloved female figure is little more than a pretext. We easily recognise this structure, it is found for instance in such popular 'male bonding' movies as *Kramer v. Kramer* or *Ordinary People*, where Momma is eventually evicted by father and son who then settle into a covertly incestuous, manly American dyad.[4] Sedgwick cites the Freudian Oedipus complex as another symmetrical triangle of son-mother-father and Gayle Rubin's development of the theories of Lévi-Strauss and others into what Rubin terms the male 'traffic in women'.[5]

I have already shown in earlier chapters that the *récit*, despite its strikingly oedipal formulation, is not consistent with the usual reading of that triangle. Heterosexual desire in it is very often fraught with jealousy, the woman is almost always attached to another man like the oedipal mother, and yet the protagonist does not engage cathectically with the other man: rivalry is swallowed, repressed, neglected. Werther likes to think of Albert as different from himself, prosaic, unworthy of Lotte, but he does not really hate him, any more than Dominique hates M. de Nièv.es, who is scarcely noticed, or than René or Jérôme really reject God. At the same time, they do not entirely love the rival, there is always a reluctant theism or a disgruntled remarking of the intervention of a grown-up, the annoying presence of a third party. Jealousy is, then, a sense of bitterness and disruption given fictional occasion by the figure of the 'other man' but not really focused on him. In Proust, as we have seen, the aggression of desire is essentially directed against the woman, specifically against her subjectivity and her desire, written on her body, invested in her mind. In *La Confession d'un enfant du siècle*, there is even jealousy without any rival, in which animosity is exercised against Brigitte during the first few months apparently purely for its own sake. The oedipal triangle does not seem to be operating on the Freudian model. It could be objected that what we are reading is the narrative which follows the breakdown of the Oedipus complex, when the boy has relinquished his claim on the mother in virtue of his realisation that the father has her, has the phallus and might castrate him; at this stage he would be repressing his parricidal jealousy and feeling comradeship rather than rivalry, identification rather than hatred. But that will not work. Jealousy is too obviously present in the texts; sexuality is not repressed but crucial; this is not a world of latency. Essentially, the other man is the object of neither parricide nor identification; he is the pretext of an intense battle with the mother.

It seems to me that we must understand the *récit* by looking more closely at the difference between the use of the male figures as doubles and the female figure as mirror; and to do this I want to return to Freud's essay on the uncanny, to the aesthetic observation with which it closes. As I discussed in Chapter 2, realism is the contextual precondition of the uncanny in fiction. I want to suggest that in the *récit*, which my examples have shown is at a sort of borderline between the Gothic and realist novels, situated if you like at the end of Romanticism's adolescence, there is a rather unexpected conjunction of these effects. The doubles – generally taken, with reason, as a marker of the Gothic imagination – are not uncanny in their effect; the woman, more firmly embedded in a realistic concreteness and alterity to the hero, is. It is because she is outside him that she affects the protagonist (and his double the implied reader) as mysterious, terrible or magical; the male figures, on the other hand, are ambiguous but biddable projections of himself.

It does not really matter which man we take as the projecting ego; the author and protagonist are interchangeable in this structure. What matters is that there be a given male self and a collection of male figures who act fictionally for him and around him. The model

I propose is that the relation of self to doubles is that of the man to the penis/phallus. I shall look at this relationship further in a moment. The figure of the woman as mirror is uncanny because she is not the projection of his unconscious but an other that opposes it. To borrow a concept from Winnicott, she is the not-me that the child wishes to take as transitional object and that resists such appropriation which, if it is to work, must be tacit and seamless.[6] Or, again using Winnicott, she is the not-good-enough mother who does not submit with loving precision to the game of mirrors, perhaps because she is unhappy with the child-care ruling that 'success in infant care depends on the fact of devotion, not on cleverness or intellectual enlightenment' (p. 12). Mothers, unlike analysts, are not supposed to know.

Everything begins with the beginning of psychoanalysis, a moment Stephen Heath marks as a change from sight to hearing: 'Charcot sees. Freud hears'.[7] Or to be exact, Charcot watches and exhibits the woman, Freud listens to the woman in the consentual privacy of surgery and couch. Or we could shift the start of psychoanalysis to a point somewhat later when, with the abandonment of the seduction theory, Freud stopped listening to the women who told him they had been raped by their fathers and instated a brand-new 'voyeur's theory'[8] in which the child's seeing influences a whole transferential future. As I have argued elsewhere, in this shift Freud coopts the maternal, reversing what he later called 'the advance in intellectuality' from matriarchy to patriarchy, 'when men decided to put their inferences upon a level with the testimony of their senses' (9, p. 113; and 13, pp. 360-1) and deduce paternity instead of observing maternity. For just as everything follows from this moment of looking – even, absurdly, the female Oedipus complex – the seeing of Freud makes him, after all, a bad listener to women and forever baffled by their utterance.

The importance of the penis/phallus is axiomatic in psychoanalysis. When Lacan opts to adorn the phallus with the crowning dimension of 'lack' he takes nothing from its centrality, extending it rather, for now it is magical, floating unattached to anyone, the signifier men do not have and women cannot quite be, but which everybody pursues everywhere. 'In this family *Kula* ring, women go one way, the phallus the other', notes Rubin (p. 192): the traffic in women and the pursuit of the phallus is the patriarchal double helix we all occupy.

I must continue to call the magical member the 'penis/phallus' because, as many commentators have observed, the phallus is conceivable only by reference to the real male genital, which is itself unimaginable without the symbolic cathexis of its magical shadow. In the examination I now propose of male narcissism, the double status of this genital is essential. Indeed, it has numerous identities, as various and ambiguous as the doubles in the *récit*. I want to look especially at two aspects of its significance: its status in relation to the male ego, and its axiomatic separability from that ego.

When Freud calls the little boy 'the small bearer of the penis' (7, p. 321), this is no casual metonymy. It is difficult to see which has primacy, the male whose genital is so special, or the genital itself whose context he is privileged to be. Men's narcissism is focused on their genital. Beauvoir notes: 'one can understand . . . that the length of the penis, the power of the urinary jet, erection and ejaculation become for him the measure of his own value. Thus the phallus is everywhere a fleshly incarnation of transcendence'.[9] From a toy, it becomes a tool and a fetish, the emblem of all use-value and exchange-value. In Derrida, the phallus is equated with the Logos, that unitary and originary presence whose delusion centres Western philosophy; and feminists such as Irigaray and Cixous agree in placing it with the Logos on one side of the binary opposition masculine/feminine. Whether as in the latter avatar or in the infinite mobility of Lacan's Phallus the male genital is perceived as essentially a rigid erection or a movable feast, it is both a darling delusion and constitutional of 'the man'. We must not ignore what a compensatory reversal this is: for real men, the phallus is an occasional state of the penis, for modern theory the relation is inverted: the father is dispensable while his Law and his phallus are everywhere. But what the fetish carries over from the organ is all the ambivalence of the penis which is not always a phallus.

Men's genital is fundamentally unreliable: it may become erect too often for the blushing adolescent or not often enough for the embarrassed adult. Like the doubles of the *récit*, it is both adored and disliked, for it may act or unconscionably fail to act, or act too soon; women's clitoris, by contrast, produces orgasms which are reliable and multiple. The multiplication of doubles denotes, then, both a series of differently-felt avatars of the penis/phallus and also a plurality of *jouissance* that men can only envy.[10]

Secondly, what both the doubles and the 'traffic in the phallus' indicate is that the man must logically conceive of his genital as something separable from himself. If, as Beauvoir observes, it is the emblem of transcendance, then the question is: will it take him with it, or fly off and leave him bereft? In my analysis of *Lorenzaccio*, I showed that the 'other self' embodied in the hero's planned assassination is a phallic self which he imagines clothed in a false femininity that, like Sartre's 'viscous', may cling, may become it and take it fatally from him. The mask that cleaves to the face is the same as the quicksand, vagina dentata etc., in which men's imagination articulates its dread of losing the penis/phallus.[11] For the more insistently the organ is valued, the more awful *and inevitable* is its loss. The castration complex does not require a glimpse of the undressed mother or girl, it is an inherent consequence of the narcissistic investment in the male genital. Karen Horney sees this over-valuation as itself based in anxiety: in her scheme, an instinctive desire directs the penis towards a vagina and the sight of the mother's genital makes the boy realise with shame that his penis is too small; this 'early wound to his self-regard' (p. 358) makes him withdraw his libido from his mother and direct it to his genital; thus his narcissism is based on a 'scar' (p. 359) – the converse, note, of Freud's diagnosis of a woman's narcissism as being based in 'a wound' (7, p. 337) that, without compensatory move, leads to her accepting the true fact of her 'inferiority'. Whether or not we agree with Horney that male narcissism is a secondary development, it is clear that the extreme valuation of the penis/phallus is inextricably linked to its vulnerability.

Patriarchy is grounded in the given of male narcissism and it is accurately reflected in the Lacanian flying signifier of the phallus which must begin as a fleshly attachment to the man's body but, for the unconscious, is never safely rooted there. Transcendence in action is conceived as penetration, and to penetrate the other (the woman's genital) is perhaps to give her what he values most. Or rather, *pace* Cixous, it is not to give the thing but perhaps to have the thing stolen from him. This is the reason that, as we perceived in discussing Musset, the image of phallic self and that of the female soul as separable part of the male self are much the same thing. What comes forth from him may, after all, be appropriated, dissolved, owned by her.

This brings us back to the first problem. The dissemination of doubles in the *récit* suggests a stable, unitary ego from which the 'shadows' proceed, the male phallogocentric originating self. But the doubles, as much as they proliferate to protect, embody and praise the self, also always diminish it, prove its vulnerability and are its repeated castrations. For this reason, they are both an essential effort and necessarily secondary, for the project is doomed to failure. It is the engagement with the woman – more dangerous and more vital – on which all is staked.

In going on to discuss the phenomenon of 'penetration', I shall be looking at the minor artform of pornographic photography, but before I do, let me make a parenthesis on the representability of the penis/phallus. Annette Kuhn points out that 'the tendency for men to feature more often in hardcore than in softcore pornography may be explained to some extent in terms of the relatively strong cultural taboo on representations of male sexual organs and of sexual activities involving men – though this of course begs the question of why the taboo exists in the first place'.[12] It is, of course, partly explained by the now familiar fact that representation is a one-sided activity in which men look and women are seen, but that does not seem entirely to account for the fact that, say, Action Man and King Kong, so relentlessly masculine, do not have a penis. My own favourite instance is that infinitely mobile plasticine figure Morph, who changes shape all the time but when it is itself consists only of a trunk, a head, two arms and two legs – ergo, a little girl – yet is always referred to as 'he' in the way parents point out birds, fish and monkeys at the zoo (unless they have obvious infants nestling close) as if they must be male. The reason, I think, is that these embodiments are presented as being themselves the phallus, maleness in motion; and that if they were seen to have a separable homunculus between their legs, where would the transcendental process stop? For it has to stop; that is the whole point.

Penetration is not (though apparently in coitus it feels like) infinite flying; it is a quest for an end-point, for desire desires the end to desire. Orgasm is very nice, but it is also supposed to be a resolution that allows people to get up and start living again. Now women's *jouissance* is not like that, and this is perhaps its most interesting difference from that of men: there is no reason to stop, so Masters and Johnson verify, 'until physical exhaustion intervenes'.[13] The first two sentences of this paragraph, a familiar argument from many male analysts of sexuality, apply only to male desire, but as far as that goes, they seem reasonable. Penetration as the specific expression of male desire, then, is an action directed towards stasis, a quest to arrive somewhere where it can stop.

This is precisely the logic of the Derridean 'supplement': the penis/ phallus makes men 'whole', the norm of human completeness, yet it is also extra, extraneous, capable either of carrying away its owner (the myth of men's uncontrollable lust) or of flying off altogether (castration, abandonment and loss). The woman's role in this system, as exemplified in pornography, is correspondingly complex. She is required to be a lack, to exhibit her castration as the 'fact' Freud deems it, for two reasons: firstly, to imply, by a suspect and certainly unstable myth of complementarity, that the man who looks at her is phallic, the convex for her concave; secondly to disprove, by what Sartre calls the 'appeal [appel]' of her open genital, that she is actually complete in herself, has no such anxious homunculus attached to her body, is really not and cannot be castrated. Horney observes reasonably that, unlike the boy, the girl 'preserves her physical integrity' (p. 356); there is nothing to wound her narcissism in a knowledge of the female genital that, naturally, she has had ever since she perceived herself as a subject. It is because she is a whole without supplement that the male gaze needs to make her, instead, a 'hole', something he is invited to fill by penetration.

Pornography has, interestingly, retraced the steps of civilisation, for while it originated in writing (pornography = writing about prostitutes) it is nowadays considered to be worth censoring only if it is in the visual media of photography or film. This is an instance of what linguists call 'secondary orality';[14] it is also, if you like, a reversal of the 'advance in intellectuality' which closely follows Freud's own, going back to a moment of looking that can never finish being repeated because the male fixation on the woman's body as castrated is, in itself, irresoluble.

Proust is not alone in revealing male desire as epistemophilia – the vulgarest pornographic pictures do the same. The 'transcendance', the penetration of the phallus into the woman's body, which pornography repetitively invites is a kind of 'investigation' by rape.[15] Kuhn isolates two typical poses in softcore photographs: the topos in which 'the spectator sneaks a look at her enjoyment of an apparently unselfconscious moment of pleasure in herself: the Peeping Tom's favourite fantasy' (p. 30) and the '"come-on"' (p. 41) in which, eyes directed outwards and lips slightly parted, the woman is presented as inviting entry. What the first does indirectly and the second directly is call upon the spectator to rend open the flat surface of the page, denying that behind it there is no one, no real woman. Disavowing the reality both of woman and of two-dimensional representation (and this, as Susanne Kappeler argues, is its real crime against women),[16] pornographic photography suggests that you, the man, can actually enter this woman in your quest to know.

In the *récit*, similarly, woman is mysterious. The myth of female enigma is essential to preserve the male monopoly on knowledge: Freud's 'riddle' (2, p. 146), Lacan's 'the women don't know what they are saying' and even the gentle Winnicott's distinction between mother and analyst. If the man is to be 'the subject presumed to know', women must seem epistemologically penetrable, but not easily so: there is no end-point to this knowledge, it must forever be restarted. For after all the viewer of pornographic pictures, like the reader of the uncanny, knows in advance what he is going to see. Kuhn shows that, in hardcore porn, where pictorial representation is often reduced to a view of the open cunt and, conversely, men are pictured (though rarely with an erection), there is 'a relatively limited range of possibilities for male fantasy' (p. 46). Here more focusedly, the looker seeks what he already knows he will find, bending over the shady pool into which Narcissus gazed. What he wants to do is imagine himself penetrating inside, travelling beyond the obliging surface, to the destination – the womb – in which he will find himself.

This penetrative imagination *is* castration: the self is separated, by this fantasy, into lost ego and travelling phallus. Castration is accepted (temporarily) as the price of a more urgent desire: to arrive at the rediscovery of the prenatal self, fit object for narcissistic love, safe and true. If the unstable and perpetual wish is to know woman as other, it is because there alone can the man find himself.

But that self is fluid, the pool (however glassy its surface) is still the place where self-love drowns. Fluid – the 'female medium' of course – not just in the sense of a metaphor but also in the literal sense of being changeable and intangible. Women's wombs contain not only male foetuses but also female ones. It is possible that, at the end of the journey, the phallic traveller will find not a tiny self, but a tiny female. And here we come to the woman's side of the story.

Psychoanalysis has found this fact of nature hard to countenance:

not only does the Oedipus complex work properly only for sons, but the hysterics whose case-histories Freud reproduces have mothers he scarcely mentions. Feminism, on the other hand, has a natural interest in the mother-daughter dyad: examining female-authored texts as an alternative to the old authorship/paternity myth, reclaiming mothers as 'sisters' or looking at the actual operation of the pre-oedipal relation between mothers and daughters. It is a curious anomaly that the best-known feminist texts written on motherhood are by women who have sons and only are daughters.[17] I shall return to the pre-oedipal dyad in a moment; first I want to conclude the discussion of male narcissism by seeing the precise way in which women function in it as mirrors.

In pornographic photography, the woman is presented as a flat mirror: the man is invited to 'break in', smashing it and her, traversing her surface by the fiction of the 'come-on'. The poetry of surface all comes back to this: for all her rich independence as a character, Mademoiselle de Maupin flaunts delusory costume so that d'Albert can strip her of it. Sandra Gilbert draws a contrast between the motif of costume in male- and female-authored modernism: the men's texts 'balance self against mask, true garment against false costume',[18] while in the women's texts 'that fundamental self for which, say, Yeats, uses nakedness as a metaphor is itself merely another costume . . . [they] see what literary men call "selves" as costumes and costumes as "selves"' (pp. 195-6). In the same collection of essays, Froma I. Zeitlin shows how in Aristophanes's *Thesmophoriazousae*, male characters (and actors) don women's clothing in a safe parody that will end in the revelation of the phallus under the clothes where 'comedy is playing with the extreme limit of its own promiscuous premises where all can now converge in the ambiguities of intersexuality' (p. 139): here, as is sometimes argued with regard also to film and pornography, men look for the 'phallic mother' underneath the garments. This certainly may occur, but I prefer to argue that (as in *Mademoiselle de Maupin* where, precisely, the Shakespearian convention of men acting women is 'happily' undermined) what the spectator looks for is the woman's hole beneath her outer surface which he can enter and 'occupy'. Costume and mirrors are essential to the secondary narcissism that patriarchy confers on women.

We are supposed to (and we do, well-taught) spend our time gazing at ourselves in mirrors. Female narcissism revolves around surface phenomena: poses, clothing, make-up.[19] It is meant to create ever more elaborate surfaces for the male gaze to penetrate. It is not designed to cover up our 'lack' – though Freud symptomatically lists side by side women's narcissistic vanity and their humilated urge to clothe the shame of castration (2, p. 166) – but to present it as an available picture which, like the page, can be torn down, torn through. That this 'narcissism' is not a matter of self-love is proved by the fact that none of us is ever satisfied with what she sees in the mirror. Anorexia is only the most extreme instance of the fact that, as Rosalind Coward puts it, 'women's relation to their self-image is . . . likely to be dominated by discontent' (p. 79).

A particularly interesting example of this can be found in Virginia Woolf's confessional writings.[20] The narrator has described her shame at looking in the mirror and the feeling that 'my natural love for beauty was checked by some ancestral dread' (p. 79); a few pages later we read about 'the moment of the puddle in the path; when for no reason I could discover, everything suddenly became unreal; I was suspended; I could not step across the puddle; I tried to touch something . . . the whole world became unreal' (p. 90, ellipses Woolf's). In *The Waves*, this scene is developed further in the voice of Rhoda:

> I came to the puddle. I could not cross it. Identity failed me. We are nothing, I said, and fell. I was blown like a feather, I was wafted down tunnels. Then, very gingerly, I pushed my foot across. I laid my hand against a brick wall. I returned very painfully, drawing myself back into my body over the grey, cadaverous space of the puddle. This is life then to which I am committed (p. 43)

Rhoda is an isolated figure – 'the world is entire, and I am outside of it' (p. 15) – whom other people see as 'authentic' (p. 78) or 'wild' (p. 167) but who hates mirrors for what she sees in them 'is not my face . . . I have no face' (pp. 29 and 150). On her first night in school she resolves to 'seek out a face, a composed, a monumental face, and will endow it with omniscience, and wear it under my dress like a talisman' (p. 23). But the face worn under the dress is the hole men look for, and the shallow, murky puddle beneath her feet, which she must leap over, is as exposing of that face as the mirrors nasty little boys carry up stairs behind their teachers. To cross the puddle, for Woolf or her surrogate, is an unbearable reminder of the function of all mirrors in which women are meant to espy their beauty without 'ancestral dread'. Neither face is allowed to be 'omniscient'.

Women are not supposed to know or look at their genital; in this sense shame does adorn the outside, fitting it only for the penetration of the male gaze. Or rather, they must not look into it; feminism's cooptation of the speculum out of the hands of paternal doctors is a response to that taboo: it allows a female self-knowledge that goes beyond the 'hole', focusing, in Irigaray's argument, 'a new despecularisation of the maternal and the feminine'.[21] In an allied argument, other feminists suggest that the metaphor of the mirror can bespeak a renewed relation between women that avoids the mediation of men.[22] Sexual separatism is one way to go through the looking glass to another side.

If there is a primary narcissism of women, repressed by the castration complex of their brothers and fathers, it is the knowledge that their body is complete as it is, not castrated. This knowledge is invested in the mother-daughter bond, for all its risks and dangers. If the *récit*, from *René* to *Journal d'un curé de campagne*, is haunted by the dyad of mother and daughter, that is because this is where men's knowledge stops, where narcissism is at a loss, for here (they seem to suspect) is a desire not fraught by separation.

Much has been written on this relationship, but the argument is problematic. What is certain is that nothing which looks at mothers from the viewpoint of the child only (son or daughter) gives an adequate picture of the experience of a mother-child relation. Those who argue, like Chodorow, Dinnerstein and many others, that mothers cathect their male and female children differently can only bring evidence from the 'feelings' of women who reproduce the conditioning effect vulgarly embodied in pink and blue bootees.[23] There has been little inclination so far to theorise this supposed distinction in a way that provides an adequate understanding of it.

All that is clear thus far is that there is a universal disinclination to credit mothers with either knowledge or desire. This applies not only to the 'fathers' who write advice and theory on motherhood, but also to adults of both sexes who find it extremely difficult not to theorise from the position of the child. Everyone, daughters as well as sons, wants a 'good-enough mother' and lugs around an image of the all-powerful, all-giving, wonderfully nurturant creature who has no subjectivity of her own. The impossibility of maternal knowledge and maternal desire is, after the myth of women's bodily incompleteness, the most influential disavowal of the patriarchal system. In the confessional *récit*, it permeates both thematics and plot.

The protagonists we have looked at in this book readily exemplify the effects of what John Bowlby calls 'maternal deprivation', partial or complete: 'partial deprivation brings in its train anxiety, excessive need for love, powerful feelings of revenge, and, arising from these last, guilt and depression . . . Complete deprivation . . . has even more far-reaching effects on character development and may entirely cripple the capacity to make relationships with other people'.[24] He goes on to insist, with gentle firmness, that a good mother is one whose 'love and pleasure' (p. 18) in her infant is available in the same way as she 'provides the needed food substances in her own milk in exactly the right combination without having to make a chemical analysis and work to a formula'. The logical slide from such complexities as feeling and sexuality to the supposedly 'natural' production of maternal milk is typical of the shifty way that phantasy intervenes to pull the viewpoint always away from the possibility of maternal intelligence.

Mothers must know without knowing and desire without desiring. If the 'cuddling and playing, intimacies of suckling [and] the rituals of dressing and washing' that Bowlby approves as innocent modes of maternal pleasure cross a certain line, then we have the blameworthy phenomenon of maternal seduction that Freud calls in to replace the unpalatable theory of father-rape. In rejecting the original seduction theory, Freud not only exonerates fathers from incestuous action but makes them 'victims of childhood fantasy' (Chodorow, p.160), leaving mothers, caught between ignorance and responsibility, as the real seducers. There follows the familiar reasoning in which mothers are always to blame and there is a negligible difference between a mother's devotion and neglect, both equally pernicious in their effects. For psychoanalysis's axiom of infantile sexuality is predicated on the desexualisation of paternal relations and the seductiveness of the mother-machine. She must be a machine because she must at all costs not be that complete, intelligent thing, a woman, just as the child is profoundly unimaginable as female. The mother makes the child 'phallic' (a wholly 'masculine' narcissism) by being 'phallic', that is, by seeming a mirror.

It is Winnicott who develops the Lacanian hint that the mother is the infant's first mirror. In an article of 1960, he theorises the relationship between mothers and preverbal infants by comparing it with the ideal attitude of analyst to patient.[25] But the key difference is that, while each ideally provides a passive reflection in which the child/patient can perceive and develop a self, the analyst 'needs to be aware' (p. 593) and in control of the transferential process, whilst the best mother is often the most 'uninstructed'.

The exactitude of mirroring whereby the mother is both entirely adaptive and instantly ready to let the child go depends by definition on her ignorance of what she is feeling and doing. No doubt many mothers delight in the sense of instinctively providing what Kristeva calls 'the reassuring clothing [enrobement] within the preverbal mirroring of the mother' (p. 42). But if the male analysts are to be believed, this takes place without any of the intentionality of desire. When Winnicott asks that the 'mirroring' of mothers 'shall not be taken for granted' (*Playing*, 131), he means by psychoanalysts, not by mothers. This mirroring is ideally a kind of self-effacement:

> What does the baby see when he or she looks at the mother's face? I am suggesting that, ordinarily, what the baby sees is himself or herself. In other words the mother is looking at the baby and what she looks like is related to what she sees there. All this is too easily taken for granted. I am asking that this which is naturally done well by mothers who are caring for their babies shall not be taken for granted. I can make my point by going straight over to the case of the baby whose mother reflects her own mood or, worse still, the rigidity of her own defences. In such a case what does the baby see?

If the mother fails to reflect the baby, 'the mother's face is not then a mirror' (p. 132) and 'a mirror [will become] a thing to be looked at but not to be looked into'. Penetration is of the essence; the mother's face must be the open hole wherein the child sees itself. She can reciprocate but not initiate. It seems to me that the crime for which the protagonists of the *récit* condemn the mother to death is that, by intentionality, she is felt to evade them; her look is not the mirror they wish it to be. The transference performed in the text, where the heroine replays the sins of the intentional mother, is a punishment for the crime of knowing. Juno, reappearing as Echo, is divided and silenced.

Transference is what we all do; counter-transference is what the 'knowing' analyst is supposed to do, however motherly he or she may be. There are disagreements about the precise definition of this term;

that is, about how far counter-transference can be differentiated from the supposedly initiating transference of the patient. Essentially, analysts should be able to coopt and exploit their counter-transference by means of awareness and reasoning in such a way that it feeds profitably into knowledge of the patient, not into knowledge of themselves. Laplanche and Pontalis base this argument on Freud's remark that "'everyone possesses in his own unconscious an instrument with which he can interpret the utterances of the unconscious in other people'".[26] Everyone may possess it but it is not given to everyone to make the unconscious conscious in this way. It is the prerogative of the analyst; and even if analysts may be like mothers, mothers in their mirroring are not thought capable of counter-transference.

Kristeva puts the psychoanalytic position thus: 'we direct towards the mother not only our needs for survival but above all our earliest mimetic aspirations. She is the other subject, an object that guarantees my being as a subject'.[27] The juxtaposition of 'subject' and 'object' here shows how the mother's subjectivity is strictly limited in her role as mirror by the desire of the child. Her subjectivity is precisely what makes her an object. Both her knowledge and her desire are retroactively specified (just as they are in the *récit*) and if they exceed this specification, they are murderous and soon murdered.

I want to suggest an alternative reading of the mother-infant dyad, one closer to the mutuality of speech than that of sight, and in doing so to depart from the position of Narcissus, exemplified in the *récit*, and move across to that of Echo. In the *récit*, the insistent topos of the childbed death represents an unconscious disappointment at not being born a girl. The ubiquitous female couples are presumed to have – and occasionally allowed to voice – a reciprocity which is felt to be impossible for mothers and sons. It is well known that orthodox Jewish men thank God daily that they were not born a woman; the woman's asymmetrical prayer is humbly to thank God for making her 'according to his will'. Now clearly this difference derives from the avowed privilege of being male; but we could reread it to suggest that the negative formulation of the man's prayer is necessary to shore up every day the compensatory bonding of the male God with his progeny, while the woman's prayer represses a completeness that binds her to the (unspoken) desire of the mother. I shall return shortly to this exclusion of motherhood from monotheistic theology.

Freud describes the mother-son relationship as the only one that is truly benign. But in his whole scheme, the only form of parent-child incest never mentioned is that between mothers and daughters. Father-daughter and son-mother incest both contain the element of political violence conditional on the use – fantasised or actual – of the penis/phallus; mother-daughter incest is potentially a genuine mirroring exchange of desire.

Chodorow and others distinguish between the attitudes of mothers to daughters and sons as between a narcissistic relation that focuses on pre-oedipal closeness and a sexual relation that is oedipal, focused on possession and separation. This assumes a differentiation between the narcissistic and the sexual that is too clear-cut. I would suggest, on the contrary, that the mother's attitude to a child of either sex is to perceive it as a transitional object, an other midway between 'me' and 'not-me', and that her sensual knowledge of it is made up of a mixture between self-love and desire. Cixous describes motherhood thus: 'the child is the other, but the other without violence' (p. 166). Precisely, this is a sexual relation unlike other sexual relations in that it is not political.

Mothers may, of course, exploit or dislike their children. Eichenbaum and Orbach argue cogently that since every mother is a daughter too, she inevitably brings transferential impulses with her to parenthood. But if we are to get a saner and clearer idea of the special intensity of the pre-oedial tie, we must restore to it the dual element of maternal knowledge and desire.

Neil Hertz's essay on the Dora case focuses on Freud's compulsive wish to discover 'how much of Dora's knowledge came to her "orally"'.[28] He argues that Freud was anxious not to blur the lines between what Dora knew and what he himself knew, for that would impugn 'the status of Freud's knowledge and of his professional discourse' (pp. 234-5). Specifically, he tries to investigate 'the possibility of oral sexual intercourse' (p. 235) between Dora and Frau K. The speaking of the two women together – women's language when men are not present – is itself a discourse of desire. Similarly, the protagonists and the authors of the *récit* do everything to prevent the bonding of women, for all the mother-daughter dyad returns to haunt them, for they suspect that in the unknown speech of women together there is a 'betrayal' more threatening than any heterosexual rivalry. The penultimate narrator of *Mademoiselle de Maupin* wonders not just what Madeleine and Rosette did to each other but also what they said.

'For if she begins to tell the truth, the figure in the looking glass shrinks': women's speech is the destruction of male specular desire. The speaking face is not his face any more but her own, and to hear her (properly, that is, without interpretation) would be to find a hole no longer inviting but uttering. I want to complete my discussion by looking not simply at the significance of women's voice as occulted in patriarchy, but at its place in the strange relationship of speech and writing.

Let us not forget that the *récit* straddles the borderline between these two modes of language. It is a writing that tends towards the first/second-person conditions of 'discourse' but employs the preterite typical of the 'story'. It is haunted by an original scene of birth-separation but presents a world always already marked by paternal mediation. The *hantise* of the mother-daughter pair suggests an envied potentiality of speech which is never possible between mother and son; instead, the boy offers the father a text in order to consummate the second-best bond of the symbolic order.

In current feminist thought, especially but not only in French, women are everywhere exhorted to take up language. Specifically, we are encouraged to write, whether with the 'white ink' of our milk or more violently in our blood;[29] Irigaray's 'womanspeak' is similarly fluid and similarly moves rapidly from an act of coming out of the mirror by a 'mimetic' reading of men's texts to a reentry 'into the house of the philosopher' (*Ce Sexe*, p. 147) which must be in the form of writing.[30] The equation of body and utterance has been criticised by many commentators,[31] but what is perhaps the oddest aspect of this bodily essentialism is its tendency to by-pass speech for writing.

Robin Lakoff, in her early analysis of 'women's language', seems to have found nothing bizarre in communicating her findings – all matters of speech-mannerisms – in a written form; perhaps because, as Deborah Cameron points out, this is what linguists do all the time.[32] But if the distinctions, such as they are, between women's and men's language are perceptible only in speech, the solution to centuries of silence appears to be in writing. It seems to be a single step from Kristeva's preverbal *sémiotique* to the Lacanian puns of Mary Daly's *Gyn/Ecology* which are perceptible only on the printed page.

There are many kinds of orality and literacy: private speaking is very different from public speaking and it is the latter that excludes women, far more grievously than, say, novel-writing which (as Jane

Austen knew) can be carried on in the drawing-room and slipped under a blotter. And naturally, if we want to be 'heard' we need to be published and read. But the reason for the by-passing of speech is less obvious than this: it has to do with the fact that speech, for all its origin in the pre-oedipal dyad of mutual mirroring, is understood in current theory (under the minus-sign of course) to be male.

This is how Echo is currently silenced. There is in the present-day climate of *le postmoderne* a curious new version of patriarchal imperialism. We all know that logocentrism is phallocentric: speech is the (impossible) originary presence which denotes unity, singleness, the phallus. Cixous lists the binary politics by which women are repressed, shut off into the status of other: 'Man/Woman . . . Speech/ Writing . . . Logos/writing' (*La jeune Née*, p. 116-7). A similar equa-tion is central in Derrida's *Eperons*, where we find the conception of phallogocentrism coopted by a 'masterful' man.[33] Alice Jardine, in her study of 'gynesis' – 'the putting into discourse of "woman" as that process diagnosed in France as intrinsic to the condition of modernity'[34] – shows how postmodern theorists in France are coopt-ing 'the space "outside of" the conscious subject [which] has always connoted the feminine in Western thought' (p. 114). Thus the 'other' space called Writing is now the site of the feminine, where men want to be. And yet, as she points out, 'the myth of presence is, first of all, the myth of nature-before-culture, the natural goodness of the Maternal' (p. 128). In Lacan, after all, the ternary structure typical of writing belongs to the father's dissolution of the mother-child dyad. What seems to have happened is that, in the deconstruction of logocentrism, speech and the maternal have together disappeared. The 'other' writing performed by Derrida, de Man et al., and by the French women theorists who reject the label 'feminist', has taken over centre-stage, filling the *'void'* (Jardine, p. 154) left by the demise of the phallic Subject. 'The undecidability intrinsic to writing . . . is located in a feminine place' (p. 186). Somehow, in all this, the problem of women's exclusion from language is lost.

Speech is first acquired in that linguistic 'mirroring' in which each, mother and child, is for the other a transitional object. Language-learning is a kind of play, the beginnings of cultural creativity. A recent study describes how the mother (or mother-figure) both follows and initiates in the earliest development of the child's lan-guage.[35] She coos when it coos, she 'understands' its babbling, she feeds it the stimuli which make it capable of understanding a massive number of words before it can speak any. This, rather than the silent mirror, is what the originary dyad is all about. A mother surely never offers the infant a completely voiceless gaze; from the very beginning, she talks to her speechless child.

The earliest relation of speech between mother and infant is, then, part of the sexuality which is without violence. If the breast gives forth milk, the face gives forth speech. The 'oral sexual intercourse' that psychoanalysts, philosophers and authors of *récits* are afraid of is the mutuality they left behind for the women and their daughters, while they oedipally struggled away and defined desire in their own terms.

In the unconscious of adult men, the speech that is a mutuality of mother and child – daughter or 'minus-daughter' – haunts the assertion of the logos.[36] 'God generally speaks only to men', Kristeva accurately observes.[37] Writing too is familiarly thought of as an oedipal chain from father to son: both Barthes and Bloom see the creation of new texts from old as an intertextual relation of paternity.[38] In this, they follow the structure of Judaic monotheism which, in attributing creation and providence to a single masculine deity, overrides even the minimal mediation of the mother's body allowed by patriarchy. The fraught passion in Bloom's system of 'strong poets' is all that remains admissible of the incest between father and son. In the *récit*, especially those discussed in Chapter 6, the same chain reaches upwards, and is flawed not by aggression but by undesire. I have already suggested that this selfconscious bonding of male to male is predicated on a repressed envy and disappointment at the son's felt exclusion from the original mirroring dyad. For if monotheism was crazy (and clever) enough to found the whole of Western culture on the logical absurdity of male parthenogenesis, it remains true that the only asexual reproduction in nature is down an exclusively female line.

Narcissus drowns of self-love, conjuring up a male other in order to make up for the impossibility of mirroring. The specular relation of love-at-first-sight is a *pis-aller* for the speech he tries not to hear between Juno's knowledge and Echo's desire.

Is such mirroring possible between mother and daughter? Not necessarily, perhaps almost never. It may well be, as I have suggested, that there is nothing really different in the way mothers behave towards their daughters and their sons – certainly a child's position in the chronological order of the family may be as important a factor as sex – and that every child is to its mother a more or less equidistant transitional object. Nevertheless the silencing of women's speech is both symptom and cause of an obsession with the supposed privilege of the women's mutual doubling which surfaces in the echoes of the confessional *récit*. Narcissus goes down to Hades leaving Echo's voice on earth; Orpheus the poet goes down to rescue his wife and leaves her voiceless behind; but Ceres, in her visit to the underworld, brings forth her beloved daughter (for the bright part of the year) from the author's skull where Pluto had immured her.

Notes to Chapter 1

Throughout this book, all translations from French and German, unless otherwise attributed, are my own, and reference is given to the original text. Further references to a cited text will appear after quotations; passages without page reference are from the last-cited page. Unless otherwise stated, all italics are the author's and all ellipses mine.

1 Ovid, *Metamorphoses*, I, trans. F. J. Miller, London, 1916, p. 147. I am indebted to James Diggle for his help with the nuances of this text.

2 The last-quoted phrase replaces that of Miller's translation.

3 Jean Laplanche, *Vie et Mort en Psychanalyse*, Paris, 1970, p. 108. For a full discussion of the post-Freudian refutation of 'primary narcissism', see Victoria Hamilton, *Narcissus and Oedipus*, London, 1982.

4 Caren Greenberg, 'Reading Reading: Echo's Abduction of Language', in eds. S. McConnell-Ginet et al., *Women and Language in Literature and Society*, New York, 1980, pp. 300-09.

5 Jacques Lacan, *Le Séminaire, XX: Encore*, ed. J.-A. Miller, Paris, 1975, p. 68.

6 T. S. Eliot, *Collected Poems 1909-1962*, London, 1963, 1974, p. 71 and p. 82, note to line 218.

7 Henri Bergson, *Le Rire*, Paris, 1940, pp. 7 and 11.

8 See H. Dörrie, 'Echo und Narcissus: Psychologische Fiktion in Spiel und Ernst', *Das altsprachliche Unterricht*, 10, 1, 1967, p. 56.

9 Hamilton, op. cit., p. 125.

10 John Brenkman, 'Narcissus in the text', *Georgia Review*, 30, 1976, p. 301.

11 Sigmund Freud, 'The "Uncanny"', *The Pelican Freud Library*, 14, eds., J. Strachey and A. Richards, trans. J. Strachey, Harmondsworth, 1985, p. 368. Quotation from Freud throughout this study will be from this series.

12 See for example the following studies: John Ellis, *Narration in the German Novelle*, Cambridge, 1974, 1979; Martin Swales, *The German Novelle*, Princeton, 1977; Roger Paulin, *The Brief Compass*, Oxford, 1985.

13 See especially Joachim Merlant, *Le Roman personnel de Rousseau à Fromentin*, Paris, 1905.

14 Naomi Segal, *The Unintended Reader*, Cambridge, 1986, pp. x-xi.

15 Jean-Paul Sartre, *L'Etre et le néant*, Paris, 1943, p. 706.

16 Cf. Shoshana Felman, 'Women and Madness: The Critical Phallacy', *Diacritics*, 5, 4, p. 8: '"woman" . . . is the exact metaphorical measure of the narcissism of man'; and Luce Irigaray, *Speculum de l'autre femme*, Paris, 1974.

17 Gérard de Nerval, *Œuvres*, I, Paris, 1958, p. 590.

18 Stendhal, *Le Rouge et le noir*, Paris, 1955, p. 357. M. H. Abrams notes without embarrassment how the term sometimes comes to be used for writing more like lamps than mirrors: 'emphasis on the intellectual location of artistic ideas accustomed critics to the concept of the work of art as a mirror turned around to reflect aspects of the artist's mind; occasionally, it even passed over into statements characterising art as a form of expression, or communication . . . Often the reflector is reversed, and images a state of mind rather than of external nature', *The Mirror and the Lamp*, Oxford, 1953, 1981, pp. 45 and 50.

19 Otto Rank, *The Double*, trans. H. Tucker, Chapel Hill, 1971; originally published 1914.

20 Jean Paulhan, in Michel Raimond, ed., *Les Critiques de notre temps et Gide*, Paris,

1971, p. 38; Pierre Lafille, *André Gide romancier*, Paris, 1954, p. xviii.
21 For details of all critical works cited in this section, see Bibliography.

Notes to Chapter 2

1 André Gide, *Oscar Wilde: in memoriam*, Paris, n.d., p. 46.
2 Emile Benveniste, *Problèmes de linguistique générale*, I, Paris, 1966.
3 Throughout this book, I shall use the following terms for the first-person speakers of the texts: 'the frame-narrator' for the 'I' who speaks in the frame-narrative; 'the narrator' for the 'I' of the protagonist telling his story; 'the hero' for the younger self of the narrator.
4 Antoine-François Prévost d'Exiles, *Histoire du Chevalier des Grieux et de Manon Lescaut*, ed. F. Deloffre and R. Picard, Paris, 1965, pp. 4 and 6. For a much fuller discussion of *Manon Lescaut*, see my *The Unintended Reader*.
5 Charles-Augustin Sainte-Beuve, *Mes Poisons*, Paris, 1926, p. 98; Auguste Dupouy, *Carmen de Mérimée*, Paris, 1930, p. 11. Pierre Trahard, however, views this comparison as 'external and artificial', *Prosper Mérimée de 1834 à 1853*, Paris, 1928, p. 223.
6 All quotations from *Carmen* are from Prosper Mérimée, *Romans et Nouvelles*, II, ed. M. Parturier, Paris, 1967; this reference, p. 401.
7 Mario Praz, *The Romantic Agony*, trans. A. Davidson, Oxford, 1933, 1970, p. 247.
8 A few examples will illustrate this: while eighteenth-century critics tended to brand her a 'whore' or a 'tart', readers of the Romantic period often opted to see her as an animal or a minx: Cellier, who himself types her 'this funny little animal, more than half wild', quotes Saint-Victor: '"she no more knows she is doing wrong than a Tahitian girl is aware she is naked"' (p. 258) and the rather more exasperated Barbey d'Aurevilly: 'that cowardly, base and superficial Manon Lescaut ... Even a she-dog can be sincere' (p. 267). In twentieth-century eyes, she has appeared rather more mechanical: 'no more than part of the machinery' (Turnell, p. 51), 'almost totally without initiative' and operating by 'a sort of psychological automatism' (Deloffre and Picard, p. cxxi), or else she is a cross between hippie and small-time whore: 'a good time girl' (Greshoff, p. 166), a 'combination of adult feminine beauty and childlike irresponsibility' (Mylne, *Manon Lescaut*, p. 27), 'the banal character of a girl [fille] greedy for pleasure' (Jaccard, p. 9). For full references, see Bibliography I.
9 Deloffre and Picard, p. cxlviii.
10 Virginia Woolf, *A Room of One's Own*, London, 1929, 1977, p. 35.
11 Mary W. Shelley, 'Frankenstein', in *Three Gothic Novels*, ed. P. Fairclough, Harmondsworth, 1968, p. 410.
12 Prosper Mérimée, *Théâtre*, ed. G. Sigaux, Paris, 1963, p. 2.
13 The two pictures are reproduced in Gérard Milhaud, 'Un théâtre sous le masque', *Europe*, 53, 557, 1975, facing p. 50.
14 Auguste Filon, *Mérimée*, Paris, 1898, p. 72; Ernst Falke, *Die Romantische Elemente in Prosper Mérimées Roman und Novellen*, Halle, 1915, p. 157; Albert J. George, *Short Fiction in France, 1800-1850*, Syracuse, 1964, p. 130; Jacques Chabot, *L'autre Moi*, Aix-en-Provence, 1983, p. 211.
15 With disarming use of vulgar Freudian imagery, Charles Du Bos describes the frame-opening of Carmen as 'a spacious, airy vestibule whose dimensions lead one to expect at least a *palazzino*', *Notes sur Mérimée*, Paris, 1920, p. 59; he finds

Don José's narrative disappointingly 'cramped'.

16 The subject of this story was considered so 'improper' that Mérimée was relieved to find, when he read it aloud at Fontainebleau, that none of the ladies seemed to understand it. For safety's sake, he hoped to substitute, in the general reader's mind, a deadly glance for the logically necessary rape: 'do you think the reader, less timorous than you, will accept this old-wives' tale, at a *glance?* In this case it would be a mere look from the bear that drove the poor woman mad and vouchsafed to her noble son his sanguinary instincts' (letter to 'L'Inconnue' of 29 Sep 1868).

17 The critics tend to agree: Daniel Leuwers is harsh on the rape-victim, whom he considers a 'castrating mother' ('Une lecture de "Lokis"', *Europe*, 53, 557, 1975, p. 74); Chabot too finds it impossible to take the countess seriously: 'we are witness not so much to the abduction of an innocent young woman by an ill-mannered bear as to the judicial murder of a rather likeable animal' (p. 298); for him too she is simply 'a bad mother who wants to kill her son'.

18 In 'The Uncanny', 14, p. 374; Mérimée's own definition of the 'recipe' for writing a *conte fantastique* is interestingly close to this: after an opening of minute realism, 'the transition from the strange to the marvellous is imperceptible, and the reader will find himself in the realm of the fantastical without even noticing that the real world has been left far behind', quoted in R. C. Dale, *The Poetics of Prosper Mérimée*, The Hague and Paris, 1966, pp. 94-5).

19 See Jan Willem Hovenkamp, *Mérimée et la couleur locale*, Nijmegen, 1928.

20 See Carl Gustav Jung, 'Anima and Animus', *The Collected Works of C. G. Jung*, trans. R. F. C. Hull, 7, London, 1953, pp. 186-209.

21 Prosper Mérimée, *Carmen*, ed. M. Cégretin, Paris, 1966, 1980, pp. 62 note 5 and 59 note. 4.

22 For a witty version of the watch as phallic symbol, see G. Legman, *Rationale of the Dirty Joke*, I, London, 1972, pp. 82-5.

23 *A pastesas*, Mérimée's footnote tells us, means 'to rob skilfully, to steal without violence' (p. 383). Carmen rightly sees Don José's stupidity as an inability to control his aggression; she fails to note that his violence is allied to sexuality and therefore must, in the end, be turned against her.

Notes to Chapter 3

1 Quotations from Goethe are from *Werke: Hamburger Ausgabe in 14 Bänden*, ed. B. von Wiese and E. Trunz, Hamburg, vol VI, 1951.

2 Gerald Storzer points out a similar relation in *Atala* and *René:* 'the woman loved is the instrument by which the hero preserves intact his illusory and subjective world', 'Chateaubriand and the Fictional Confession', in ed. R. Switzer, *Chateaubriand*, Geneva, 1970, p. 125.

3 The two texts have been published together since 1805; most critics stress their twinship. Hélène Monod-Cassidy, however, breaks the sibling-tie: '*Atala* is daughter to the *philosophes*, while *René* is a son of Werther', 'Amours sauvages, amours chrétiennes: quelques prédécesseurs peu connus d'*Atala*', ed. Switzer, op. cit, p. 243.

4 François-René, vicomte de Chateaubriand, *Atala, René, Les Aventures du dernier Abencérage*, ed. F. Letessier, Paris, 1962.

5 Atala, curiously, has not only white skin but golden hair: 'often Atala's long

tresses, plaything of the morning breeze, would spread their golden veil across my eyes' (p. 146); one wonders how it could have taken so long to discover that she was not pure Indian.

6 Chateaubriand, *Essai sur les révolutions; Génie du christianisme*, ed. M. Regard, Paris, 1978, p. 599.

7 Some of the many examples of this are pp. 92, 103, 121, 126, 137-8, 138, 147 and 148. See also *Les Natchez*, in Chateaubriand, *Œuvres complètes*, III, Paris, n. d., p. 321: 'Indian law permits a woman to release a prisoner by adopting him as her brother or her husband'; both these options seem to be available to Atala. Several critics point out (sometimes in order to avoid the embarrassing possibility of autobiographical reference) that the theme of incest was common and popular in eighteenth-century fiction. On the question of the relations between Chateaubriand and his sister Lucile, the final word should surely be the following : 'it is perfectly possible after all that nothing "happened" between Chateaubriand and Lucile (did anything happen between Vautrin and Rastignac or between Balzac et Sandeau?). *But what is certain is that something happens in the text*', Pierre Barbéris, *A la Recherche d'une écriture: Chateaubriand*, Paris, 1974, p. 260.

8 Naomi Schor, *Breaking the Chain*, New York, 1985, p. 145.

9 See for example Hugo von Hofmannsthal, *Gesammelte Werke in Einzelausgaben: Aufzeichnungen*, ed. H. Steiner, Frankfurt, 1959, pp. 220 and 213. For a discussion of the double meaning of this term, see my *The Banal Object*, London, 1981, pp. 55-6.

10 Charles-Augustin Sainte-Beuve, *Chateaubriand et son groupe littaraire sous l'Empire*, Paris, 1948, p. 310.

11 In the passage from the *Défense du Génie du Christianisme* reproduced in the Preface of 1805, Chateaubriand refers with nervous circumlocution to the theme of incest, linking it to that of suicide and attributing both to René's habits of thought: 'indeed, the problem starts with René's foolish dreams and his wild behaviour completes it: by the former, he leads astray the imagination of a weak woman; by the latter, wanting to put an end to himself, he forces this unfortunate creature to come back to him; thus . . . the punishment proceeds from the fault' (p. 178). What he does not say is that René's fault causes Amélie's punishment.

12 Barbéris, op. cit., pp. 86-7, notes that René is known in this text not by the 'name of the father' but by his relation of brotherhood to Amélie; he comes to America to find not a wife, Céluta, but a father, Chactas. Thus, like my other protagonists, he speaks of the woman in order to join the order of the fathers.

13 Freud, 'Family Romances', 7, pp. 217-25. See also *Moses and Monotheism*, 13, pp. 246-52; and Otto Rank, *The Myth of the Birth of the Hero*, trans. F. Robbins and S. E. Jelliffe, New York, 1952. For a literary use of their arguments, see Marthe Robert, *Roman des origines et origine du roman*, Paris, 1972.

14 See Freud, *Beyond the Pleasure Principle*, 11, pp. 283-7; Anika Lemaire, in *Jacques Lacan*, Brussels, 1977, pp. 149-50, quotes an article by Conrad Stein suggesting that this game marks 'the earliest accession to the order of language' and thus that the signs 'fort' and 'da' would represent 'the Name-of-the-Father, though the latter only later comes to have the symbolic content attributed to it by Lacan'. In my *The Unintended Reader*, p. 254, I suggest that this scene is concerned, precisely, with the quarrel between child and mother, in which no rivalry with the father is relevant; it is the felt threat of the mother's independent self which causes the infant's first experiment with language.

15 Kathleen O'Flaherty points out 'a disparity between René's age and his physiological, emotional and mental development . . . the phenomena which René experiences from his sixteenth to his twenty-first year correspond approximately to

Chateaubriand's own evolution between eleven and seventeen', 'Adolescence in the Work of Chateaubriand', ed. Switzer, op. cit., p. 276.

16 Letessier finds 'more plausible' Chateaubriand's own note of 5 January 1804: '"here I am at the top of Vesuvius, sitting writing *at* the mouth of the volcano"' (p. 200, footnote 1, italics Letessier's). See also Raymond Lebègue, *Aspects de Chateaubriand*, Paris, 1979, p. 241.

17 Shortly before her death, Lucile wrote Chateaubriand a letter which ends: 'I could take as my life's emblem the moon in a cloud, with this motto: "Often obscured [obscurcie], never tarnished"': the image of a darkened or tarnished reflector surely suggests that in her mind too she had been a (perhaps willing) mirror for her brother; quoted in E. Michel, *Chateaubriand*, Paris, 1911, p. 24.

18 Friedrich Nietzsche, *The Birth of Tragedy* and *The Case of Wagner*, trans. W. Kaufmann, New York, 1967; this and the next quotation: p. 60, italics Nietzsche's.

19 Goethe, *Hamburger Ausgabe*, III, ed. E. Trunz, Hamburg, 1949, 1954, p. 364.

20 Benjamin Constant, *Adolphe*, ed. J-H. Bornecque, Paris, 1960, p. 119.

21 *Adolphe*, pp. i-iii: in the first edition of the *Journaux intimes*, we read: 'I am beginning a novel which will be my story'; the correct version, in context, is: '"wrote to Charlotte. Begun a novel which will be our story"'.

22 Surprisingly few commentators seem to notice this; exceptions are Han Verhoeff, *'Adolphe' de Constant*, Paris, 1976, pp. 65-74, and Eve Gonin, *Le Point de vue d'Ellénore*, Paris, 1981, pp. 159-60.

23 Gonin, despite an admirably conscientious attempt to piece out Ellénore's side of the story, has no quarrel with this characteristic. Her account does not explore the possibility that what is hidden of the woman is not simply a pure will to love, but more complicated motives and desires.

24 Godelieve Mercken-Spaas, *Alienation in Constant's 'Adolphe'*, Berne, Frankfurt and Las Vegas, 1977, p. 33, shows that all the families in *Adolphe* are 'mutilated': Ellénore's own insecure background is reproduced in her abandonment of her children.

25 Charles Baudelaire, 'Le Voyage'; I translate: 'the universe is as large as his vast appetite'.

26 The desire to replace not so much the man as the children is a variant of the Oedipus complex that Freud mentions in his discussion of the 'family romance' and elsewhere. We find versions of it here, in *Werther*, in all those novels of adultery – *Le Rouge et le noir*, *L'Education sentimentale*, *Pierre et Jean* – where a beloved child falls ill just around the time the affair begins; in history, it is a marked feature of the marriage of D. H. Lawrence; and the childlessness of some heroines of the *récit*, such as Madeleine or Alissa (not to mention Madeleine Gide) also represent it.

27 For a detailed analysis of Ellénore as Adolphe's mirror, see Verhoeff, op. cit., pp. 58-65.

28 Maurice Blanchot, *La Part du feu*, Paris, 1949, p. 236. For an adulatory view of the stance of pity, see Charles Du Bos, *Grandeur et misère de Constant*, Paris, 1946, eg., p. 25: Adolphe is 'a man . . . who . . . succeeds in transcending the individual in himself by his feeling for the existence of other people and by his religious cult of suffering'; Georges Poulet, *Benjamin Constant par lui-même*, Paris, 1968, p. 87: 'the suffering of others . . . the whole novel of Adolphe is marked by this ethical preoccupation. The only solution to the problem of the suffering one causes is to take this suffering upon oneself [assumer soi-même cette douleur]'. But to assume it is to coopt it; in these views Ellénore may be a saint, but she can never have an ethical preoccupation, that being a prerogative of her partner. Mercken-Spaas, op. cit., pp. 55-6, identifies Adolphe's pity as a version of *amour*

propre; Verhoeff, op. cit., sees both Adolphe's supposed indifference and his pity (often suspended by the narrator) as symptomatic of aggression and contempt.

29 Ernest Jones, *The Life and Work of Sigmund Freud*, edited and abridged by L. Trilling and S. Marcus, Harmondsworth, 1961, 1977, p. 54. This is what Freud later theorises as 'reaction-formation', eg. in 'Instincts and their Vicissitudes', 11 p. 126.

30 Verhoeff summarises this nicely, op. cit., p. 70: 'Adolphe is kept by a kept woman – the relations between a mother and her child'.

31 Constant attenuated the original of this cry, uttered by Charlotte von Harden-burg, as reported in his *Journaux intimes*, 12 December 1807: 'she said: "That voice, that voice, it's the voice that hurt me. That man has killed me"' (p. 327, note 66). Unlike Ellénore, Charlotte did not die, but became Constant's none too happy wife.

32 Alfred Fabre-Luce comments less abstractly on Constant, *Benjamin Constant*, Paris, 1939, p. 235: 'he always enjoyed analysing himself in front of the object of his passion: this was perhaps his greatest sexual pleasure, a most refined form of masturbation'.

Notes to Chapter 4

1 This motif reappears in many European modernists' work. See Hofmannsthal, op. cit., p. 47: 'We must hide the depths. Where? On the surface', or p. 40: 'nothing is present on the inside that is not simultaneously perceptible on the outside'; Valéry: *'The most profound thing in man is his skin'*, 'L'Idée fixe', *Œuvres*, Paris, 1960, p. 215; Rilke: 'is not everything surface? . . . There is nothing but a single, manifold surface, everywhere moving and modifying','Auguste Rodin', *Gesammelte Werke: IV*, Leipzig, 1930, pp. 382-3. More recently, in Sartre, we find a fascination with surface in the discussion of the caress as 'appropriation', knowledge without absorption: *L'Etre et le néant*, pp. 668-9. All these writers, from different viewpoints, endorse Gautier's impatience with the 'depth' theory of significance.

2 Théophile Gautier, *Emaux et camées*, ed. J. Pommier and G. Matoré, Lille and Geneva, 1947, p. 132.

3 Albert Boschot, *Théophile Gautier*, Paris, 1933, p. 133, notes that the original Madeleine Maupin, who sang at the Opéra in between swashbuckling adventures and affairs with both sexes, had an '"ambiguous" contralto voice'.

4 Richard B. Grant, one of the rare critics to spare Rosette any attention, notes that the latter is named after her dress 'as if to suggest that for him she is her body and exterior garments', *Théophile Gautier*, Boston, 1975, p. 37. Indeed, for d'Albert the idea is that – exactly as in the poem 'A une robe rose' – the woman's body and her costume should be indistinguishable, both pure surface.

5 Théophile Gautier, *Mademoiselle de Maupin*, ed. M. Crouzet, Paris, 1973, p. 49.

6 As I noted in my *The Unintended Reader* (p. 246), there are plenty of instances of active incorporation to be found in nature: let anyone try breastfeeding. D'Albert's positive image of the magnet can be negatively matched by all those male nightmares of female quicksands, the vagina dentata, etc. discussed by Horney. As for the active pursuit of a passive goal, Freud is happy to admit this (2, p. 149) but does not puzzle out how the aim remains passive if the aimer is so active. Gautier has the same fantasy: for the brief time they spend in bed, Madeleine is all trembl-

ing schoolgirl and d'Albert wins the orgasm Olympics.

7 Jean Richer, *Etudes et recherches sur Théophile Gautier*, Paris, 1981, p. 11, brings together these three motifs, when he notes Gautier's obsession with 'the themes of the mirror and travesty, together associated with the light-darkness polarity and the conception of the Androgyne'.

8 Carl Gustav Jung, 'Anima and Animus', *The Collected Works of C. G. Jung*, 7, London, 1953, pp. 186-209.

9 Alfred de Musset, *Lorenzaccio*, Paris, 1976, p. 118.

10 See Georges Poulet, *Trois Essais de mythologie romantique*, Paris, 1966, pp. 83-134.

11 On this scene, see Richer, op. cit., pp. 14-15 and 223: he suggests a source in a New Year ritual in which a young man dresses up as a girl called Rosetta. The bestial couple Titania/Bottom apparently fascinated Gautier (and we can find a further parallel in Mérimée's *Lokis*). Richer does not observe the subversion of the erotic myth, though, in d'Albert's attack of over-excitement.

12 See *René*, p. 232, where this opening phrase is almost exactly repeated: Amélie, seen here at her most erotic, has just been transformed from sister into nun.

13 This image of the female eye as phallic appears frequently in these texts as elsewhere: Carmen's 'evil eye' or, especially, the eye of Julie in *Dominique* which is defined as both pursuing and engulfing.

14 A similar image is used of Lorenzaccio in André Lebois, *Vues sur le théâtre de Musset*, Paris, 1966, p. 99: 'this swordless man has at his disposal a perfect scalpel, which he uses to search [fouiller] through his heart and his loins'; here too there is a displacement of the phallic into a kind of cruel feminine knowledge.

15 Fernandez Sanchez, op. cit., p. 6, points out that this pose is also the one in which Madeleine first sees d'Albert on her arrival at Rosette's chateau.

16 Alfred de Musset, *La Confession d'un enfant du siècle*, ed. G. Barrier, Paris, 1973; this edition follows the MS of 1836, indicating the omissions of 1840 in square brackets. A study of the suppressed passages in the first forty or so pages shows interestingly that they tend to carry an imagery of castration – the amputation on p. 19; on p. 22: 'they had been dipped into the contempt of life like young swords'; demolition and sudden ageing on p. 24; 'this lugubrious forest [of potencies]' on p. 26; and on p. 32, the plummeting of 'the staunchest minds' into the darkness.

17 See Charles Maurras, *Les Amants de Venise*, Paris, 1904, p. 236: 'the whole point of the book is this secret, "Brigitte's secret", which also remained a secret for the author'.

18 Rivers of ink have been spilt over the question of what went wrong in the original Sand-Musset affair; what seems to be hinted between the lines here – that Sand's fluency and diligence as a writer irritated her lover – may well have been the case, as she is said to have leapt out of bed while he was fit only for sleep in order to get on with the work that was paying for the Venice holiday. While not wishing to add to the heaps of scholarly gossip, I am interested in the suggestion, in Charlotte Haldane, *Alfred*, London, 1960, pp. 67-71, that Musset's jealousy was aroused (bizarrely one might think) by Sand's famous 'frigidity'. Haldane gives a pre-feminist diagnosis of Sand's sexual problem – 'her unsatisfied femininity [was] constantly frustrated by the male element in her personality' (p. 103) – but it seems more probable that Musset was alarmed by what he took to be proof of his lack of skill; for the anxious phallic myth, women's lack of *jouissance* is little less threatening than their full enjoyment. Toesca, op. cit., p. 140, suspects that Musset got something quite specific out of the crisis: 'in Venice, the drama of jealousy took shape. Alfred de Musset plunged into his element'; Henry D. Sedgwick, *Alfred de Musset 1810-1857*, London, 1932, p. 61, agrees that 'his

passion of self-pity [was] the strongest emotion that he knew'.

19 Such epithets were exchanged in the Musset-Sand correspondence, but equally often they called each other 'brother' (Sand habitually wrote with the masculine adjective); see the letters quoted by Barrier, *Confession*, p. 361, note 1 to p. 219.

20 The Christian imagery undergoes several narratorial transformations; for example, in a passage suppressed in 1840, Octave beside the cheery prostitute drinks 'a more bitter chalice than the angels brought to Christ, turning their heads aside, on the Mount of Olives' (p. 86); on p. 93, Octave finds himself 'marked with a burning stigmata'; in two images of St. Thomas he first confronts Jesus as the repentant doubter, then seems to be investigating himself; finally, he sees Brigitte as wearing 'that diadem of blood thorns that is the crown of resignation' (p. 295); the replacement of her 'rosière's' garland perhaps?

21 Mary Elizabeth Coleridge, 'The Other Side of the Mirror', quoted by Sandra Gilbert and Susan Gubar, *The Madwoman in the Attic*, London, 1979, 1984, pp. 15-16, and Annette von Droste-Hülshoff, 'Das Spiegelbild', *Gedichte*, Stuttgart, 1978, pp. 35-6.

Notes to Chapter 5

1 All reference to works by Nerval is to *Œuvres de Gérard de Nerval*, ed. H. Lemaître, Paris, 1966; see also *Aurélia*, p. 798.

2 Uri Eisenzweig, *L'Espace imaginaire d'un récit*, Neuchâtel, 1976, pp. 114-9, contrasts these pairings as respectively metaphoric and metonymic.

3 Sarah Kofman, *Nerval, le Charme de la répétition*, Lausanne, 1979, pp. 71-89; on p. 85 she too describes the relation of triad to pair as a form of 'circulation' though for different reasons. L.-H. Sébillotte, in *Le Secret de Gérard de Nerval*, Paris, 1948, sees the central trauma of Nerval's life, which informs the breakdown represented in *Aurélia*, as an experience of impotence during the affair with Jenny Colon; his reading of *Sylvie* therefore tends to discount the figures of Sylvie and Adrienne and to see the hint of son-mother desire rather as a screen to render the actress's figure sexless than a pointer to the key original. This argument illustrates how possible it is to isolate any one of the three women as the central one, grouping the others together under the sign of irrelevance. Christopher Prendergast, *The Order of Mimesis*, Cambridge, 1986, pp. 153-63, argues that, though Adrienne is 'the most privileged' figure, she is herself a substitution in a chain without inauguration.

4 Michel Jeanneret, *La Lettre perdue*, Paris, 1978, pp. 82-3, argues that if the hero's *histoire* is about wandering and failure, the narrator's *récit* (using Genette's categories) demonstrates a regulative control; but this ignores the fact that our knowledge of the hero is only through the narrator, and by-passes the irony of the critique, which properly belongs to neither of them.

5 Many critics comment on this image, for example, Georges Poulet, *Trois Essais de mythologie romantique*, Paris, 1966, p. 24; Jeanneret, op. cit., p. 24; Ross Chambers, *Gérard de Nerval et la poétique du voyage*, Paris, 1969, p. 240; Bettina L. Knapp, *Gérard de Nerval*, Alabama, 1980, p. 215; Prendergast, op. cit, p. 153; but they and other writers who observe the protagonist's narcissism do not take up the significance of the verb 'craigner'.

6 Janet Todd, *Women's Friendship in Literature*, New York, 1980, p. 65.

7 The edition by Lemaître erroneously has 'que' here; I correct it following Gérald

Schaeffer, *Une double Lecture de Nerval*, Neuchâtel, 1977, p. 127, note 14.

8 Alissa, as we see in the next chapter, has identical eyebrows; in both young women the feature is read as signifying innocence and enquiry. In Sylvie, innocence develops into enquiry; in Alissa's case, enquiry is stifled and replaced by an enforced and extreme version of innocence.

9 Arthur Symons, *The Symbolist Movement in Literature*, London, 1899, pp. 22-3.

10 All quotations are from Victor Hugo, *Les Contemplations*, ed. L. Cellier, Paris, 1969; this reference, from a letter of November 1855, is on p. xiii.

11 This pun has of course been taken over and developed recently by Hélène Cixous.

12 All quotations from *Dominique* are from ed. B. Wright, Paris, 1966; this reference, p. x.

13 See Jean Pierre Richard, *Littérature et sensation*, Paris, 1954, p. 223: 'through *Dominique*, Fromentin seems almost to be glorying in his own failure'. Jacques Vier, *Pour l'étude de* Dominique, Paris, 1958, p. 53, links the unconsummated passion to the mystique of modesty when he observes: 'a breath of renunciation animates the whole work'.

14 I have tried to remain close to the original wording wherever possible in translating texts, but in Sir Edward Marsh's 1948 translation of *Dominique*, London, 1986, p. 39, there is a very direct assumption of the childbed death: 'the effort to nurse me cost my mother her life'.

15 Roland Barthes, 'Fromentin: "Dominique"', in *Le Degré zéro de l'écriture; Nouveaux essais critiques*, Paris, 1953, 1972, p. 161.

16 The protagonist does of course replace Madeleine with his shadowy wife, and this lends his 'idealism' a certain irony; see Maija Lehtonen, *Essai sur* Dominique *de Fromentin*, Helsinki, 1972, pp. 44-5; and Claude Herzfeld, Dominique *de Fromentin*, Paris, 1977, p. 105.

17 Olivier's gaze too is phallic – 'the direct gaze with which he covered himself as with a raised sword, whenever he found himself in the presence of new faces, especially women's faces' (p. 188) – but it is a self-protective look which attacks rather than drawing in. Julie's gaze is much more powerful: 'she slowly fixed upon Olivier the blue-black enamel of her lightless eyes' (pp. 188-9), training on him 'a scrutiny capable of uprooting even Olivier's solid self-confidence'. In this scene female desire is presented as castrating the male gaze.

18 Albert Thibaudet, *Intérieurs*, Paris, 1924, p. 175, seems in uncritical sympathy with this jealousy when he gives his explanation of Madeleine's anti-biographical sterility: 'this is because [children] would have complicated and weakened this work, getting in the way of the love story'. See also Chapter 3, note 26.

19 I am indebted to my colleague Jane Bewick for pointing out that Madeleine is frequently shown clothed in a veil (e.g., on her arrival home in Ormesson; at the wedding) or viewed through a cloud of dust (at the prizegiving), obscured (in the painting) or ghost-like (on Dominique's last arrival at Nièvres; at dinner after the scene of the embrace). Here, in the pretext for throwing herself at Dominique, she is at once putting aside a covering and, if you like, offering the hymen for penetration. The humble task of folding the shawl is particularly well-chosen: protected by its everyday function, she will choreograph a set of movements where, from the symmetrical gestures of mirror-image folding, the two must finally come close enough to touch hands.

Notes to Chapter 6

1 James Joyce, *A Portrait of the Artist as a Young Man*, ed. R. Ellmann, Bungay, 1964, p. 219.

2 Letter to Louise Colet of 9 December 1852, Gustave Flaubert, *Correspondance*, II, ed. J. Bruneau, Paris, 1980, p. 204.

3 Letter to Scheffer, reprinted in André Gide, *Œuvres complètes*, IV, ed. L. Martin-Chauffier, Paris, n. d., pp. 616-7.

4 From a letter to Christan Beck of 16 November 1909, quoted in J. C. Davies, *Gide: L'Immoraliste and La Porte étroite*, London, 1968, p. 25.

5 Letter from Gide to Jammes of 7 July 1902, *Francis Jammes et André Gide, Correspondance 1893-1938*, ed. R. Mallet, Paris, 1948, p. 197.

6 Unless otherwise stated, all quotations from Gide's fiction are from André Gide, *Romans*, Paris, 1958; this quotation, p. 153.

7 Pierre-Quint cites an almost identical remark made to him by Gide apropos of the conflict between his homosexuality and his marriage: "'it *frightens* me to think that every desire, every potentiality [puissance] that I do not satisfy during my life would torture me to let them survive'", Léon Pierre-Quint, *André Gide: l'homme – sa vie – son œuvre*, Paris, 1952, p. 27. For Gide's awareness of his suppression of the homosexual theme ('the most wounding edge of the sword') from the text, see *Et nunc manet in te*, in André Gide, *Journal 1939-1949. Souvenirs*, Paris, 1955, p. 1135.

8 A letter from Jammes of June 1902 notes this with some brutality, describing Michel as 'a pathetic lunatic whose very vices are half-hearted, a failure even as a sadist and pederast in vain . . . your hero has just one fault that makes him uncongenial to me: that is, his total lack of immorality. He searches for it without ever finding it. He commits acts that *get nowhere*', quoted in *Romans* pp. 1515-6.

9 Barbéris, op. cit., notes the motif of the 'single night' in Chateaubriand, where the sexual act is unrepeatable and ideally followed by the murder of the woman. In Gide, a less aggressive version of this *Liebestod* is found in the attempted suicide of Olivier in *Les Faux-monnayeurs*. We can also see analogies in other *récits*: the brevity of the 'charm' of love in *Adolphe* and *La Confession d'un enfant du siècle*; avoidance of consummation in *Sylvie* and *Dominique*; the direct incest-taboo in *René* and *La Porte étroite*; only the heroes and heroines of *femme fatale* narratives actually seem to enjoy sex, and defer a little the inevitable murder that follows.

10 *Journal 1939-1949. Souvenirs*, p. 593: 'since then, whenever I have sought pleasure [le plaisir], I have been chasing after the memory of that night'. The sense of relief, reflected in the eager citing of his prodigious number of orgasms, is understandably absent in *L'Immoraliste*.

11 Cf. a similar image in the 'nightmare' reproduced in Gide's first publication, *Les Cahiers et les poésies d'André Walter*, Paris, 1952, p. 179. Here the woman appears in a seamless ecclesiastical robe, very straight and gently smiling; a monkey hops in and raises her skirt; the narrator looks in horror: 'under the dress there was nothing; it was black, black as a hole; I sobbed in despair. Then, with both hands, she siezed the base of her dress and flung it over her head. She/it turned inside out like a bag. I saw no more; the night closed in on her. . . I was so scared that I woke up; the night was still so black that I did not know if it was not still the night of the dream' (ellipses Gide's). Here, the black hole of the 'castrated' woman turns into the whole world as maternal sac.

12 The epithet 'affreux' occurs with gathering frequency in the last pages of *L'Im-*

moraliste, representing the Medusan fascination that Marceline's sick appearance exerts on Michel, and is also found in *La Porte étroite*, where it expresses sexual abhorrence of changes in Alissa.

13 *Romans*, pp. 1549 and 1552. Apropos of these remarks of Gide's, this reaction is fairly typical: 'to picture the self-destructive mysticism of a woman must have seemed to him a high achievement of creative imagination, and a genuine escape from self', Albert J. Guerard, *André Gide*, Cambridge, Mass., 1959, p. 122.

14 For a typical view of Gide's own relationship to his mother, see Wallace Fowlie, *André Gide: his life and art*, New York and London, 1965, p. 28: here the writer's 'unmanliness' is blamed on the 'strong-willed and almost virile matriarch'.

15 The parallels between *La Porte étroite* and *Dominique* are striking; there are grounds for assuming influence, since Gide chose Fromentin's *récit* in 1913 as one of his ten favourite French texts (*Romans*, p. xi), but there is also an element of coincidence, extending even to the women's names in fiction and life: Madeleine and Julie[tte]. Gide's text is closer to Fromentin's biography than the latter's fiction, however, in making the unloved sister herself in love with the protagonist.

16 Cf. a letter from Madeleine to Gide, quoted in Jean Schlumberger, *Madeleine et André Gide*, Paris, 1956, p. 115: even after agreeing to their marriage, she observes, 'we must remember always to part from time to time, so that we can have each other's letters – they are irreplaceable, all the more since we are so afraid to speak to each other . . . Oh what funny, foolish people we are!' (ellipses Schlumberger's). For what happened to these 'irreplaceable letters' see *Et nunc manet in te* and Schlumberger's commentary; for a connexion between this conflict and Gide's narrative technique, see my own '"Parfois j'ai peur que ce que j'ai supprimé ne se venge" – Gide and women', *Paragraph*, 8, 1986, pp. 62-74.

17 Almost the identical sentence occurs in *La Symphonie pastorale*, p. 925: 'Lord, it seems to me sometimes that I need her love in order to love you'.

18 References are to Alain-Fournier, *Le grand Meaulnes*, Paris, 1971.

19 See my 'The Adulteress's Child – a sidelight on Pierre et Jean', *French Studies Bulletin*, 17, 1985/6, pp. 6-8.

20 References are to Andra Breton, *Nadja*, Paris, 1964.

21 References are to Georges Bernanos, *Œuvres romanesques*, Paris, 1961, ed. G. Picon et al.

22 For details of this thematics, see my *The Banal Object*, pp. 111-6.

23 See the screenplay of the film *Sartre*, directed by A. Astruc and M. Contat, Paris, 1977, p. 59.

24 References to Camus's fiction are to Albert Camus, *Théâtre, Récits, Nouvelles*, ed. R. Quilliot, Paris, 1962. This remark is from Camus's preface to the American edition of *L'Etranger*, signed 1955.

25 References are to Marcel Proust, *A la Recherche du temps perdu*, three vols, ed. P. Clarac and A. Ferré, Paris, 1952.

26 Rebecca West, *The Return of the Soldier*, first published 1918, London, 1980, p. 167: '"his mother was not his sort. She wanted a stupid son, who would have been satisfied with shooting"'.

Notes to Chapter 7

1 See Christopher Prendergast, op. cit., p. 163. As one might aphoristically amplify his point: if there is no *hors-texte*, there is also no *Urtext*.

2 It is often argued, eg., by Nancy Chodorow, *The Reproduction of Mothering*, Berkeley, Los Angeles and London, 1978, that women never separate from their mothers as totally as men.

3 Eve Kosofsky Sedgwick, *Between Men*, New York, 1985, p. 76.

4 For an evergreen analysis of male bonding in American fiction, see Leslie Fiedler, *Love and Death in the American Novel*, New York, 1960.

5 Gayle Rubin, 'The Traffic in Women: Notes on the "Political Economy" of Sex', in ed. R. Reiter, *Toward an Anthropology of Women*, New York and London, 1975, pp. 157-210. See also Luce Irigaray, *Speculum de l'autre femme*, Paris, 1974, and *Ce Sexe qui n'en est pas un*, Paris, 1977. In the former, Irigaray proves dazzlingly that Freud goes so far as to conceive female homosexuality as a transaction between males (pp. 122-9) and to design the whole of female psychosexual development so as to make us Jocasta (p. 136).

6 Donald W. Winnicott, *Playing and Reality*, Harmondsworth, 1971, 1985, especially pp. 1-30 and 130-8.

7 Stephen Heath, 'Difference', *Screen*, 19, 3, 1978, p. 58. See also Heath, *The Sexual Fix*, London, 1982, pp. 33-49.

8 Hélène Cixous, 'Sorties', in Catherine Clément and Hélène Cixous, *La jeune Née*, Paris, 1975, p. 151.

9 Simone de Beauvoir, *Le deuxième Sexe*, 1, Paris, 1949, p. 64.

10 The recent spate of novels, chiefly by women, in which a heroine ends the text by a climactic first experience of orgasm (see Heath, *The Sexual Fix*, or Maurice Charney, *Sexual Fiction*, London and New York, 1981) is a curious reversal of this distinction; it is as if women must be shown to envy the unique 'Big O' which men have always had: once will now after all be enough!

11 See Karen Horney, 'The Dread of Woman', *International Journal of Psycho-analysis*, 13, 1932, pp. 348-60.

12 Annette Kuhn, *The Power of the Image*, London, Boston, Melbourne and Henley, 1985, p. 45; see also Rosalind Coward, *Female Desire*, London, 1984, p. 229: 'controlling the look, men have left themselves out of the picture because a body defined is a body controlled'.

13 Cited from Masters and Johnson's findings by Mary Jane Sherfey in ed. J. Baker Miller, *Psychoanalysis and Women*, Harmondsworth, 1973, p. 139.

14 See Walter J. Ong, *Orality and Literacy*, London and New York, 1982, p. 11. Ong has a nice way of parodying the oxymoron 'oral literature' by comparing it with the upside-down definition we would get if we asked someone to define a horse in terms of a car: such a negative definition of the 'wheelless automobile' (pp. 12-13) strikes me as rather similar to the psychoanalytic view of women as 'castrated men'.

15 Laura Mulvey, 'Visual Pleasure and Narrative Cinema', *Screen*, 16, 3, 1975, p. 14.

16 Susanne Kappeler, *The Pornography of Representation*, Cambridge, 1986.

17 For example, Adrienne Rich, *Of Woman Born*, London, 1977; Julia Kristeva, 'L'Héréthique de l'amour', *Tel quel*, 74, 1977, pp. 30-49; and Mary Kelly's visual *Post-Partum Document*, London, 1983.

18 Sandra M. Gilbert, 'Costumes of the Mind: Transvestism as Metaphor in Modern Literature', in ed. E. Abel, *Writing and Sexual Difference*, Brighton, 1982, p. 196;

Froma I. Zeitlin, 'Aristophanes' *Thesmophoriazousae*', Abel op. cit; see also Kuhn, op. cit., p. 73.

19 Cf. Sandra Gilbert and Susan Gubar, *The Madwoman in the Attic*, Cambridge Mass. and London, 1982, p. 34: 'the "killing" of oneself into an art object – the pruning and preening, the mirror madness'; John Berger, *Ways of Seeing*, London and Harmondsworth, 1972, p. 54: 'nudity is placed on display . . . Nudity is a form of dress'.

20 Virginia Woolf, *Moments of Being*, ed. J. Schulkind, St. Albans, 1978; also Woolf, *The Waves*, London, 1931, 1977.

21 *Speculum*, p. 182; see also *Ce Sexe*, p. 150, where Irigaray contrasts the male use of women as a *'plane mirror'* with a new *'intervention of the speculum and the concave mirror'*.

22 For example, Elisabeth Lenk, 'The Self-Reflecting Woman', in ed. G. Ecker, *Feminist Aesthetics*, London, 1985, p. 57; Radicalesbians, quoted in Hester Eisenstein, *Contemporary Feminist Thought*, London and Sydney, 1984, p. 52. In Sartre's *Huis Clos*, too, the lesbian Inès offers her eyes as mirror to the 'narcissistic' Estelle.

23 This argument is put eloquently in Chodorow, op. cit.; it is also noted in Dinnerstein, *The Mermaid and the Minotaur*, New York, 1976, p. 68: 'the mother is likely to experience a more effortless identification, a smoother communication, with a girl baby than with a boy baby'; Coward, op. cit., p. 228: 'a difference based just on the strangeness of the [boy's] body'; Luise Eichenbaum and Susie Orbach, *Understanding Women*, Harmondsworth, 1983, p. 57: 'built into a mother's experience with a son is the knowledge that he will become his own person in the world'. The fact that each argument proceeds from different premises makes it difficult to see how the certainty is arrived at.

24 John Bowlby, *Child Care and the Growth of Love*, Harmondsworth, 1953, 1965, p. 14.

25 Donald W. Winnicott, 'The Theory of the Parent-Infant Relationship', *International Journal of Psycho-analysis*, 41, 1960, pp. 585-595.

26 J. Laplanche and J-B. Pontalis, *The Language of Psycho-analysis*, London, 1973, p. 93.

27 Julia Kristeva, *Pouvoirs de l'horreur*, Paris, 1980, p. 43.

28 Neil Hertz, 'Dora's Secrets, Freud's Techniques', in ed. C. Bernheimer and C. Kahane, *In Dora's Case*, London, 1985, p. 234. In this connection, it is curious that the many commentators in this collection who note the biased reading Freud makes of Dora's knowledge of oral sex – he assumes that Frau K. and Dora's presumably impotent father performed fellatio when logically it would have been cunnilingus – fail to infer the possibilty of cunnilingus (at least as a fantasy) between her and Frau K. Hertz quotes Freud's observation that the throat and oral cavity were '"precisely in her case . . . in a state of irritation"' (p. 228), but draws no conclusion from this. Jane Gallop reads Freud's euphemistic bit of French – '"j'appelle un chat un chat"' (p. 209) – as calling 'a pussy a pussy'. But this phrase, precisely, doubles the word 'pussy' and hints, not at a male-female act but at one of two women together.

29 Hélène Cixous, 'Le Rire de la méduse', *L'Arc*, 61, 1975, pp. 39-54, and Susan Gubar, '"The Blank Page" and the Issues of Female Creativity', Abel, op. cit., pp. 73-93.

30 In *Ce Sexe*, p. 129, Irigaray's interviewer suggests that *'if "womanspeak" is possible, writing is an effect of it'*, but she gets an evasive response.

31 For instance in Beverley Brown and Parveen Adams, 'The Feminine Body and Feminist Politics', *m/f*, 3, 1979, pp. 35-50; Jane Gallop, *'Quand nos lèvres s'écrivent: Irigaray's Body Politic'*, *Romanic Review*, 74, 1, 1983, pp. 77-83.

32 Robin Lakoff, *Language and Women's Place*, New York, 1975, p. 1: 'language is more amenable to precise reproduction on paper and unambiguous analysis than are other forms of sexist behaviour'; Deborah Cameron, *Feminism and Linguistic Theory*, Basingstoke and London, 1985, pp. 165-6.

33 Jacques Derrida, *Spurs/Eperons*, Chicago and London, 1978, 1979, p. 96; Derrida's version of the female-body-as-writing is the particularly unappealing 'graphic of the hymen', pp. 98, 100 and 110. For a description of Derrida as 'master', see Jonathan Culler, 'Jacques Derrida', in ed. J. Sturrock, *Structuralism and Since*, Oxford, 1979, p. 155.

34 Alice Jardine, *Gynesis*, Ithaca and London, 1985, p. 25.

35 David Crystal, *Listen to your Child*, Harmondsworth, 1986.

36 Even earlier, there is a kind of linguistic exchange which is a perfect example of affectionate misreading: when the pregnant woman first perceives the foetus's kicking (called 'quickening' in folk-language, but several weeks after foetal formation is complete and certainly some time after the child has started to kick) she cannot help receiving it as a first initiative of 'conversation' from the signalling child; the latter is of course just exercising its limbs.

37 Julia Kristeva, *Des Chinoises*, Paris, 1974, p. 21.

38 Roland Barthes, 'La Mort de l'auteur', *Mantéia*, 5, 1968, p. 15; Harold Bloom, *The Anxiety of Influence*, New York, 1973.

Bibliography

I

Chateaubriand

Barbéris, Pierre, *Chateaubriand: une réaction au monde moderne*, Paris, 1976

——, *A la Recherche d'une écriture. Chateaubriand*, Tours, 1974

Bérenger, Henry, *Chateaubriand*, Paris, 1931

Bertaut, Jules, *La Vie privée de Chateaubriand*, Paris, 1952

Bertrin, Georges, *La Sincérité religieuse de Chateaubriand*, Paris, 1900

Chateaubriand, François-René, vicomte de, *Atala, René, Les Aventures du dernier Abencérage*, ed. F. Letessier, Paris, 1962

——, *Œuvres complètes*, III, Paris, n.d.

——, *Essai sur les révolutions, Génie du christianisme*, ed. M. Regard, Paris, 1978

Chinard, Gilbert, *L'Exotisme américain dans l'œuvre de Chateaubriand*, Paris, 1918

Duhamel, Roger, *Témoins de leur temps: Chateaubriand, Barrès, Brasillach*, Ottawa, 1980

Evans, Joan, *Chateaubriand*, London, 1939

Giraud, Victor, *Le Christianisme de Chateaubriand*, Paris, 1925

——, *La Vie romanesque de Chateaubriand*, Paris, 1932

Knight, Diana, 'The Readability of René's Secret', *French Studies*, 37, 1, 1983, pp. 35-46

Lebègue, Raymond, *Aspects de Chateaubriand*, Paris, 1979

Le Fèbvre, Yves, *Le Génie du christianisme*, Paris, 1929

Lemaître, Jules, *Chateaubriand*, Paris, 1912

Le Savoureux, H., *Chateaubriand*, Paris, 1930

Lescure, M. de, *Chateaubriand*, Paris, n.d.

Levaillant, Maurice, *Le véritable Chateaubriand*, Oxford, 1951

——, *Chateaubriand, prince des songes*, Paris, 1960

Martin-Chauffier, Louis, *Chateaubriand ou l'obsession de la pureté*, Paris, 1943

Maurois, André, *Chateaubriand*, London, 1938

Michel, Evariste, *Chateaubriand: Interprétation médico-psychologique de son caractère*, Paris, 1911

Mirecourt, Eugène de, *Chateaubriand*, Paris, 1867

Moreau, Pierre, *Chateaubriand*, Paris, 1927

——, *Chateaubriand, l'homme et l'œuvre*, Paris, 1956

Monod-Cassidy, Hélène, 'Amours sauvages, amours chratiennes: quelques prédecesseurs peu connus d'*Atala*', in ed. R. Switzer, *Chateaubriand*, Geneva, 1970, pp. 245-51

O'Flaherty, Kathleen, 'Adolescence in the Work of Chateaubriand', in Switzer, op. cit., pp. 273-81

Painter, George D., *Chateaubriand, a Biography, I (1768-93)*, London, 1977

Porter, Charles, *Chateaubriand, Composition, Imagination and Poetry*, Saratoga, 1978

Richard, Jean Pierre, *Paysage de Chateaubriand*, Paris, 1967

Servien, Pius, *Lyrisme et Structures Sonores*, Paris, 1930

Storzer, Gerald H., 'Chateaubriand and the Fictional Confession', in Switzer, op. cit., pp. 123-131

Switzer, Richard, ed., *Chateaubriand*, Proceedings of the Commemoration of the Bicentenary of the Birth of Chateaubriand 1968, Geneva, 1970

——, *Chateaubriand*, New York, 1971

Constant

Alexander, Ian W., *Benjamin Constant:* Adolphe, London, 1973
Constant, *Benjamin, Adolphe,* ed. J.-H. Bornecque, Paris, 1960
Bastid, Paul, *Benjamin Constant et sa doctrine,* Paris, 1966
Berthoud, Dorette, *Constance et grandeur de Benjamin Constant,* Lausanne, 1944
Blanchot, Maurice, *La Part du feu,* Paris, 1949
Bressier, Henri, *Benjamin Constant et les femmes,* Geneva, 1973
Cordey, Pierre and Jean-Luc Seylaz, eds., *Benjamin Constant,* Actes du Congrès Benjamin Constant 1967, Geneva, 1968
Deguise, M. P., 'Benjamin Constant sous le regard d'autrui', Cordey and Seylaz, op. cit., pp. 109-17
Du Bos, Charles, *Grandeur et misère de Benjamin Constant,* Paris, 1946
Dumont-Wilden, L., *La Vie de Benjamin Constant,* Paris, 1930
Ettlinger, Josef, *Benjamin Constant, Der Roman eines Lebens,* Berlin, 1909
Fabre-Luce, Alfred, *Benjamin Constant,* Paris, 1939
Glachant, Victor, *Benjamin Constant sous l'œil du guet,* Paris, 1906
Gonin, Eve, *Le Point de vue l'Ellénore,* Paris, 1981
Gouhier, Henri, *Benjamin Constant,* Paris, 1967
Hasselrot, Bengt, *Nouveaux Documents sur Benjamin Constant,* Copenhagen, 1952
Holdheim, William W., *Benjamin Constant,* London, 1961
Jallet, J., 'Adolphe, la parole et l'autre', *Littérature,* 2, 1971, pp. 71-88
Jasinski, Béatrice W., *L'Engagement de Benjamin Constant,* Paris, 1971
King, Norman, 'Structures et stratégies d'*Adolphe*', in ed. E. Hofmann, *Benjamin Constant, Madame de Staël et le groupe de Coppet,* Oxford, 1982, pp. 267-85
Léon, Paul, *Benjamin Constant,* Paris, 1930
Mercken-Spaas, Godelieve, *Alienation in Constant's* Adolphe, Berne, Frankfurt and Las Vegas, 1977
Nicolson, Harold, *Benjamin Constant,* London, 1949
Poulet, Georges, *Etudes sur le temps humain,* Edinburgh, 1949
— —, *Benjamin Constant par lui-même,* Paris, 1968
Roger, Noëlle, *Les Amours de Corinne,* Paris, 1931
Rudler, Gustave, 'L'âme et le caractère', in *Centenaire de Benjamin Constant,* Lausanne, 1930, pp. 9-35
Thompson, Patrice, *La Religion de Benjamin Constant,* Pisa, 1978
Todorov, Tzvetan, *La Poétique de la prose,* Paris, 1971
Verhoeff, Han, *'Adolphe' et Constant,* Paris, 1976
Wernli, Annaliese, *Le Thème de la liberté dans l'itinéraire de Benjamin Constant,* Zurich, 1968

Fromentin

Barthes, Roland, 'Fromentin: "Dominique"', *Le Degré zéro de l'écriture; Nouveaux Essais critiques,* Paris, 1953, 1972, pp. 156-69
Eckstein, Marie-Anne, *Le Rôle du souvenir dans l'œuvre de Fromentin,* Zurich, 1970
Evans, Arthur, R., *The Literary Art of Eugène Fromentin,* Baltimore, 1964
Giraud, Victor, *Eugène Fromentin,* Niort, 1945
Greshoff, C. J., *Seven Studies in the French Novel,* Cape Town, 1964
Herzfeld, Claude, Dominique de *Fromentin,* Paris, 1977
Lehtonen, Maija, *Essai sur* Dominique de *Fromentin,* Helsinki, 1972.
Lethbridge, Robert, 'Fromentin's "Dominique" and the Art of Reflection', *Essays in*

Bibliography

French Literature, 16, 1979, pp. 43-61

Mickel, Emanuel J., *Eugène Fromentin*, Boston, 1981

Richard, Jean Pierre, *Littérature et Sensation*, Paris, 1954

Sagnès, Guy, editor, *Colloque Eugène Fromentin*, Lille, 1979

Thibaudet, Albert, *Intérieurs*, Paris, 1924

Vier, Jacques, *Pour l'étude de* Dominique *de Fromentin*, Paris, 1958

Gautier

Barrès, Maurice, *Les Maîtres*, Paris, 1927

Benesch, Rita, *Le Regard de Théophile Gautier*, Zurich, 1969

Boschot, Albert, *Théophile Gautier*, Paris, 1933

Delvaille, Bernard, *Théophile Gautier*, Paris, 1968

Dillingham, Louise Bulkley, *The Creative Imagination of Théophile Gautier*, Princeton and Albany, 1927

Du Camp, Maxime, *Théophile Gautier*, Paris, 1895

Fauchereau, Serge, *Théophile Gautier*, Paris, 1972

Fernandez Sanchez, Carmen, '"Mademoiselle de Maupin" et le récit poétique', *Bulletin de la Société Théophile Gautier*, 3, 1981, pp. 1-10

Grant, Richard B., *Théophile Gautier*, Boston, 1975

Jasinski, René, *Les Années romantiques de Théophile Gautier*, Paris, 1929

Lloyd, Rosemary, 'Rereading *Mademoiselle de Maupin*', *Orbis Litterarum*, 41, 1986, pp. 19-32

Marcel, Henry, *Essais sur Théophile Gautier*, Paris, 1903

Matoré, Georges, *Le Vocabulaire et la société sous Louis-Philippe*, Geneva, 1951

Palache, John Garber, *Gautier and the Romantics*, London, 1927

Payr, Bernhard, *Théophile Gautier und E. T. A. Hoffmann*, Berlin, 1932

Poulet, Georges, *Trois Essais de mythologie romantique*, Paris, 1966

Richardson, Joanna, *Gautier, his Life and Times*, London, 1958

Richer, Jean, *Etudes et Recherches sur Théophile Gautier prosateur*, Paris, 1981

Smith, Albert B., *Ideal and Reality in the Fictional Narratives of Théophile Gautier*, Gainesville, 1969

Starkie, Enid, *From Gautier to Eliot*, London, 1960

Symons, Arthur, *Studies in Prose and Verse*, London, 1904

Tennant, P. E., *Théophile Gautier*, London, 1975

Van der Tuin, H., *L'Evolution psychologique, esthétique et littéraire de Théophile Gautier*, Amsterdam, 1933

Voisin, Marcel, *Le Soleil et la nuit*, Brussels, 1981

Gide

Ames, Van Meter, *André Gide*, Norfolk, 1947

Archambault, Paul, *Humanité d'André Gide*, Paris, 1950

Arland, Marcel and Jean Mouton, eds., *Entretiens sur André Gide*, Paris and The Hague, 1967

Bastide, Roger, *Anatomie d'André Gide*, Paris, 1972

Bettinson, Christopher, *Gide: a study*, London, 1977

Boisdeffre, Pierre de, *Vie d'André Gide*, Paris, 1970

Brée, Germaine, *Gide*, New Brunswick, 1963

Collignon, Jean, 'Gide's Sincerity', *Yale French Studies*, 7, 1965, pp. 44-50

Bibliography

Cordle, Thomas, *André Gide*, New York, 1969

——, 'Gide and the Novel of the Egoist', *Yale French Studies*, 7, 1965, pp. 91-7

Davies, J. C., *Gide: L'Immoraliste and La Porte étroite*, Southampton, 1968

Delay, Jean, *La Jeunesse d'André Gide*, 2 vols, Paris, 1956 and 1957

Du Bos, Charles, *Le Dialogue avec André* Gide, Paris, 1923

Falk, Eugene E., *Types of Thematic Structure*, Chicago and London, 1967

Fayer, Mischa Harry, *Gide, Freedom and Dostoevsky*, Vermont, 1946

Fowlie, Wallace, *André Gide: his life and art*, New York and London, 1965

Freedman, Ralph, *The Lyrical Novel*, Princeton, 1963

Freyburger, Henri, *L'Evolution de la disponibilité gidienne*, Paris, 1970

Gabory, Georges, *André Gide: son œuvre*, Paris, 1924

Gide, André, *Romans; Récits et Soties; Œuvres lyriques*, ed. M. Nadeau et al., Paris, 1958

——, *Oscar Wilde: in memoriam*, Paris, n.d.

——, *Et nunc manet in te* suivi de *Journal intime*, Neuchâtel and Paris, 1947

——, *Journal 1939-1949; Souvenirs*, Paris, 1954

Guerard, Albert, *André Gide*, Cambridge, Mass, 1951, 1969

Holdheim, W. Wolfgang, *Theory and Practice of the Novel: a study on André Gide*, Paris, 1968

Ireland, G. W., *André Gide: a Study of his Creative Writings*, Oxford, 1970

Lafille, Pierre, *André Gide romancier*, Paris, 1954

Littlejohn, David, *Gide: a collection of Critical Essays*, Englewood Cliffs, 1970

Macauer, Maurice, *Gide: l'indécision passionnée*, Paris, 1969

Maisani-Léonard, Martine, *André Gide ou l'ironie de l'écriture*, Montreal, 1976

Mann, Klaus, *André Gide and the Crisis of Modern Thought*, London, 1948

March, Harold, *Gide and the Hound of Heaven*, Philadelphia, 1952

Marchand, Max, *Le Complexe pédagogique et didactique d'André Gide*, Oran, 1954

Martinet, Edouard, *André Gide: l'amour et la divinité*, Paris and Neuchâtel, 1931

Masson, Pierre, *André Gide: voyage et écriture*, Lyon, 1983

Nersoyan, H. J., *André Gide: the Theism of an Atheist*, Syracuse, 1969

O'Brien, Justin, *Portrait of André Gide: a Critical Biography*, London, 1953

——, 'Gide's Fictional Technique', *Yale French Studies*, 7, 1965, pp. 81-90

O'Neill, Kevin, *André Gide and the* Roman d'Aventure, Sydney, 1969

Painter, George, *André Gide: a Critical Biography*, London, 1968

Parnell, Charles, 'André Gide and his *Symphonie pastorale*', *Yale French Studies*, 7, 1965, pp. 60-71

Pasco, Allan H., 'Irony and Art in Gide's *L'Immoraliste*', *Romanic Review*, 64, 3, 1973, pp. 184-203

Pierre-Quint, Léon, *André Gide*, Paris, 1952

Raimond, Michel, ed., *Les Critiques de notre temps et Gide*, Paris, 1971

Rossi, Vinio, *André Gide: the Evolution of an Aesthetic*, New Brunswick, 1967

Schildt, Göran, *Gide et l'homme*, Paris, 1949

Schlumberger, Jean, *Madeleine et André Gide*, Paris, 1956

Stoltzfus, Ben, *Gide's Eagles*, Carbondale and Edwardsville, 1969

Sonnenfeld, Albert, 'On Readers and Reading in *La Porte étroite* and *L'Immoraliste*', *Romanic Review*, 67, 3, 1976, pp. 172-86

Thomas, Lawrence, *André Gide: the ethic of the artist*, London, 1950

Trahard, Pierre, La Porte étroite *d'André Gide*, Paris, 1968

Bibliography

Mérimée

Arbalet, Paul, *Trois Solitaires: Courier-Stendhal-Mérimée*, Paris, 1934
Autin, Jean, *Prosper Mérimée*, Paris, 1983
Baschet, Robert, *Du Romantisme au Second Empire: Mérimée 1803-1870*, Paris, 1958
Billy, André, *Mérimée*, Paris, 1959
Bowman, Frank Paul, *Prosper Mérimée*, Berkeley and Los Angeles, 1962
Chabot, Jacques, *L'autre Moi*, Aix-en-Provence, 1983
Dale, R. C., *The Poetics of Prosper Mérimée*, The Hague and Paris, 1966
Du Bos, Charles, *Notes sur Mérimée*, Paris, 1920
Dupouy, Auguste, *Carmen de Mérimée*, Paris, 1930
Falke, Ernst, *Die Romantische Elemente in Prosper Mérimées Roman und Novellen*, Halle, 1915
Filon, Augustin, *Mérimée*, Paris, 1898
Freustié, Jean, *Prosper Mérimée (1803-1870)*, Paris, 1982
Gobert, D. L., 'Mérimée revisited', *Symposium*, 26, 2, 1972, pp. 128-46
Hovenkamp, Jan Willem, *Mérimée et la couleur locale*, Nijmegen, 1928
Johnstone, G. H., *Prosper Mérimée*, London, 1926
Leuwers, Daniel, 'Une lecture de "Lokis"', *Europe*, 53, 557, 1975, pp. 70-76
Mérimée, Prosper, *Carmen*, ed. M. Cégretin, Paris, 1966, 1980
——, *Romans et Nouvelles, II*, ed. M. Parturier, Paris, 1967
——, *Théâtre*, ed. G. Sigaux, Paris, 1963
Milhaud, Gérard, 'Un théâtre sous le masque', *Europe*, 53, 557, 1975, pp. 47-59
Raitt, Alan W., *Prosper Mérimée*, London, 1970
Sainte-Beuve, Charles-Augustin, *Mes Poisons*, Paris, 1926
Sivert, Eileen Boyd, 'Fear and Confrontation in Prosper Mérimée's Narrative Fiction', *Nineteenth Century French Studies*, 6, 3 and 4, 1978, pp. 213-230
Symons, Arthur, *Studies in Prose and Verse*, London, 1904
Tilby, Michael J., 'Language and sexuality in Mérimée's *Carmen*', *Forum for Modern Language Studies*, 15, 3, 1979, pp. 255-63
Smith, Maxwell A., *Prosper Mérimée*, New York, 1972
Trahard, Pierre, *Prosper Mérimée et l'art de la nouvelle*, Paris, 1952
——, *Prosper Mérimée de 1834 à 1853*, Paris, 1928

Musset

Affron, Charles, *A Stage for Poets*, Princeton, 1971
Allem, Maurice, *Alfred de Musset*, Grenoble and Paris, 1947
Barine, Arvède, *Alfred de Musset*, Paris, 1893
Crossley, Ceri, *Musset: Lorenzaccio*, London, 1983
Dolder, Charlotte, *Le Thème de l'être et du paraître dans l'itinéraire spirituel d'Alfred de Musset*, Zurich, 1968
Fabig, Angelika, *Kunst und Künstler im Werk Alfred de Mussets*, Heidelberg, 1976
Gans, Eric L., *Musset et le 'drame tragique'*, Paris, 1974
Gastinel, Pierre, *Le Romantisme d'Alfred de Musset*, Paris, 1931
Geyer, Wilhelm, *Alfred de Musset in seinem dramatischen Werk*, Giessen, 1923
Gochberg, Herbert S., *Stage of Dreams*, Geneva, 1967
Guillemin, Henri, *La Liaison Musset Sand*, Paris, 1972
Haldane, Charlotte, *Alfred*, London, 1960
Henriot, Emile, *Alfred de Musset*, Paris, 1928
——, *L'Enfant du siècle*, Paris, 1953

Lafoscade, Léon, *Le Théâtre d'Alfred de Musset*, Paris, 1901
Lainey, Yves, *Musset ou la difficulté d'aimer*, Paris, 1978
Lebois, André, *Vues sur le théâtre de Musset*, Paris, 1966
Lefèbvre, Henri, *Alfred de Musset, dramaturge*, Paris, 1955
Lindau, Paul, *Alfred de Musset*, Berlin, 1877
Masson, Bernard, *'Lorenzaccio' ou la difficulté d'être*, Paris, 1962
——, *Musset et le théâtre intérieur*, Paris, 1974
——, *Musset et son Double*, Paris, 1978
Maurras, Charles, *Les Amants de Venise*, Paris, 1904
Merlant, Joachim Claude, *Le Moment de Lorenzaccio dans le destin de Musset*, Athens, 1955
Pommier, Jean, *Variétés sur Alfred de Musset et son théâtre*, Paris, 1944
——, *Autour du drame de Venise*, Paris, 1958
Sand, George, *Elle et Lui*, ed. H. Guillemin, Neuchâtel, 1963
Sedgwick, Henry Dwight, *Alfred de Musset 1810-1857*, London, 1932
Sices, David, *Theater of Solitude*, Hanover, New Hampshire, 1974
Tilley, Arthur, *Three French Dramatists*, Cambridge, 1933
Toesca, Maurice, *Alfred de Musset ou l'amour de la mort*, Paris, 1970
Van Tieghem, Philippe, *Musset, l'homme et l'œuvre*, Paris, 1944

Nerval

Béguin, Albert, *Gérard de Nerval*, Paris, 1945
Bénichou, Paul, *Nerval et la chanson folklorique*, Paris, 1970
Cellier, Léon, *De 'Sylvie' à Aurélia*, Paris, 1971
Chambers, Ross, *Gérard de Nerval et la poétique du voyage*, Paris, 1969
Constans, François, *Gérard de Nerval devant le destin*, Paris, 1979
Dédéyan, Charles, *Gérard de Nerval et l'Allemagne*, Paris, 1957
Ducray, Camille, *Gérard de Nerval*, Paris, 1946
Durry, Marie-Jeanne, *Gérard de Nerval et le mythe*, Paris, 1956
Eisenzweig, Uri, *L'espace imaginaire d'un récit: 'Sylvie' de Gérard de Nerval*, Neuchâtel, 1976
Gascar, Pierre, *Gérard de Nerval et son temps*, Paris, 1981
Grossvogel, Anita, *Le Pouvoir du nom*, Paris, 1972
Jeanneret, Michel, *La Lettre perdue*, Paris, 1978
Knapp, Bettina L., *Gérard de Nerval*, Alabama, 1980
Kofman, Sarah, *Nerval, le charme de la répétition*, Lausanne, 1979
Le Breton, Georges, *Nerval, poète alchimique*, Paris, 1982
Marie, Aristide, *Gérard de Nerval*, Paris, 1955
Mauron, Charles, *Des Métaphores obsédantes au mythe personnel*, Paris, 1963
Peyrouzet, Edouard, *Gérard de Nerval inconnu*, Paris, 1965
Poulet, Georges, *Trois Essais de mythologie romantique*, Paris, 1966
Prendergast, Chrisopher, *The Order of Mimesis*, Cambridge, 1986
Proust, Marcel, *Contre Sainte-Beuve*, Paris, 1954
Rhodes, S. A., *Gérard de Nerval 1808-1855*, London, 1952
Richard, Jean Pierre, *Poésie et profondeur*, Paris, 1955
Richer, Jean, *Gérard de Nerval et les doctrines ésotériques*, Paris, 1947
——, *Gérard de Nerval*, Paris, 1950
——, *Nerval: Expérience et création*, Paris, 1963
——, *Nerval au royaume des archétypes*, Paris, 1971
Rinsler, Norma, *Gérard de Nerval*, London, 1973

Bibliography

Schaeffer, Gérald, *Une double Lecture de Nerval*, Neuchâtel, 1977
Sébillotte, L.-H., *Le Secret de Gérard de Nerval*, Paris, 1948
Sowerby, Benn, *The Disinherited*, London, 1973
Symons, Arthur, *The Symbolist Movement in Literature*, London, 1899

Prévost

Cellier, Léon, 'Le mythe de Manon et les romantiques français', *Actes du Colloque d'Aix-en-Provence*, 50, Aix, 1965, pp. 255-68
Donohoe, Joseph I. Jr., 'The Death of Manon: a Literary Inquest', *L'Esprit créateur*, 12, 2, 1972, pp. 129-46
Gossman, Lionel, 'Male and female in two short novels by Prévost', *Modern Language Review*, 77, 1982, pp. 29-37
Greshoff, C. J., 'A note on the ambiguity of *Manon Lescaut*', *Forum for Modern Language Studies*, 3, 1967, pp. 166-71
Hazard, Paul, et al., *Etudes critiques sur* Manon Lescaut, Chicago, 1929
Jaccard, J.-L., *Manon Lescaut, le personnage-romancier*, Paris, 1975
Josephs, H., 'Manon Lescaut: a rhetoric of intellectual evasion', *Romanic Review*, 59, 1968, pp. 185-97
Kory, O. A., *Subjectivity and Sensitivity in the Novels of the Abbé Prévost*, Paris, 1972
Lotringer, S., 'Manon L'Echo', *Romanic Review*, 63, 1972, pp. 92-110
Mathé, R., *Manon Lescaut: Abbé Prévost*, Paris, 1970
Mauron, Charles, '*Manon Lescaut* et le mélange des genres', *Actes du Colloque d'Aix-en-Provence*, 50, Aix, 1965, pp. 113-8
May, Georges, *Le Dilemme du roman au XVIIIe siècle*, New Haven and Paris, 1963
Miller, Nancy K., *The Heroine's Text*, New York, 1980
Mylne, Vivienne, *The Eighteenth-Century French Novel*, 2nd edition, Cambridge, 1981
— — , *Prévost: Manon Lescaut*, London, 1972
Poulet, Georges, *Etudes sur le temps humain*, I, Paris, 1972
Prévost d'Exiles, Antoine François, *Œuvres, I: Mémoires et aventures d'un homme de qualité qui s'est retiré du monde*, ed. P. Berthiaume and J. Sgard, Grenoble, 1978
— — , *Histoire du Chevalier des Grieux et de Manon Lescaut*, ed. F. Deloffre and R. Picard, Paris, 1965
Roddier, Henri, *L'Abbé Prévost: l'homme et l'œuvre*, Paris, 1955
Rousset, Jean, *Narcisse romancier*, Paris, 1973
Sgard, Jean, *Prévost romancier*, Paris, 1968
Showalter, English, *The Evolution of the French Novel 1641-1782*, Princeton, 1972
Singerman, Alan J., 'A *fille de plaisir* and her *greluchon*: society and the perspective of *Manon Lescaut*', *L'Esprit créateur*, 12, 2, 1972, pp. 118-28
Stewart, P., *Imitation and Illusion in the French Memoir-novel 1700-1750*, New Haven and London, 1969
Todd, Janet, *Women's Friendship in Literature*, New York, 1980
Trahard, Pierre, *Les Maîtres de la sensibilité française au XVIIIe siècle (1715-1789)*, I, Paris, 1931
Turnell, Martin, *The Art of French Fiction*, London, 1959
Winandy, Rita, 'Prévost and Morality of Sentiment', *L'Esprit créateur*, 12, 2, 1972, pp. 94-102

II

Abel, Elizabeth, ed., *Writing and Sexual Difference*, Brighton, 1982
Abrams, M. H., *The Mirror and the Lamp*, Oxford, 1953, 1981
Alain-Fournier, *Le grand Meaulnes*, Paris, 1971
Ardener, Shirley, ed., *Perceiving Women*, London, 1975
Astruc, Alexandre and Michel Contat, directors, *Sartre*, Paris, 1977
Balzac, Honoré de, *La Comédie humaine*, ed. P.-G. Castex et al., Paris, 1976
Barthes, Roland, *Le Degré zéro de l'écriture*, Paris, 1953, 1972
——, 'La Mort de l'auteur', *Mantéia*, 5, 1968, pp. 12-17
Barzun, Jacques, *Classic, Romantic and Modern*, London, 1943, 1961
Beauvoir, Simone de *Le deuxième Sexe*, 2 vols, Paris, 1949
Benveniste, Emile, *Problèmes de linguistique générale*, 2 vols, Paris, 1966, 1974
Berger, John, *Ways of Seeing*, London and Harmondsworth, 1972
Bergson, Henri, *Le Rire*, Paris, 1940
Bernanos, Georges, *Œuvres romanesques*, ed. G. Picon et al., Paris, 1961
Bernheimer, Charles and Claire Kahane, eds., *In Dora's Case*, London, 1985
Bishop, Lloyd, *The Romantic Hero and his Heirs in French Literature*, New York, Berne, Frankfort, Nancy, 1984
Bloom, Harold, *The Anxiety of Influence*, New York, 1973
Bowlby, John, *Child Care and the Growth of Love*, Harmondsworth, 1953, 1983
Brenkman, John, 'Narcissus in the Text', *Georgia Review*, 30, 1976, pp. 293-327
Breton, André, *Nadja*, Paris, 1964
Brown, Beverley and Parveen Adams, 'The Feminine Body and Feminist Politics', *m/f*, 3, 1979, pp. 35-50
Burke, Carolyn, 'Irigaray through the Looking Glass', *Feminist Studies*, 7, 2, 1981, pp. 288-306
Cameron, Deborah, *Feminism and Linguistic Theory*, London, 1985
Camus, Albert, *Théâtre, Récits, Nouvelles*, ed. R. Quilliot, Paris, 1962
Chodorow, Nancy, *The Reproduction of Mothering*, Berkeley, Los Angeles, London, 1978
Clément, Catherine and Hélène Cixous, *La jeune Née*, Paris, 1975
Clement, N. H., *Romanticism in France*, New York, 1939, 1966
Coward, Rosalind, *Female Desire*, London, 1984
Cruickshank, John, 'The Novel of self-disclosure', in J. Cruickshank, ed., *French Literature and its Background*, 4, Oxford, 1969
Crystal, David, *Listen to Your Child*, Harmondsworth, 1986
Culler, Jonathan, *On Deconstruction*, London, Melbourne and Henley, 1983
Daly, Mary, *Gyn/Ecology*, London, 1978
Demoris, René, *Le Roman à la première personne*, Paris, 1975
Derrida, Jacques, *De la Grammatologie*, Paris, 1967
——, *Spurs/Eperons*, Chicago and London, 1978, 1979
Dinnerstein, Dorothy, *The Mermaid and the Minotaur*, New York, 1976
Dörrie, Heinrich, 'Echo und Narcissus: Psychologische Fiktion in Spiel und Ernst', *Das altsprachliche Unterricht*, 10, 1, 1967, pp. 54-75
Droste-Hülshoff, Annette, *Gedichte*, Stuttgart, 1978
Ecker, Gisela, ed., *Feminist Aesthetics*, London, 1985
Eichenbaum, Luise and Susie Orbach, *What do Women Want?*, Glasgow, 1983
——, *Understanding Women*, Harmondsworth, 1985
Eisenstein, Hester, *Contemporary Feminist Thought*, London and Sydney, 1984
——, and Alice Jardine, eds., *The Future of Difference*, Boston, Mass., 1980

Bibliography

Eliot, T. S., *Collected Poems 1909-1962*, London, 1963, 1974

Ellis, John, *Narration in the German Novelle*, Cambridge, 1974, 1979

Felman, Shoshana, 'Women and Madness: the Critical Phallacy', *Diacritics*, 5, 4, 1975, pp. 2-10

Fieder, Leslie, *Love and Death in the American Novel*, London, 1960, 1966

Flaubert, Gustave, *Correspondance* II, ed. J. Bruneau, Paris, 1980

Foucault, Michel, *Histoire de la sexualité* I, Paris, 1976

Freud, Sigmund, *The Pelican Freud Library*, vols 1-14, trans. J. Strachey, ed. J. Strachey and A. Richards, Harmondsworth, 1973-

Furst, Lilian, *Romanticism*, London and New York, 1969

Gallop, Jane, *Psychoanalysis and Feminism: the Daughter's Seduction*, London, 1982

——, *'Quand nos lèvres s'écrivent:* Irigaray's Body Politic', *Romanic Review*, 74, 1, 1983, pp. 77-83

George, Albert J., *Short Fiction in France, 1800-1850*, Syracuse, 1964

Gilbert, Sandra and Susan Gubar, *The Madwoman in the Attic*, New Haven and London, 1979, 1984

Gilligan, Carol, *In a Different Voice*, Cambridge, Mass., and London, 1982

Girard, René, *Mensonge romantique et vérité romanesque*, Paris, 1961

Goethe, Johann Wolfgang von, *Werke: Hamburger Ausgabe in 14 Bänden*, ed. B. von Wiese and E. Trunz, III, Hamburg, 1949, 1954, and VI, Hamburg, 1951

Greene, Gayle and Coppélia Kahn, eds., *Making a Difference*, London and New York, 1985

Grillparzer, Franz, *Der arme Spielmann*, Stuttgart, 1979

Hamilton, Victoria, *Narcissus and Oedipus*, London, 1982

Heath, Stephen, 'Difference', *Screen*, 19, 3, 1978, pp. 51-112

——, *The Sexual Fix*, London, 1982

Hofmannsthal, Hugo von, *Gesammelte Werke in Einzelausgaben: Aufzeichnungen*, ed. H. Steiner, Frankfurt, 1959

Holmes, Glyn, *The 'Adolphe' type in French fiction in the first half of the nineteenth century*, Quebec, 1977

Horney, Karen, 'The Dread of Woman', *International Journal of Psycho-analysis*, 13, 1932, pp. 348-60

Hugo, Victor, *Les Contemplations*, ed. L. Cellier, Paris, 1969

Hytier, Jean, *Les Romans de l'individu*, Paris, 1928

Irigaray, Luce, *Speculum de l'autre femme*, Paris, 1974

——, *Ce Sexe qui n'en est pas un*, Paris, 1977

Jardine, Alice, *Gynesis*, Ithaca and London, 1985

Jones, Ernest, *The Life and Work of Sigmund Freud*, abridged by Lionel Trilling and Steven Marcus, Harmondsworth, 1962

Jones, P. Mansell, *French Introspectives from Montaigne to André Gide*, Cambridge, 1937

Joyce, James, *A Portrait of the Artist as a Young Man*, Bungay, 1964

Jung, Carl Gustav, *The Collected Works of C. G. Jung*, ed. H. Read, M. Fordham and G. Adler, London, 1953

Kappeler, Susanne, *The Pornography of Representation*, Cambridge, 1986

Kristeva, Julia, *La Révolution du langage poétique*, Paris, 1974

——, *Des Chinoises*, Paris, 1974

——, 'Héréthique de l'amour', *Tel quel*, 74, 1977, pp. 30-49

——, *Pouvoirs de l'horreur*, Paris, 1980

Kuhn, Annette, *The Power of the Image*, London, 1985

Lacan, Jacques, *Le Séminaire, XX: Encore*, ed. J.-A. Miller, Paris, 1975

Lakoff, Robin, *Language and Woman's Place*, New York, 1975

Laplanche, Jean, *Vie et mort en psychanalyse*, Paris, 1970

——, and J.-B. Pontalis, *The Language of Psycho-analysis*, London, 1980
Legman, G., *Rationale of the Dirty Joke*, I, London, 1972
Merlant, Joachim, *Le Roman personnel de Rousseau à Fromentin*, Paris, 1905
Mitchell, Juliet, *Psychoanalysis and Feminism*, Harmondsworth, 1974, 1975
——, *Women: the longest Revolution*, London, 1984
——, and Jacqueline Rose, *Feminine Sexuality*, London, 1982
Moi, Toril, *Sexual/Textual Politics*, London and New York, 1982
Mulvey, Laura, 'Visual Pleasure and Narrative Cinema', *Screen*, 16, 3, 1975, pp. 6-18
Nietzsche, Friedrich, *The Birth of Tragedy and The Case of Wagner*, trans. Walter Kaufmann, New York, 1967
Ong, Walter J., *Orality and Literacy*, New York and London, 1982
Ovid, *Metamorphoses*, I, trans. F. J. Miller, London, 1916
Paulin, Roger, *The Brief Compass*, Oxford, 1985
Praz, Mario, *The Romantic Agony*, trans. A. Davidson, Oxford, 1933, 1970
Proust, Marcel, *A la Recherche du temps perdu*, 3 vols, ed. P. Clarac and A. Ferré, Paris, 1952
Rank, Otto, *The Myth of the Birth of the Hero*, trans. F. Robbins and S. E. Jelliffe, New York, 1952
Reiter, Rayna, ed., *Toward an Anthropology of Women*, New York and London, 1975
Rich, Adrienne, *Of Woman Born*, London, 1977
Ridge, George R., *The Hero in French Romantic Literature*, Athens, Georgia, 1959
Rilke, Rainer Maria, *Gesammelte Werke*, 4, Leipzig, 1930
Robert, Marthe, *Roman des origines et origines du roman*, Paris, 1972
Ruddick, Sara, 'Maternal Thinking', *Feminist Studies*, 6, 2, 1980, pp. 342-367
Rutter, Michael, *Maternal Deprivation Reassessed*, Harmondsworth, 1972
Sartre, Jean-Paul, *L'Etre et le néant*, Paris, 1943
——, *Œuvres romanesques*, ed. M. Contat et al., Paris, 1981
——, *Les Mots*, Paris, 1964
Schenk, H. G., *The Mind of the European Romantics*, Oxford, 1979
Schor, Naomi, *Breaking the Chain*, New York, 1985
Sedgwick, Eve Kosofsky, *Between Men*, New York, 1985
Segal, Naomi, *The Banal Object*, London, 1981
——, *The Unintended Reader*, Cambridge, 1986
——, 'The Adulteress's Child – a sidelight on Pierre et Jean', *French Studies Bulletin*, 17, 1985/6, pp. 6-8
——, '"Parfois j'ai peur que ce que j'ai supprimé ne se venge" – Gide and women', *Paragraph*, 8, 1986, pp. 62-74
Shelley, Mary, 'Frankenstein', in *Three Gothic Novels*, ed. P. Fairclough, Harmondsworth, 1968
Stifter, Adalbert, *Bunte Steine*, Munich, n.d.
Storm, Theodor, *Immensee und andere Novellen*, Stuttgart, 1979
Swales, Martin, *The German Novelle*, Princeton, 1977
Valéry, Paul, *Œuvres*, Paris, 1960
West, Rebecca, *The Return of the Soldier*, London, 1980
Winnicott, Donald, 'The Theory of the Parent-Infant Relationship', *International Journal of Psycho-analysis*, 41, 1960, pp. 585-595
——, *Playing and Reality*, Harmondsworth, 1974, 1980
Woolf, Virginia, *The Waves*, London, 1931
——, *Moments of Being*, ed. J. Schulkind, St. Albans, 1976
Zola, Emile, *Le Roman expérimental*, Paris, 1880

Index

Index

Index